REAL OLD TORY POLITICS

REAL OLD TORY POLITICS

The Political Diaries of Sir Robert Sanders,
Lord Bayford, 1910–35

Edited with an introduction by

JOHN RAMSDEN

ISBN 0 9508900 0 6

British Library Cataloguing in Publication Data

Bayford, Robert Sanders, *Baron*
   Real old Tory politics.
   1. Great Britain—Politics and
   government—1910–1936
   I. Title II. Ramsden, John Andrew
   941.083   DA576

ISBN 0-950890-00-6

PUBLISHED BY THE HISTORIANS' PRESS,
9 DAISY ROAD, LONDON E18 1EA.

Produced by Alan Sutton Publishing Limited
17a Brunswick Road, Gloucester GL1 1HG
and printed in Great Britain

CONTENTS

ACKNOWLEDGEMENTS

I owe a special debt of gratitude to the late Mrs V.E. Butler, the daughter of Lord Bayford, both for generously giving permission for the publication of the diary and for giving me a great deal of information about her father by letter and in conversation. I should thank the Conservative Research Department which has provided the diary with a London home for the past several years and thank Mr Geoffrey Block and Mrs Peggy Critch, formerly of the Conservative Research Department Library who combined to make working on the text there such a pleasant experience. I am also grateful to the University of Birmingham for permission to quote from the papers of Sir Austen Chamberlain.

The Historians' Press gratefully acknowledges the assistance of The Twenty-Seven Foundation in supporting the series of which this volume forms a part. This volume is published with the help of grant from the late Miss Isobel Thornley's Bequest to the University of London.

Like any diarist, Sanders abbreviated names in the text, and used nick-names to refer to friends, but there is little difficulty in identifying these. The only name which might lead to real confusion was Sanders' own: although his christian names were Robert and Arthur, he was widely known from his Oxford days as 'Peter'. A number of letters to him printed here therefore begin 'Dear Peter'. Other shortened or familiar names are listed below; politicians and others referred to by surname are identified by footnote on their first appearance in the text.

A.J.B.'	Arthur James Balfour, later Earl Balfour
'Aubrey'	Aubrey Herbert
'Austen'	Sir Austen Chamberlain
'Bal'	Lord Balcarres, later 27th Earl of Crawford
'Bobby'	Sir Bolton Eyres-Monsell, later Viscount Monsell
'Bonar' or 'B.L.'	Andrew Bonar Law
'C.B.'	Sir Henry Campbell-Bannerman
'Edmund' or 'E.T.'	Lord Edmund Talbot, later Viscount Fitzalan; also 'Lady Edmund' for Viscountess Fitzalan
'F.E.'	F.E. Smith, later Earl of Birkenhead
'G.Y.' or 'George'	Sir George Younger, later Viscount Younger
'Hamar'	Sir Hamar Greenwood, later Viscount Greenwood
'Jack'	Sir John Gilmour
'Jix' or 'J. Hicks'	Sir William Joynson-Hicks, later Viscount Brentford
'L.G.' or 'George'	David Lloyd George
'Leslie'	Sir Leslie Wilson
'Linky'	Lord Hugh Cecil, later Lord Quickswood
'Lucy' or 'L.'	Lucy Sanders, Lady Bayford
'Neville'	Neville Chamberlain
'Pike'	H. Pike Pease, later Lord Daryngton
'Rufus'	Sir Rufus Isaacs, later Marquess of Reading
'Stanley' or 'S.B.'	Stanley Baldwin
'T.P.'	T.P. O'Connor
'The Viscount'	Viscount Valentia, later Lord Annesley
'The Bull'	General Sir E.H. Allenby, later Viscount Allenby
'Willie' or 'Willie B.'	W.C. Bridgeman, later Viscount Bridgeman
'Winston' or 'W.C.'	Winston Churchill
'Worthy' or 'W. Evans'	Sir Laming Worthington-Evans

INTRODUCTION

Sir Robert Sanders and his Political Diary

Sir Robert Sanders, Lord Bayford, was never a dominating national leader, but for fifteen years his political career took him close to the sources of power and influence. Like the diaries of C.P. Scott for the Liberal Party or Beatrice Webb for the Labour Movement, the diary of Sir Robert Sanders is therefore of primary value to historians for the light it sheds on contemporary politics.[1] However, again like Scott or Beatrice Webb, Sanders was an active and interesting political figure in his own right. He was widely seen as 'a Tory of the old school' or as 'the epitome of the country gentleman in politics' with all the implications, both favourable and unfavourable, that such epithets are intended to convey. This caricature was in some senses true, and was justified by much that Sanders himself said and did, but it is more misleading than helpful in assessing him as a political figure. This introduction seeks to describe Sanders' career so that readers of his political diary may know something of the man himself. Such knowledge cannot be exclusively derived from the diary, for even in the privacy of his diary Sanders was remarkably modest and restrained. This moderation was a marked characteristic of his political career and so some compensation may be necessary in assessing his own actions and views.[2]

Sanders' early years appear to justify his later identification as the archetypal country gentleman. He was born in 1867, the son of Arthur Sanders of Fernhill, Isle of Wight, and spent his childhood in the Isle of Wight and in Surrey. He was educated at Harrow and at Balliol College, Oxford (1886-90). Here the divergence between the typical career and Sanders' own became more noticeable. At Harrow he was Head Boy - a position reserved for one with academic as well as social and sporting status. At Oxford he was noted as a keen hunting man; his hunting friends included J.W. Hills, George Lane-Fox and Lord Willoughby de Broke, all political colleagues in later years. However, his apparently exclusive interest in hunting was also misleading, as Hills later recalled:[3] 'He was a mystery to us at the University. He hunted and amused himself, no one

1

ever knew him to study, but in the end he surprised us all by getting a First.' The answer to the mystery was Sanders' modesty and his capacity for hard work. He acquired his First in Jurisprudence after taking Classical Moderations, an appropriate combination for a future politician. In 1891 he was called to the Bar at the Inner Temple but never practised as a barrister. He had been independent since, on his father's death in 1886, he had inherited property in south London which provided him with a comfortable income. There is no indication at this time of his having political ambitions, but, during the next few years, he settled in Somerset - the county which was to be the essential background to his political career and his home for the rest of his life. His daughter, the Hon. Mrs V.E. Butler, has described this development:[4]

Having finished with examinations, my father concentrated his energies on hunting. One of his Oxford friends, the Hon. L.J. Bathurst, had become Master of the Exmoor Foxhounds, and my father divided his time between hunting with him there and at Cirencester. It was on Exmoor that he met my mother, Lucy Halliday, whose father, a local landowner, was a contemporary at Winchester and at the Bar of my father's father, and was chairman of the Devon Quarter Sessions. They married in 1893 and took a house in Leicestershire, for the hunting.

. Then in 1895, at the age of 28, he became Master of the Devon and Somerset Staghounds, and went to live in Somerset, at Exford in the centre of Exmoor. He came there as no stranger - the Exmoor Foxhounds covered part of the same country as the Staghounds, and he had frequently hunted with both. Several of his Oxford friends lived in the neighbourhood and my mother's old home was only some twelve miles from Exford.

He remained Master till 1907 and established himself during those years as a man belonging to Somerset. He soon earned the reputation among hunting people of being a first rate Master of Hounds, showing excellent sport, and he also gained the trust and affection of the Exmoor farming community, who, living isolated lives in harsh climatic conditions (before the advent of cars, radio or television), found their main recreation and excitement in staghunting.

But, as at Oxford, he did not allow hunting to absorb all his energies. He joined the North Devon Yeomanry, with many of the local farmers serving in his squadron. Having been appointed a magistrate, he attended regularly both his local Bench and at Quarter Sessions. In 1900, he fought his first Parliamentary election at the Liberal stronghold of Bristol East. The following year Somerset County Council elected him as an alderman; there were no party politics on the council, which was composed largely, like the magistracy, of the local gentry. Aldermen were still chosen (as they must have been at the inception of County Councils in 1888), not from former elected members, but from other persons who were considered likely to give useful service to the county. Although my father had lived in the county for only six years, he evidently passed this test.

Thus, when in 1903 he was adopted as prospective Conservative candidate for the Bridgwater division (which included parts of Exmoor), he was already widely known in the constituency and by the leading people in the county, and was generally regarded as a Somerset man.

Unfortunately, even Bridgwater did not withstand the Liberal landslide of 1906, and Sanders was defeated by seventeen votes. He at once threw himself into the task of improving the local organisation, blamed by the press for his defeat. In January 1910 he made his third attempt, entering Parliament with the largest majority in the county.[5] On entering the House of Commons he started a political diary and kept it regularly until he left in 1929.

The diary shows his immediate disappointment with the limited role of the backbencher; the debates were soon described as 'dull' and the routine business of passing legislation clearly failed to evoke much interest in a man predisposed to more vigorous activity. Many of the new Conservative M.P.s of 1910 felt the same frustrations with parliament. After a vigorous campaign against a Liberal government they regarded as corrupt and almost revolutionary, they had succeeded in winning as many seats as the Liberals, only to find that Labour and the Irish M.P.s kept the Liberals in power. Conservative admiration for the constitution reached its lowest ebb in these years when they were powerless to prevent what appeared to them to be a social and political revolution. The unusual bitterness that characterised politics was partly an effect of the Conservative recognition of their impotence in face of a determined government. Sanders was fortunate though in soon being involved more actively in the organisation of politics, and consequently was not so exposed to these frustrations. Just over a year after entering the House, he was appointed a junior opposition whip, probably through the good offices of the then Chief Whip, Sir Alexander Acland-Hood, who sat for the neighbouring West Somerset Division. Sanders was surprised by such early promotion but threw himself into the work of the Whip's Office with enthusiasm and began to enjoy parliamentary politics a great deal more. He was to spend half of his political career as a whip and so suited was he for the task that he was widely tipped to become Chief Whip for the Coalition Government in 1921. The Whip's Office was a good listening post for a man interested in the latest political news and speculations, not least because the whips acted as a team and shared information with each other as a matter of course.

The information thus gathered had a distinctly optimistic flavour at a time when the party was going through a very sticky patch, but it is an invaluable source nonetheless.

The work of the Whip's Office from 1911 to 1914 was the promotion of a continuous battle in parliament to harry and if possible defeat the Liberal Government. This was then more likely than it may now seem for two reasons: first, it was only a few years since a government had last resigned without an election defeat (in 1905) and secondly, the Liberal Government had to rely on the relatively unpredictable support of Labour and Irish Members. The job of the Unionist whips was to press the Government at its weak spots, to use parliamentary rules to obstruct as much as possible, and to create disorder in the House of Commons. At worst, this activity would be good for Unionist morale, in the country as well as in parliament, and it would certainly slow down the progress of government legislation. At best it might cause the government to resign or to call a general election which the Unionists expected to win. In all of this Sanders took an active part, and so involved did he become with the rules and standing orders of the House that soon after the war he was tipped not only as a possible Chief Whip but also as a possible Speaker. He also took part in the more clandestine manoeuvres by which the whips were trying to catch the government out with a snap vote. Many such attempts were made and some succeeded; they did not bring the government down but they certainly kept it on edge and hindered its legislation. Without Unionist obstruction there would probably have been some form of Plural Voting Bill passed before 1914, with incalculable political repercussions. The Whip's Office took all these activities very seriously and seems to have genuinely believed in the possibility of turning the government out. As the diary shows, Sanders himself was not so sanguine, but the optimism which he records as the general mood of the party goes far towards explaining its attitude to politics in these years.

The outbreak of World War I necessitated Sanders' removal from Westminster, for by 1914 he was Lieutenant Colonel of the Royal North Devon Hussars. For the first year of the war, while his regiment was in camp at Clacton-on-Sea, he could occasionally return to Westminster. In 1915 and 1916 he commanded the regiment on active service at Gallipoli and elsewhere in the Mediterranean. Two diary entries and a few letters from the Chief Whip, Lord Edmund Talbot, are the only evidence of any political involvement in the first half of the war.

However, Edmund Talbot was trying to recall some active M.P.s from the Front because of the shortage of manpower at Westminster,[6] and it was at his request that Sanders returned to politics in the spring of 1917. Although he moved back into the Whip's room, his real position changed, for he soon became a sort of unofficial *party* Chief Whip in opposition to the Government Chief Whips, one of whom was a Conservative. As such his function was to organise party opposition to the government policy to which the leaders of the party had assented: in the most extreme case, the passage of the Representation of the People Bill, he was opposing a Conservative Minister, Hayes Fisher. This activity threw Sanders into close contact with Sir George Younger, Chairman of the Conservative Party Organisation, and in 1918 Sanders himself became Deputy Chairman. He also continued as a whip and formally became a member of the government when appointed Treasurer of the Household (later a Junior Lord of the Treasury), but there was little doubt that his primary loyalty was to the party rather than to the government. The whips as a whole were in an unusual position during the Coalition; they were normally professional partisans with clearly visible opponents but at this time an acute conflict of interests could arise. Since the government had an overwhelming parliamentary majority, it was perhaps inevitable that the whips should devote some of their energies to internal intrigue rather than to organising against the opposition. Sanders certainly took a lead in this, as he was obliged to do as Deputy Chairman of the party, and provided an important link between the government, the whips and the Central Office. However, it was his open partisanship which apparently prevented him from moving up to be Chief Whip in 1921. Although the Coalition Government had two Chief Whips, one Conservative and one Liberal, it was apparently unacceptable to Lloyd George that the Conservatives should be represented by Sanders. This was perhaps as great a mistake for Lloyd George as it was a serious blow for Sanders, for it may be claimed with justice that a more vocal and less compromising Conservative Chief Whip than Leslie Wilson might have helped Austen Chamberlain to avoid the near-disaster of 1922.

As a senior whip and Deputy Chairman of the party, Sanders joined the ranks of the party managers, a small and informal group of men who directed the organisation of the party in the country. The group was to a large extent formed by self-selection, for very few senior politicians had the time and the inclination to involve themselves in the nuts and bolts of organisation. From 1911, as a junior whip, Sanders had exercised certain regional responsibilities,[7] in his case in the south west, but from 1917 he was involved on a national scale. Once again, the man of action found an appropriate channel for his political energies and he continued as an active political organiser well into the 1930s. Thus in 1929 he headed a small secret committee which investigated the causes of the general election defeat in Central Office; in 1933 he became an active Chairman of the Association of Conservative Clubs; in 1927 he was Chairman, and in 1934 President, of the National Union. However, the immediate business for party managers in 1917 was more pressing and more controversial. Sanders' first main job was to adapt the party to the changed circumstances which followed the passing into law of the Representation of the People Act. This involved the winding up of local associations and the creation of new ones to conform to the new constituency boundaries; it also involved the placing and replacing of parliamentary candidates, and all of this in wartime. More important though were the secret negotiations regarding the allocation of seats between the Coalition partners for the coming general election. Sanders was especially involved with trying to find seats for the embryonic British Workers' League, a Coalition front-organisation which, it was hoped, would win the votes of 'patriotic labour' to the government. The private negotiations went on through the summer of 1918 and provided the basis for the distribution of coupons at the December 1918 general election.

Victory at that election increased rather than decreased the problems of the party managers, for their electoral bargain had been made for the duration of one parliament only. All the party managers were therefore under constant pressure from supporters in the country, and the Conservatives had the added disadvantage of having to deal with Lloyd George – whom they neither liked nor trusted. Although most Conservative front-benchers could agree to work with Lloyd George, in the short term at least, Conservatives in the country were hostile to the man as well as to many of his policies. The party managers were never able to communicate this distrust effectively to their leaders. As Younger later recalled, 'a constant eye had to be kept on L.G. and his supporters, with unpleasant rows at intervals.'[8] In all of this, Sanders played a leading role and his diary charts the course of intrigue and negotiation within the Coalition over the years 1918 to 1922. The party managers also had their hands full with the more routine parts of their job, for bye-elections went very badly indeed, and sections of the party appeared to be on the point of breaking away altogether.[9]

Sanders' own political career took another step forward in March 1921 when he became Under Secretary at the War Office. He was one of few men with personal military experience to occupy a political office at the War Office in these years and, perhaps for this reason, seems to have got on well with the Generals. Under the Secretary of State, Sir Laming Worthington-Evans, Sanders was made responsible for applying to the War Office the cuts necessitated by the fall of the 'Geddes Axe'. He was able to offset some of the prejudice of the professional soldiers who would have liked to make all of the cuts in the territorial forces.

In the political crisis of July–October 1922, Sanders was in close touch with Conservatives who wanted to throw over the Coalition.[10]

He took a leading part in . . . the revolt of the Under-Secretaries. . . . He was the first speaker at their meeting on August 3 with Austen Chamberlain and Lord Birkenhead, and, in the words of one who was present, explained 'with great clearness' the difficulties he was finding with his leading supporters on account of their hostility to the Coalition. When on Monday October 16, a last desperate effort of conciliation by means of a meeting at Downing Street . . . broke down, it was Sir Robert Sanders who asked, as the meeting was about to separate: 'Do you want any resignations?' Lord Birkenhead, who replied, said: 'Not yet.'

Sanders had earlier hoped for Bonar Law's return to politics as a means of re-uniting the party; at the Carlton Club Meeting, he voted against the Coalition and in favour of a Conservative government under Law. As a result of that government coming into office, Sanders at last got the preferment that he had been denied the previous year. He became Minister of Agriculture and Fisheries, and a member of the Cabinet. In the following month, at the general election, he held his seat at Bridgwater by only 119 votes, a warning of what was to happen in the next year.

During the short-lived Bonar Law/Baldwin administration of 1922–3 the Ministry of Agriculture was something of a hot seat. The farmers had been demanding government action to protect British agriculture from ruination in a time of falling world prices. Indeed, the failure to meet this demand had been one of the Coalition Government's costliest mistakes. However, the new Conservative Government was in an even worse quandary, for it believed that in tariffs it had the answer to the farmers' needs, but was restrained from introducing them because of Bonar Law's pledge against 'food taxes' at the 1922 general election. Sanders had always been an advocate of tariff reform, but he had also accepted the tactical necessity of giving the pledge against food taxes in 1913 and in 1922.[11] He saw no point in having the ideal policy if it split the party and kept it in opposition. Now, as Minister of Agriculture, he was expected to administer the party's non-policy, and, not surprisingly he became a keen advocate of a reversal of course over tariffs. Once he had secured the inclusion of food in the government's tariff proposals, he became a supporter of Baldwin's decision to call a tariff election in 1923. At that election, the Conservatives lost their overall majority, but they remained the largest party and were ultimately able to reap the benefit of a Labour minority government and a divided Liberal Party. For Sanders the election defeat of 1923 was more serious, for he lost at Bridgwater and this greatly curtailed his political career. Like so many other politicians, the brief intermission away from Westminster meant that Sanders permanently lost his place on the political ladder. He soon gave up the Bridgwater seat, was adopted instead for the Wells Division and won it easily in the 1924 general election. However, the year of opposition had been a vital one in the reorganisation of the party and the re-thinking of its policy.[12] Although he was only 57 when he was elected for Wells, Sanders seemed to be part of a past political generation. Younger men, first elevated because of the lack of front-bench talent in the 1922–3 government, were now promoted over his head. Moreover, the 1924 Cabinet also included five ex-Coalition Ministers who had refused to join Law in 1922 but had held their seats in 1923. In his characteristic way, Sanders did not complain, and his diary gives no hint of the disappointment he must have felt.

On his return to the back benches, Sanders felt the same frustration that he had experienced in 1910. Debates were again 'dull' – and indeed after the epic struggles of 1911–14 and 1918–23, the debates of the 1924–9 Parliament *were* dull. Not only was he forced to remain unwontedly inactive, but he was also cut off from the springs of political information and influence. In search of employment, he became Chairman of a Standing Committee of the Commons, and accepted an offer that he be nominated in due course for the Speakership.[13] When this fell through in 1928, he again acepted his fate without complaint, but decided to retire from the Commons. He did not stand at the 1929 general election – although he was an active campaigner on behalf of others – and in the dissolution honours he was created Lord Bayford. Without the chance of active involvement, he chose not to be involved at all; he had entered politics through choice not through necessity, and he preferred to devote his talents to other areas of service to the community rather than see them wasted. National politics therefore occupied a decreasing part of his life, but he became more actively involved in local affairs, most especially with the County Council. He became Chairman of the County Councils' Association in 1933, and was Chairman of the Somerset County Council from 1937 to his death. He still hunted regularly and his few appearances at the House of Lords were in connection with rural matters. After his retirement politics seems to have depressed him somewhat, as several diary entries indicate. Leigh Maclachlan noted a comment in Lord Bayford's last letter to him (in August 1939): 'All recent news seems very beastly.'

Lord Bayford died in February 1940. Maclachlan commented: 'a gallant and very honourable English gentleman has passed from our ken'.[14] This comes very close to Sanders' political reputation, both as he appeared to others and as he appears through the pages of his diary. He was certainly held in high regard by supporters and opponents alike. A mainly hostile report in the Liberal *Star* in 1914 included the following passage:[15]

Delightfully and consistently Tory . . . and as might be expected of a genial West Country squire, he is popular with everyone. He is an interesting survival of an old-world Toryism that is loved and lost. Clean-shaven, ruddy of complexion, with a healthy outdoor glow, he was a striking contrast to the new Tory leader who sat beside him [Bonar Law].

In some respects this is fair, but in contrasting Sanders – as typical of the traditional squirearchy – with the new meritocratic Toryism of Bonar Law, it misses the point by a wide margin. From Somerset, the position could look very different, and the *Somerset County Gazette* could actually cite Sanders as an example of the new Toryism:[16]

> Imperturbable coolness and exceptional power of concentration on the matter in hand are two of Mr Sanders' most striking characteristics. He is typical of the revolution that is coming over English life and politics – the revolution that is gradually throwing open the career to talent and causing men to be judged by what they are and do, and not by the non-essentials.

If Sanders was categorised as a country squire then it was mainly because of his own life and his own words. He lived a country life whenever he could, and continued to hunt as much as possible, even when a Minister. He also spiced his speeches with the images of the hunting field, and clearly enjoyed jokes about his interest in hunting. However, his opponents' assumption that his partiality for the country automatically involved hostility towards the towns, industry and the modern world was false. In his adoption speech at Bridgwater in 1903, Sanders had begun his comments on tariff reform with a fashionable disclaimer of intellectualism but went on with words that may have surprised many of his listeners:[17]

> Now, as Mr Stanley kindly said, I am a University man myself, but, although I am a University man, I do not wish to advocate the government of England by the professors (hear, hear and applause) and it has been a fact that whenever any great change has been proposed the professors have been against it. When Galileo discovered that the world went round the sun all the professors were against it, and they put him in prison for saying it, but the world went round the sun just the same (laughter) and so I think that in a question like this we ought to attach more importance to the opinions of business men (applause) who have had to deal with this question not in the lecture room and in the study but in the workshop and in the counting house.

He went on to make a highly flattering reference to Joseph Chamberlain, not only for introducing the policy of tariffs but also for his past services to the country. A politician who counted Joe Chamberlain as a hero in 1903 was clearly no typical squire. But by this time the old antagonism of 'Land'

versus 'Capital' had ceased to count for much in the Conservative party;
the difference continued only in life-style and political ideals rather than as
a clash of separate economic interests. Sanders certainly held such an ideal
of what a country gentleman in politics should be like, and his reputation
with others demonstrates how close to it he came, but his was never an
ideal which excluded all other forms of political life as necessarily inferior
or impossible. Thus, he reported in 1911 on the election of Bonar Law as
leader of the Party, laying stress on the gentlemanly nature of the
proceedings:[18] 'It was, however, a curious feature that while Walter Long
was speaking of the decision almost as the Swan Song of the country
gentleman, he and Chaplin the two country gentlemen cut far the finest
figures in the proceedings.' He was frequently pleased and surprised at the
gentlemanliness of the Conservative party in times of crisis.

Sanders' attitude to his party was one of total loyalty, and in this he was
consistent throughout his career. In the adoption speech quoted above, he
went on to state his view of party politics:[19]

> Well, as a matter of principle, I see no objection to these proposals, but
> as a matter of tactics I think we ought to leave this matter in the hands of
> the leaders of the party. I belong to none of these new leagues. I belong
> to only one league, and that league is good enough for me. It is called
> the Conservative party (loud applause) and as a member of the
> Conservative party I am anxious to support the leaders of the Conserva-
> tive party (hear, hear) and when Mr Balfour and Mr Chamberlain have
> agreed that a particular course of action is the best for the cause which I
> have at heart, then, as a member of the Conservative party, I feel that in
> any little way I can I ought to support them (hear, hear and applause).
> After all, the question of tactics should be left to the generals. It is not
> for the common soldier to assert himself whatever his private opinions
> on the question of tactics may be.

Few politicians would have made such an uncomplicated statement of
unquestioning loyalty, but the same point was repeated in relation to the
government's licensing policy: he did not know what it would be, but was
prepared to trust that a Conservative government would do the right thing.
Fewer politicians still would have stuck to this view of politics over 30 years
or more, as Sanders did. Criticism of the leaders of the party or of major
elements of its policy were not to be heard either in his home or in his
diary. The reason for such total loyalty was twofold, as he explained at
Bridgwater:[20]

> I am quite ready to support the tactics that Mr Balfour and Mr
> Chamberlain have thought most necessary for the welfare of the party,

because I think we ought to attach the very greatest importance to the unity of the Unionist party (applause). We must remember that it is not only this fiscal question that we have before us, but that there are other social questions as well, and that for the dealing with those other questions the unity of the party is absolutely essential. Of course, our first object is to keep the Conservatives in, but, perhaps, as important an object is to keep the other side out.

Loyalty was thus to leaders – in the plural as representing the top echelons of the entire party, but loyalty was first to the party itself, as a contemporary commentator noted:[21]

In a word, he is for the party first and last, for Unionism as he understands it, for Unionism as the instrument of sober considered progress, upon familiar lines, yielding here a little and there a little to the fierce clamour of the new time with its new, strange voices, but keeping ever to the great trunk road of which Pitt was the engineer in the days of long ago.

With this attitude to his party, the 'team-game' aspect of politics came easily to him; his attitude no doubt helped to make him a good whip and a good party manager. In the convention of the day, he talked of Liberals as 'the rads' (radicals) and, although there was little personal antipathy, there was a deep institutional and traditional hostility. This partially explains the ambiguous attitude of Sanders, and of other Conservatives who shared his views, towards the Lloyd George Coalition. He was all in favour of an electoral arrangement which would help to keep his party in power, but was not keen on his party making sacrifices. The distribution of coupons for the 1918 election was a great advantage to the Conservatives over the whole country, but it meant that some constituencies had to be sacrificed to the Liberals, and he did not like enforcing this compromise, as Maclachlan recalled:[22]

Deputation after deputation came pouring in from constituencies whose candidatures had been assigned to Lloyd George Liberals. At last, after one particularly painful interview, Sir Robert Sanders, looking thoroughly upset, turned to the writer and said, 'You must see any further deputations there may be. I won't be a party to turning down any more of these good fellows.'

He clearly identified completely with the local party leaders and – in this case – sympathised with them too much. As he had said when first introduced to his Bridgwater supporters: 'I believe we are all on one side.'

Within this general loyalty to the party, there were naturally different feelings towards different Conservatives. If he had heroes, then they were men like Walter Long and others of that political style, although he also had great admiration for Andrew Bonar Law and for Stanley Baldwin, his Harrow contemporary. The few politicians for whom he had no time at all were the ambitious careerists, in his own party especially Churchill and F.E. Smith. He did not much like Asquith, while for Lloyd George there was a sort of amused admiration, and a total distrust.

The diary which Sanders began to keep after he was elected to the Commons in 1910 was not his only diary and not his first. He kept a diary of hunting and one of his war experiences: all were quite separate and so the diary in which he recorded political events was exclusively a political diary. It was written up about once a fortnight, although less often in times of parliamentary recess and more often in times of political crisis. For most of his political career, he was close to sources of information and gossip, so much of this was recorded, but he clearly felt no obligation to fill the diary if current news did not interest him much. The result is that the diary, spanning entries from 1910 to 1935, covers only just over 300 pages in manuscript. It is therefore possible to print it in full here, as a complete historical record.[23] Along with the diary were kept a number of political letters and, where relevant to the material in the diary, they have been inserted in the text at the appropriate place.

Any diarist shows a bias towards some sources of information and to some subjects. It may be as well to indicate what overt interests were influential in the selection of material here. Sanders' personal concern was mainly with general political matters, and with the organisation of party politics in particular. The Whip's Office, the Central Office and committees of the National Union therefore provided most of his sources of information. However, much was also gleaned from casual conversation with other Members of Parliament, of all parties. It is for these reasons that, after his retirement in 1929, the sources of information dried up and the diary becomes much less informative. The areas of policy in which Sanders specialised were electoral, agricultural, and military, all areas in which his interest had long pre-dated his arrival at the top in politics. Thus, he was speaking on proposals for electoral reform in 1913, long before he had any close connection with the Central Office, and he was concerned with the interests of the countryside long before and long after he was Minister of Agriculture. In relation to social matters, his attitude was slightly ambiguous, for while he favoured moderate and enlightened reform, he did not favour the identification of the party with the image of reform itself. In 1913, he voted for the principle of Women's Suffrage, but was pleased to see that it was defeated in the Commons, if only to show the militants that violence would not coerce parliament into action.[24] He was in favour of wages boards in agriculture in the same year, but was amused by the antics of the Unionist Social Reform Committee, who were trying to foist this policy on the party. In general, although he was no obscurantist opponent of social reform, he had little sympathy for its leading advocates, whether they were 'our Social Reformers' before 1914, or the 'Y.M.C.A.' in the 1920s. Reform might be necessary and desirable, but it need not be an ideal in itself.

Sanders' main concern, as befitted a man of action in the irritatingly sedentary occupation of politician, was with the practical rather than the ideal. He was little concerned with the intricacies of party dogma and much more with the actuality of what was being done or what might be done next.[25]

> He does not appeal to the gallery. He does not scan far horizons. He does not declare any vision of a promised land. He has no passionate fervour for humanity, and he is too honest to pretend to any. He is a practical politician, with no dithy-rambs. He loves the intricacies of the campaign more than the visionary gleam, the actual more than the potential, present facts more than future fancies. He is the man without a dream. But he is the type of man who brings the dreams of others to pass . . . Other men will prophesy; he will perform. Other men will create the atmosphere of change; he will give it form and change.

Thus, he was one of the few Conservatives of the 1920s who called the Labour party by that name rather than 'the socialists'. His attitude to 'the Labourmen' was generally one of amused tolerance rather than fear or panic. His own view of politics as a world where a tactical compromise had more importance than an abstract ideal gave him much in common with the early Labour leaders. He never attributed to them more extreme intentions than they actually had, and perhaps went too far the other way in assuming that they were simply career politicians: he remarked in 1920 that the only ambition of a Labour leader was to get himself a job in the government machine. Those who thought in terms of the clash of ideologies expected extreme measures from the Labour Government of 1924, but Sanders more correctly expected them to demonstrate their moderation rather than their socialism.

All of these attitudes are fully displayed in the diary itself, not through an overt selection of material, but through the informal selection process of any diarist. Information is evaluated by each politician in a different way, and the information recorded in this diary reflects Sanders himself, his environment, his background, and his friends. The man reflected in the diary was a politician of considerable ability and complete honesty, a highly partisan figure but one who saw no need to obscure or hide his partisanship. At the outset of his national career, a local observer summed him up this way:[26]

> Mr Sanders is a man of many friends, and even his bitterest political opponents readily pay tribute to the excellence of his motives, the sincerity of his beliefs, and the elusive personal charm which he possesses to so considerable degree. A man whose conduct and whose aims are regarded by common consent as above suspicion.

It is not surprising that he was a politician who was so highly respected by friends and opponents alike.

INTRODUCTION NOTES

1 Beatrice Webb, *Diaries 1924–32* (1956) and T. Wilson (ed.) *The Political Diaries of C.P. Scott* (1970).
2 I owe a very great deal to the Hon. Mrs V.E. Butler, firstly for allowing the publication of her father's diary and letters and especially for talking to me about her father.
3 Quoted in *The Times*, 27 February 1940.
4 Letter to the author 9 August 1973.
5 *Somerset County Gazette*, 18 July 1914.
6 J.M. McEwen, *Conservative and Unionist M.P.s 1910–1939*, London Univ. Ph.D. thesis, 1959, chapter IV.
7 After the 1911 reorganisation of the party organisation, the whips were responsible with Central Office district agents for the running of provincial divisions, and especially for the arrangement of parliamentary speakers for by-elections.
8 Letter from Younger to Sanders, see p. 200.
9 Chris Cook and John Ramsden, *By-Elections in British Politics*, pp. 14–21.
10 *The Times* 27 February 1940; the writer of this supplementary obituary of Lord Bayford was clearly Leigh Maclachlan, who had been Chief Organisation Officer at Central Office in 1918. He signed himself 'L.M.'
11 Sanders' Election Address for 1922 quoted Law's pledge approvingly.
12 K. Middlemas and J. Barnes, *Baldwin, a Biography*, pp. 250–277.
13 See p. 220.
14 *The Times*, 27 February 1940.
15 *Star*, 15 June 1914.
16 *Somerset County Gazette*, 18 July 1914.

17 *Bridgwater Mercury*, 9 December 1903.
18 See p. 35.
19 *Bridgwater Mercury*, 9 December 1903.
20. *Ibid.*
21 *Somerset County Gazette*, 18 July 1914.
22 *The Times*, 27 February 1940.
23 Only nineteen pages out of a total of 317 cover the diary's last six years. The bulk of the diary entries were made in 1911–14, 1917–23 and 1924–9. The only cut in the text has been the removal of two sentences relating to a purely family matter.
24 See p. 59.
25 *Somerset County Gazette*, 18 July 1914.
26 *Ibid.*

Chapter 1   1910 'No Compromise on budget or veto'

Monday 21 February   Opening ceremony, etc. King's Speech shortest and most ungrammatical on record. Noticeable that on question of Lords veto the words 'in the opinion of my advisers' were introduced. On question of Standing Orders the old rule about interference of peers in elections abolished without a division. On address Balfour made a party speech, clever but little in it. Then Asquith announced course of business putting off Veto Bill until after finance. Stated that he had not asked and never intended to ask for guarantee from King before introducing such a measure. Speech rather coldly received by his own side. Then Redmond who rubbed it in that whatever Asquith may have meant by his Albert Hall speech the impression he gave was that he would not continue in office without those guarantees which he had not got. On that impression Asquith got the Irish vote and that impression was never contradicted till now. Redmond said that if Asquith would go for veto before finance Irish would support budget, but he did not definitely say they would otherwise vote against it. He finished by repeating what he said in Ireland, i.e. that course foreshadowed by Asquith would not have Irish support. A Labour member then moved adjournment on ground that the Labour party meant to hold a meeting to discuss what he was to say. Agreed to after some discussion. Much excitement in lobby. D. Hall made some comment to me about the Government. John Burns turned round and said: 'Oh no; the wicket is a bit sticky but we are still in.' On to Carlton to dine. General excitement there, but on the whole impression is that Redmond will be squared.

Tuesday 22 February   Lunch at Constitutional Club to those who won seats. Balfour made fine speech. Promised assistance to Government in details of finance, but no compromise on budget or veto. On to House. Debate on address continued. F.E. Smith in good form, but unnecessarily provocative. Labour members seem to hate him. Noticeable the keenness apparent on our side and the inertness on the other. But gossip is all against an immediate defeat of the Government.

Wednesday 23 February Austen Chamberlain's Tariff Amendment.
Rather a pompous speech. Kettle an Irishman most amusing. Announced
Irish would not vote either way. They want protection against England.[1]

Thursday 24 February Wind up of T.R. debate. Mond very effective on
Radical side. The big guns rather disappointing. Rads only got 31
majority.

Monday 28 February Arrived rather late and was not present for
speeches of Asquith and Redmond. But heard Dalziel, Healy and Lloyd
George. The upshot of the whole thing is that the Govvernment give in
to the Irish all along the line. Estimates etc. are to be introduced and will
take up all the time till Easter. Then veto resolutions in both Houses.
Budget indefinitely postponed. Meanwhile the income tax is not being
collected. Asquith said rather vaguely and Lloyd George more distinctly
that the Government would resign unless they were assured that their
veto proposals would become law this session. General doubt as to
whether they will stick to that pledge. But for the present the Irish are
probably squared – Hugh Cecil said to me on the way out: 'I am afraid
the Government have scored.'

Easter, 27 March Things have been very quiet in politics. Estimates etc.
quietly passed. Few divisions taken. Navy estimates show increase of five
millions. That made Beresford's attack on Admiralty fall rather flat.[2] The
Government a good deal heckled over non-collection of income tax, but
stuck to their guns. They only take vote for Civil Service supply up to
middle of May, a strong hint that they expect to be out by then. Veto
resolutions published Tuesday before Easter. Much what was expected,
except that Speaker is made sole judge as to whether a measure is financial
or not.

Tuesday 29 March Veto resolutions. Asquith very good. Balfour made
some good points in return, but rather flippant. A young Welshman,
Edgar Jones, was rather effective. Munro Ferguson spoke against the
veto but seemed to speak for himself alone. Rufus Isaacs put up for first
time as Solicitor General, very disappointing.

Wednesday 30 March Veto resolutions still on. F.E. Smith on the whole
the best debating speech of the session. Hugh Cecil very eloquent at the
end, and defended hereditary principle with an evident sincerity that
alone made such defence possible in the House. Birrell forcible and
good.

Wednesday 6 April Veto resolutions mainly debated by lawyers. Somewhat tedious. Tariff Reform debate during private members' time produced a speech from Storey which cornered the Labour members very effectively.[3] They were very visibly perturbed and published a very feeble defence in *The Times* subsequently. Tariff reform beaten by 33 votes.

Thursday 7 April First veto resolution carried by over 100. The end of the debate quite farcical. The second part of the resolution was not discussed at all. After eleven a debate on milk clauses of L.C.C. bill. Strongly opposed by agricultural members and defeated by four votes. Represented as vote for impure milk. Really vote against giving L.C.C. powers which ought to be exercised by Government or not at all.[4]

Friday 8 April Poor Law Bill on lines of minority report. Ormsby Gore made excellent maiden speech against it. Balfour blessed it more than any one else. Asquith mildly and John Burns rather emphatically against it. The latter very proud of his own work at L.G.B. Quite absurdly so. Usual conflicting rumours all this week. Generally believed that Irish have been squared and mean to support budget. Price of their support unknown. An election in June is now the usual prophecy. No one expects an election to make much difference in state of parties except Henry Hobhouse who is quite confident that Conservatives will get a majority because the people will resent Irish dictation.[5]

Monday 11 April Brought off my maiden speech about 10 o'clock. Felt very frightened but got on all right.

Wednesday 13 April Speech by Balfour at United Club luncheon declaring for a partially elected Second Chamber and reserving question of referendum. Labour members proposal to reverse Osborne judgement talked out.

Thursday 14 April Last of veto resolutions carried. Asquith made a public announcement on motion for adjournment that he would go to the King in the event of the Lords not accepting the veto resolutions. It looked as if there was going to be a row on the way out. The Irish were excited and some of them had a drop of drink in them. However, nothing actually came of it.

Monday 18 April Motion allotting time for budget. This was to have been the crucial day of the session. But Redmond was squared by Asquith's announcement. So it was known that the Government was safe. The squabble between O'Brien and Lloyd George came on. O'Brien had published a memorandum purporting to explain concessions on budget promised by Lloyd George with proviso that Cabinet must be consulted first. Lloyd George had said the statements were a lie and a breach of confidence. O'Brien spoilt his case by being too long. Lloyd George made much of the breach of confidence but hardly attempted to show that the statements were untrue. Tim Healy made a very effective speech on the relations between Redmond and the Government. Incidentally he went back on Home Rule. Opinion now puts off dissolution till July.

Wednesday 27 April   Budget passed third reading. Hustled through whole thing in three days. I spoke for a few minutes in Committee on Land Clauses.

Friday 6 May   King Edward VII died – universal feeling that the national misfortune is increased by the peculiar political circumstances of the time. The opinion generally expressed that his death was accelerated if not actually caused by political worry. Vague stories that the Queen said to Churchill: 'This is all your work.' New King and Queen reported to hold strong Conservative opinions. Papers on both sides agree that the crisis that was imminent and the general election are sure to be postponed. Compromise on Lords question urged in many quarters.

Monday 16 May   Attended reception of coffin in Westminster Hall. An impressive ceremony. The feeling of regret among all classes in London seems deeper than when the Queen died. Even children in East End show some kind of mourning. In Somerset there is less of this – Club dinners, etc. continue to be held. The County Show took place on the two days before the funeral.

Wednesday 8 June   House met again – quiet and dull. The idea of a conference on the Lords question much boomed in the papers. *The Times* especially keen on it. No one on either side seems to know much about what the future is to be. Jack Sandars prophesies a non-contentious budget, an autumn session and a January election.[6] Hood told me he did not like holding meetings as he did not know what to say. Tried to get something out of Liberal members – Trevelyan said that only row at present was likely to be over the King's Declaration business.[7] Walker from Melton did not believe in any compromise on ground that Balfour really did not see that the Liberal Party had any grievances.

One or two bits of gossip. It is said that McKenna owes his present position to the fact that he is an illegitimate son of Sir C. Dilke. Probably a mere fable, but it is difficult to explain advancement of such a very third rate man. Good story about Granard – his brother officers wrote a bogus

letter from C.B. offering him position in the Government. Granard
hurried off to C.B. C.B. said he never wrote, but that he did want a Jew
for Master of the Horse and gave him the job. Another yarn was that C.B.
appointed Whiteley his Chief Whip owing to a letter going to him that was
meant for Whitley – Whiteley accepted offer by return and so matter was
concluded.[8]

Monday 20 June Prolonged dullness in the house. Only interesting
feature Sir E. Grey's defence of Roosevelt and defiance of the Radicals
over both Egypt and Crete. Meanwhile the veto conference is an accomplished fact. Ted Gully told me he did not think anything could possibly
come of it.[9] His ground was that the rank and file of the Radical party
would not stand any modification of the Government's former position. As
regards the Irish party Lord Rathbone told me that when an election came
O'Brien would about hold his own, but no more. He predicted that Tim
Healy would lose his seat.

Tuesday 12 July Dullness has continued. Budget imposes no fresh
taxation. Introduced in a declamatory speech by Lloyd George. He gave
very little information about finance. Radical and Irish members very
nervous about the conference – held meetings and decided to memorialise
Asquith. However Elibank told them that was unnecessary as a satisfactory announcement would be made. Accordingly Asquith announced that
an autumn session would be held and the later stages of the budget would
be postponed till then. This enables the Irishmen to keep some hold on the
Government till they know if they are going to be put in the cart. I sat next
Hood at an Agents' dinner and tried to impress on him that the
Conservative backbenchers would be ready to support a wholly elected
second chamber. He said one drawback to that would be that big peers
would not subscribe largely to party funds if they had to pay election
expenses for themselves as well. F.E. Smith wrote a good letter to *The
Times* urging a settlement of the question on lines that would remove the
Radical grievance of the one-sidedness of the Lords. Conference continues
to meet, but secret as to what is going on is well kept. A little mild
excitement just now over the Woman's Suffrage Bill. It is on quite
moderate lines, practically extending municipal franchise to Parliamentary
elections. Very powerful speech against it from F.E. Smith. Quite a
masterpiece.

Wednesday July 26 Spoke on education estimates. Stage fright now
departed. A late sitting and many divisions. Got Government majority
down to 27 on one occasion.

Thursday 26 July A first rate speech by Montagu on introducing the Indian budget. Quite one of the best things of the session. Thoroughly down on the sedition-mongers. Members on both sides much perturbed over the bill to alter the King's Declaration. The No Popery drum is being beaten very hard, and in some parts of the country there certainly is strong and ignorant feeling against any alteration. Very lucky thing that the Liberal party has to make the alteration.

Friday 29 July Declaration Bill passed through all stages by large majorities. Tone of debate good throughout. Birrell made an amusing but most injudicious speech. The opposition came from Ulster and Liverpool and a few Cornish members on the Radical side. The Protestant party in the country conducted a very vigorous agitation against the Bill, and many members were a good deal frightened about it. It will probably lose the Government a few seats. On the eve of the adjournment Asquith announced that the conference was to continue and that a further announcement about it would be made in the autumn. A little chafing from the Radicals, but not a good deal. And so to the country.

CHAPTER 1 NOTES

1 A tariff reform amendment to the Address was proposed each year, with no real hope of success. Kettle suggested that its purpose was to commit not Parliament but the Unionist Party and its leader Arthur Balfour; Austen Chamberlain's motive was not simply 'to nail his colours to the mast, but to nail his captain to the mast'. *Hansard*, House of Commons, 23 February 1910.
2 Admiral Lord Charles Beresford, Conservative M.P. intermittently 1874–1900 and from 1902. A constant critic of Liberal naval policy and an inveterate advocate of naval building.
3 Samuel Storey had been Liberal M.P. for Sunderland 1881–1895 but had been elected as an Independent Conservative for the same constituency on the tariff reform issue in January 1910. He was a staunch tariff reformer and his constituency was one in which the Conservatives were thought to be especially well-organised to resist the Labour appeal for working-class votes. He retired from Parliament in December 1910.
4 This debate was on a motion to delete from the L.C.C. (General Powers) Bill a clause that would have given to the Medical Officers of Health powers to sample and control supplies of milk to London. Objections by Unionist agriculturalists were to such interference in

their industry, but there were several London M.P.s and progressive M.P.s on the Unionist side who voted with the government. *Hansard*, House of Commons, 5 April 1910.

5   This is Henry Hobhouse, Conservative M.P. 1885–1906 and Chairman of the Somerset County Council 1904–1924; not to be confused with L.T. Hobhouse or others of the family who had remained Liberals after the split of 1886.

6   Jack Sandars was Balfour's Private Secretary and political adviser whose influence in Unionist strategy was considerable (see Sir Charles Petrie, *The Powers Behind the Prime Minister*). 'Hood' was Sir Alexander Acland-Hood, Conservative M.P. since 1892 and Chief Whip 1902–1911, subsequently the 1st Lord St. Audries.

7   On June 13, Asquith did in fact announce that the government would introduce legislation to amend the King's Declaration on Accession, so as to make it less offensive to Roman Catholics.

8   Stories such as these circulated widely around and about Campbell-Bannerman but all of them are probably untrue. See John Wilson, *C.B., A Life of Sir Henry Campbell-Bannerman*, p. 464.

9   E.W.K. Gully, Secretary to the Speaker.

Chapter 2   1911 'A good deal of rough talk'

Wednesday 8 February   When Parliament assembled in November 1910 for the autumn session it was known that the conference had failed and Asquith announced an immediate dissolution. As to the reason of the failure there were many reports. The *Daily Mail* stated that the Unionist peers stated that they would rather be abolished by the country than by the conference. *The Times* had a series of articles saying that the real difficulty was Home Rule and suggesting that the Unionists should agree to some form of it. Hood told me that it was on that question that the conference broke down. Before the dissolution Lansdowne declared in Lords his programme of reform and referendum. Balfour corroborated it in a speech to the N.U. at Nottingham. Subsequently at the Albert Hall he declared for a referendum on tariff reform. That upset the *Morning Post* gang. Nicol Dunn of the *Manchester Courier* told me beforehand that such a declaration would carry Manchester. It did not. The net result of the election was No Change. After it many attacks were made on Hood and circumstantial reports put about that he would resign. He soon announced he had no intention of doing so. Lord Rothschild said he would not find money for the party as long as Hood continued.[1] A committee to look into Unionist organisation was appointed. Much good may it do! The weak point at present is Hughes.[2]

I had a fairly easy election and my majority was 1,381. Floods and rain made it very disagreeable.

House reassembled on 6 February. Colourless King's Speech. First amendment to address moved tonight by Austen Chamberlain. Quite a good speech but rest of debate not on a high level. The treaty between Canada and U.S. the great topic.[3] Little gossip about the veto. What the Lords will do probably not yet decided. Rumour says Lloyd George has cancer in the throat – don't believe it myself.

Friday 10 February   Tariff Reform Amendment defeated by 102, the Irish voting with the Government. A dull debate in which the best speech was Asquith's. He scored effectively off Chamberlain by showing that a quotation from Sir Wilfrid Laurier was unfounded.

24

Thursday 16 February   Debate on Address ended last night. Dull on the whole. Was redeemed by the Home Rule debate on the last night. That was good throughout. Asquith declared Home Rule would be the first business after the veto. Redmond accepted his definition of Home Rule, which was somewhat vague. Redmond and Carson made very good speeches. Birrell coarse and absurd. Young W.H. Redmond made his debut. Too long but quite good.[4]

Friday 3 March   Second reading of Parliament Bill carried last night by majority of 125. Debates on subject dull. Everyone wanted to speak on the subject. G. Locker Lampson got up over 30 times and was not called on. F.E. Smith made a good speech on first reading. So did Churchill. Balfour on second reading caused a 'scene' by accusing the Radical party of fraud. A meeting of Conservative members was called to urge on the party leaders the necessity of a sweeping reform of the House of Lords. It was adjourned to know if the leaders would like to have those views presented to them. At the adjourned meeting Hood announced that the Bill was practically complete, that it maintained the hereditary peers in consider-able numbers, and that the stability of the Crown depended on the maintenance of the hereditary principle. He therefore deprecated our committee passing resolutions. Hugh Cecil suggested that any one who wished could write to Lord Lansdowne on the subject. Eventually the meeting was adjourned by an unanimous vote. But there is a strong feeling among back bench Conservatives at least that these half measures of reform are likely to be a source of weakness rather than strength to the party.

Thursday 23 March   Things in the House have been dull on the whole. One all night sitting on the Budget. That was Churchill's fault. He was left in command by Asquith. Everything went well till about midnight, Simon doing the Government case very well. Then Churchill came in and tried to bully with the consequence that no more work was done. On estimates things were made rather nasty for the Government both over the Tony-pandy affair and over a curious circular that was issued by Holmes, the chief inspector of the Education Office. The circular, which was marked confidential, advised local authorities to give inspectorships to University men only. Sam Hoare got hold of this and quoted it in the House. Runciman very angry but came out of it poorly. Much gossip about new peerages. Haldane and Strachey marked down. Lord Claud Hamilton told me that he was informed by a man who went to the same tailor as Haldane that he had ordered his coronation robes. Balfour made a very brilliant speech one night about arbitration with U.S. Grey had advocated it a few nights before in a debate on Naval Estimates. Balfour strongly endorsed

Grey's words and got all the Radical side cheering him, then went on to point out that even if we had such a treaty we could not reduce our naval estimates which were in no way directed against U.S. All very well done. Pike Pease told me that Balfour only decided to speak five minutes before he rose. Arthur Lee had urged him to do so on the ground that American papers were commenting on his silence on the subject.

On Wednesday 22 March Hood sent for me and asked me if I would become one of the Unionist Whips. I was a good deal surprised as my time in the House is only a little over a year. I believe I owe it mainly to the fact that I was a successful Master of the Devon and Somerset. Hood probably considered that rather a good trial. This was kept quiet for two days. The other whips treated me very nicely, Harry Foster and Pease especially. On Friday I went to see Balfour in his room. He was very nice and charming but said nothing whatever about what he wanted me to do. He got on about history of the House of Commons and discoursed on that. When I was going to see him Balcarres said: 'Remember in dealing with him always tell him what you want done, never ask what he thinks it ought to be.' Pease's hint to me on a whip's duties was: 'Always let a man talk. Even if nothing comes of it, it relieves his feelings.' Appointment gazetted on Friday night. *The Times* and *Morning Post* rather complimentary next morning.

Thursday 30 March   Settling down to whip's duties. Generally congratulated in the House. No one seems to object at which I am rather surprised. Week spent on Revenue Bill. Discussion mainly on Land Taxes. Government had a clause down to exempt Dewsbury, Runciman's constituency, from higher scale of licence duties when the borough boundaries were extended. Such an obvious job that they had to withdraw it.

Thursday 6 April   Committee on Parliament Bill running last three days. A series of amendments of no vast importance have run rather strong. No back bench Radicals speak, but it is noticeable that their front bench men usually say something stupid which prolongs discussion that would otherwise fizzle out. One or two incidents to record. One night on motion for adjournment Malcolm raised question of new sash that officers had to get at considerable expense. One member after another on both sides of House attacked it, Hood among others. Jack Seely announced that in deference to wishes of House it should be reconsidered. So far so good. Next day it came out that this sash was a particular fad of the King's and that Malcolm was aware of the fact. Sash was withdrawn, but the King wrote a long letter to Tullibardine on subject. Another night during the debate on Parliament Bill one of our people moved an amendment that third reading of a Money Bill should be taken by ballot. Several supported motion, Hugh Cecil among others. Then Balfour got up and made a most powerful speech against motion, vehemently cheered by Radicals. In spite of that 80 of our people voted for it. Much annoyance expressed next day and whips were appealed to to get Balfour to say beforehand if he objects to any amendments. The answer is that Balfour does not make up his mind what he is going to say till he actually gets up.

Banbury has got a strongish case against the Treasury. He asked a question as to why Railway Companies had been asked to defer payment of income tax till after April 1. Hobhouse replied that it was owing to mistake of a subordinate. That all nonsense. The object is to get the money out of the old sinking fund and use it for the next budget. Speaker refused to allow adjournment to be moved, but matter to come up again. In various minor points we have certainly scored points off the Government lately.

Considerable rag last night about Clough, M.P. for Skipton Division of Yorks. He had hit a woman after his election, then made a real canting apology and finally brought an action for libel in the course of which F.E. Smith got home some nasty ones during cross-examination. Last night as he came out of the division lobby a crowd of our boys waited for him and greeted him with cheers and cries of 'Clough'. Considerable confusion in consequence and Churchill complained to Speaker who said it was most reprehensible. Radicals most annoyed.

Thursday 27 April Committee on Parliament Bill still running – Curzon made rather a strong speech at one of Pike Pease's Monday dinners, strongly urging the need of a more definite policy for the party. He hinted that the Bill for reform of Lords shortly to be introduced was as much as the Lords would at present stand, but that they might no doubt be eventually pushed further. Nothing very exciting in the House. One or two very late sittings went off quietly on the whole. Some dissatisfaction on our side at Balfour making an arrangement across the floor of the House as to amount of progress to be made in two days. Balfour's object was to get the Home Rule amendment discussed in daytime. That debate ought to have lasted longer. It concluded at dinner time when any number of our men were anxious to speak. On Thursday 20th Asquith came in after dinner in such a state that he could hardly speak two words. An amendment about the Protestant succession came on. Isaacs and Samuel were with Asquith on Treasury Bench. Balfour remarked to Lyttleton that the defence of the Protestant succession was confided to two sober Jews and a drunken Christian.

Wednesday 10 May Last day of Report stage of Parliament Bill. Whole discussion has been dull as possible. Last Thursday Lloyd George introduced insurance scheme. Spoke for two hours and a quarter and seemed none the worse. A great effort. Bill received with enthusiasm all round. Our people vied with each other in promises of support. Whether it will be so popular in the country remains to be seen. That may be doubtful, but it ought to do a lot of good.

Went down to help in North Devon election. Our people sanguine of victory at first and things seemed going very well. But when I returned just before the poll they were not so hopeful – we reduced majority by 400 but got well beaten. The organisation there very bad. As the perfection of Liberal Unionist arrangements is always rubbed into us that is rather quaint.

Lord Lansdowne's scheme for reform of House of Lords has fallen very flat. Hood says the Lords' tactics will be to move one or two important amendments and try and get every concession possible, but eventually to cave in. We cannot fight another election on the peers question. He prophesies an election in about two years. He wants the Insurance Bill to go through quickly and thinks when it gets into working order it will injure the Radicals. The financial part of Home Rule will also cause trouble.

Radical agitation both on small holdings and appointment of magistrates. On former question Carrington has given in and appointed or promised to appoint six new commissioners for gingering purposes.[5] As to magistrates Lord Chancellor much stiffer and Rads have got little change out of him so far.[6]

Tuesday 23 May   Budget introduced a week ago. Proposal to pay members £400 a year. Otherwise colourless. Amery made a good speech on it advocating Tariff Reform. Nothing much going on. Visit of German Emperor and of Colonial premiers attracting more attention than politics proper. Yesterday a committee meeting at which about 150 Conservatives were present met to discuss Insurance Bill. General idea that Bill will make a lot of enemies. Our people dare not oppose it, but hope to make party capital out of it. Not really running very straight on the subject.

Tuesday 20 June   A very slack time in the House – Whitsuntide, Ascot and then Coronation just coming on. All important business barred and seldom even a division. Meanwhile rumour is abroad that there will be a general election in July. Opinion on our side very divided as to what course the Lords ought to take on the Veto Bill. Announced today that Hood is to be a Coronation peer. Balcarres becomes Chief Whip. Steel Maitland is to look after the Central Office, while Hood remains in charge of party finance. Whether the division of authority will answer remains to be seen, but they are each of them likely to do well at their own job.[7]

Thursday 28 June[8] House at work again after the coronation. Debate on Declaration of London yesterday and today. Quite a high level. Finlay made excellent speech on our side. On the whole we have best of the debate, but the division is to be on party lines so Government Majority assumed. House of Lords discussing Veto Bill and very militant. Curious situation as to our party in Commons. A few very keen for fighting every inch – majority against it. Elibank told Balcarres that he had made no preparations for an election. Randolf Baker canvassing men with small majorities finds most of them think they would lose their seats if an early election took place. Other members with good majorities object to expenses. Courthorpe told me an election would produce a sort of strike. Fortescue showed me a whip sent round to some peers asking them to vote against all proposals for altering the powers or constitution of House of Lords. Nearly snapped the Government on Monday night – Radical majority reduced to 32. Would have run them closer had not some of our people been unable to understand mysterious notices sent to them to come to a certain spot at a certain time. Notice given today of guillotine resolution on Insurance Bill. Rather a strong measure to take after Lloyd George's original proposals for conciliation. Steel Maitland much puffed in press on taking over his Central Office duties. Rather a pity for him to go in for that style of advertisement.

Wednesday July 12   Careful investigation shows that about five out of seven of our party in House of Commons are against any policy that would cause an election. Now we learn that Balfour has been informed that the King is ready to create peers. It is desired to find out whether most of our people in the Commons wish the matter to be pressed till peers are actually created. A great many of the peers themselves are anxious that it should be done. In Commons there is much division. Walter Long is rather strong against their being created. Sir H. Craik very strong in same direction. Meanwhile Insurance Bill goes on. Guillotine idea dropped. As result of five days Clause 8 is reached. George thinks he can square the doctors but they are holding out on question of limit of income for contributors. His plan seems to be to postpone perpetually all thorny questions, but he has got in a tangle once or twice already. The divisions are mainly on party lines and the Government whips are on all the time. I have spent a week at the bye election in West Somerset. There the Insurance Bill is the one thing the audiences care about.

Tuesday 18 July   Yesterday as we were having a confab in Balcarres' room Balfour came in after much hesitation. He thought Bal was engaged, half opened the door then drew back and stood in the passage. He is quite in the dark as to what is going to be done. The Parliament Bill comes back to House of Commons on Monday next, and Balfour actually thinks that Asquith will move to accept our minor amendments while refusing the exclusion of Home Rule. He says that is their obvious tactics. Balfour has had no communication from the King or Asquith or Elibank as to what course the government mean to take. This Bal told us quite positively. Page Croft & Co. got rather laughed at for calling a meeting of stalwarts to urge the peers to die in the last ditch. Tullibardine and Gilbert Parker attended as spies. Banbury in chair. Only about 35 present and they did not all vote. I think on the whole the predominant feeling is that the Lords had better hold out and face the actual creation of peers. Bal however is against it on the ground that it would facilitate Plural Voting, Home Rule, etc. if a really large number were created. I had a talk with Hugh Cecil this morning. He is all for letting them be created. He loves the idea of a Constitutional row. He always did, even at Oxford. He says our rotten point is not to have had a clearly thought out plan of campaign all through, as the Radicals have had. He is very anxious to get up a violent agitation in Ulster in the autumn and have a secession of the northern counties worked out in every detail. He thinks someone of the position of Milner or Selborne ought to go over to run the secession.[9]

Still on Clause 8 of Insurance Bill.

Monday 24 July   Have been in West Somerset helping at the election last few days. Got Boles in by 604, a result which showed nothing much either way. Last Thursday Asquith wrote an open letter to Balfour saying he had the King's consent to creation of sufficient peers to force the Parliament Bill through. Various meetings were held on Friday among leaders on our side, and among Conservative peers. Balfour and Lansdowne want Lords to submit. Carson, F.E. Smith in Commons and Halsbury, Salisbury, Willoughby and others in Lords are for holding out. The majority of leaders is for giving in. Overwhelming back bench majority for holding out. Today Commons met to consider Lords' amendments. Asquith was deliberately howled down by our side. Hugh Cecil, Goulding and Remnant were the most persistent. Finally Asquith gave it up and moved that amendments be considered. Balfour followed. The Liberals heard him all right, but he was not very effective. Then Grey got up. Our people did not interrupt him. But he merely buttered Asquith and then moved adjournment of debate. Thereupon F.E. Smith rose. Rads would not hear him and at last the Speaker adjourned the House without question put. General opinion on our side that the row was a mistake.

Wednesday 26 July   Row renewed yesterday at question time. Hugh Cecil howled at during question time, and a good deal of rough talk. Tim Healy, who took his seat last week, said the row was the best thing the Tory party ever did. Joe Chamberlain also approved of. Smith and Carson had warned Balcarres through Ashley that it would be no use for Balfour or whips to interfere. Cripps, [illegible] and other old members of the party summoned a meeting at which Mark Lockwood proposed to write to Asquith expressing regret, but that was withdrawn as the idea had hardly a supporter. Eventually the meeting did nothing but pass a vote of confidence in Balfour. Our 'Forward' party is busy getting men to go to the Halsbury dinner tonight. Bal says whips are not to go. In Whips' room Pike and Ashley are for giving in, rest of us for standing out, Bridgeman very strongly so. Lansdowne has written an open letter to the Lords counselling giving in. Late last night Balfour published letter supporting this. Austen Chamberlain told me he did not know Balfour was writing it. It will make the position of the Halsbury dinner speakers somewhat difficult. The *Evening News* last night spoke of it as the Anti-Balfour Dinner.

Very grave rumours about the French and German business. Wilson of the General Staff has been to Paris to consult. He told Charlie that the French did not trust our Government a yard. He was called to the Cabinet to explain things. He says the only one with any guts is Lloyd George. Grey is the feeblest of the lot.[10]

Thursday 28 July[11] Bal told us after questions yesterday that we must not make too much of Balfour's letter. He wrote it mainly from a feeling of loyalty to Lansdowne. He regards the whole thing as a matter of tactics, and he did not want to stop people from going to the Halsbury dinner. If the result of Halsbury & Co's action is the creation of a limited number of peers he does not think it would do any harm; but he refuses to be a party to a 'deal'. Curzon is anxious to vote with the Government to defeat Halsbury. Bal told him that if he did so he should never be allowed to speak on a Conservative platform again. It is a fact that several peers have told Lansdowne they were ready to do so if he wished it. Smith and Carson both gave the assurance that at the dinner there should be profuse expressions of loyalty to Balfour. There were, and all the speakers professed their wish to follow him and Lansdowne when this was over.

Thursday 3 August Government still holds up Parliament Bill. Balfour announced at question time yesterday that he will move Vote of Censure on Monday on account of unconstitutional advice given to the King. Lansdowne on behalf of Curzon has given notice of same motion in the Lords for Tuesday. Our people are very pleased. Austen Chamberlain said that a resolution in practically identical terms had been suggested at a conference of the Forwards that morning. Morocco business is still critical, though the papers are very quiet about it. Bal told us that when Germany first sent a ship to Agadir Grey wanted to send a British ship there at once, but the Cabinet overruled him. Report current that if Lowther retires Jack Seely will be the next Speaker.

Saturday 5 August Now said to be settled that the Parliament Bill goes to Lords on Wednesday next without creation of Peers and takes its chance. It looks like being a very close thing. Lord Morley claims about 76. F.E. Smith told me the Forwards could raise 90. The Bishops an unknown factor. Jack Sandars told the Bishop of London that if the Bishops voted for the Parliament Bill they need not expect Conservative support on Disestablishment question. Had a talk to Pike Pease yesterday about party affairs. He believes Balfour resents Austen and F.E.'s business a great deal. He thinks it puts Austen out of the running for the reversion of leadership, and expects Walter Long to succeed. He told me a curious episode at which he had been present. At a L.U. confab after the election of 1906 Joe Chamberlain proposed that they should get Balfour turned out of the Conservative leadership and Walter Long put in his place. Lord Lansdowne immediately jumped on the proposal, and nothing came of it.

Wednesday 9 August Vote of censure debate fell rather flat. No row of any sort. Same sort of debate last night on consideraation of Lords' amendments. Hugh Cecil and Bonar Law made exceedingly good speeches. I hear Willoughby de B counts on over 110 Die Hards. Lord Burnham is betting against his getting 60. My informant is Raymond Greene. One hundred ought to win. With regard to payment of members which comes on Thursday I have been trying to get our leaders to make some sort of statement that they do not hold themselves bound to continue it. Both Austen Chamberlain and Arthur Lee say we cannot make any such announcement. Bal quite sees the point of it and has promised to speak to Balfour about it. Steel Maitland is anxious to poach some of the £400 a year for Central Office purposes.[12]

Tuesday 15 August Bill carried in Lords by seventeen last Thursday night. Thirty-one Unionists voted with government. Also ten Bishops. Query: have the Bishops done a deal with the Government over Disestablishment? Lord Morley announced on Thursday that if the Bill was not carried the Government would create peers enough to outvote any possible combination. Willoughby got 114 votes all right but it was not enough. Morley's threat turned more Unionists than was anticipated. Rosebery voted with Government. There was a sort of scramble for last word in the debate. Curzon, Halsbury, Rosebery, Selborne, all had a few last words. I think there was a good deal of court pressure to avoid the creation of peers. Payment of members is practically through. Liberal

party unanimously supported. The joy of the Labour party is almost
indecent. Our people give no hint of an intention to alter it.

A final touch to the Parliament Bill. Balfour left London for Gastein on
Thursday morning before the division in the Lords. It was known, however
that he would have to curtail his cure so as to be back in time for a golf
handicap.

The session was to have ended on 18 August. But a new sensation was
caused on Thursday 17th by the threat of a general railway strike. During
the strike of transport workers going on in London and Liverpool,
Churchill took a pretty firm attitude sending troops wherever they were
wanted. Granet of the Midland told me that he had been to see Churchill
about the prospect of a railway strike and the latter told him that he was
ready to use every soldier to protect the lines, and would call out the
reserves if necessary. On the 17th the Government tried its hand at
intervention to prevent a strike coming off. Asquith met the directors and
suggested a Royal Commission to inquire into working of conciliation
boards. Directors accepted. Asquith made same offer to men. They
declined. At 5:30 they informed the press that they had sent out notices for
a general strike. Then Ramsay Macdonald informed Elibank that he
wished to move a vote of censure on the Government. After that much
confab with Lloyd George. Asquith had not been in the House for several
days, his voice being bad. About 8 o'clock, on motion for adjournment,
George in answer to Macdonald explained that Asquith's Royal Commission meant a small body to sit and report at once. Macdonald said there
had been a misunderstanding and hoped that conferences might go on.
However, the strike started at midnight on 17th. Troops mobilised at once
very thoroughly and completely. Aston of the Stock Exchange, a leading
man on Railway Market, told me that Kitchener arranged it first stipulat-
ing for a free hand. On the G.W.R. more men came out than was
expected. On Friday House adjourned till following Tuesday. On that day
the Labour members bitterly attacked the Government. L.George turned
round on Keir Hardie with effect. The row will take a good deal of
smoothing over. Certainly the majority of the Cabinet has taken a strong
line. L.George was evidently nervous about it all through and ready to
play up the Labour men even when it came very near to going back on his
colleagues. The final round with Keir Hardie has put him in the same boat
with rest of Government. We may gain a bit by triangular contest at bye
elections but in the House the split will not help us much.[13] On the whole
the session has been a bad one for our party. Both Pike and Ed Talbot say
they have never known things in such a bad way. There is certainly a strong
feeling against Balfour's leadership. On the other hand there is no one to
take his place. My own impression is that things will improve now.

Sunday 29 October House re-assembled on October 24. During the recess the most marked thing was the strong feeling against Balfour among many of the rank and file both inside and outside the House. The foundation of the Halsbury Club was supposed to be an outward and visible sign of that feeling, though the promoters of the club denied it. Just before the reassembling of the House a shuffling of the cards took place in the Ministry by which Churchill and McKenna changed places. One incident of the shuffle was to send Strachey[14] to the Lords without office. He wrote to me privately to say that he was promised a place in the Government again very soon! Valentia 'The Viscount'[15] retired from the Whips room at the beginning of the session. He had been in it for thirteen years and was a great institution. He was a great stickler for correctness in dress, and objected to short coats or any other new fangled ideas. A bit of news about the railway strike was that Lloyd George got the directors to meet the men by publishing a telegram from the French premier to say that if the strike went on in England, France must agree to Germany's demands. Claughton came in on that against the wishes of Lord Allerton. and some of the other directors.[16] The first business of the session was a drastic guillotine motion on the Insurance Bill. Balfour made a very good speech in opposition to it. There was a good deal of discontent on the Liberal and Labour benches and a few of them voted with us. The debate cheered up our party a good deal.

Sunday 12 November Was down in the country over the South Somerset election, when on the Wednesday afternoon, 8 November, I got following letter from Willie Bridgeman marked private, dated 7 November.[17]
  I went to London early on the 9th. Found a meeting for Monday at noon had been summoned. There were four names mentioned – Austen, Long, Carson and Bonar Law. Carson said at once he would not compete. Bonar Law was urged to say the same. He refused. Things seemed close between Austen and Walter Long. Helmsley came to Bal to say there must be a vote and that he and many who supported Long would abide by the result. But from talking to members it certainly seemed to me that the Long faction would not be very loyal to Austen. There was a strong feeling against him on the ground that he had not been loyal to Balfour. The Halsbury Club business went against him too. It seemed on Thursday night about even betting between the two. I went round to the 1900 Club and was surprised to find that men there were mostly for Long. Goulding had been keen for Austen and did not want Bonar Law to compete. On his doing so Goulding said he was his oldest friend and he must back him all he could.[18] On Friday morning the *Express* came out all for Bonar Law. In the Whips' room we were making all preparations for a ballot on Monday. Just after 2 p.m. Bal summoned us all and told us of the dramatic occurrence

that both Austen and Long had independently come to the conclusion that they would both retire and would propose and second Bonar Law. He went to see the latter and said as soon as he telephoned the news people were to be told the news. I had to leave for S.Somerset before the message came. Bal himself was much against Walter Long and more or less against Bonar Law. He expressed the opinion that Bonar Law was lazy and not forthcoming enough. Walter Long was very angry because he said the Whips' room was working against him and that Pike was saying that Long's health would not stand the strain. Pike was the only whip who did any active canvassing. He was very keen for Austen.

W.C. Bridgeman to Sanders 7 November 1911

My dear Peter,
   The crisis has come. Balfour is going to announce his resignation of the leadership on the ground of health tomorrow in the City – Lansdowne is to stay and it remains for us to choose another leader.
   Bal imagined that it was his business to call a party meeting to decide – and thought that the sooner it was called the better – as intrigues would lead to deeper rifts in the party if allowed to continue for long. But now Walter Long declares it is not Bal's business and that the proper precedent is a meeting of our Privy Councillors – and also wants to defer any decision for a fortnight – so the fat is in the fire. All of us in this room (including Bal) think Austen is the right man to lead us in the Commons – and I think if the Privy Councillors don't choose him, the party would upset their decision.
   Bal is going to try and get Balfour to say that there must be a party meeting at once and the thing decided before the Nat. Union Conference, but I doubt if he will take any part. So there we are.
   Bal wanted you to know all about it. Edmund Talbot says he can't write as his hand hurts him – but is attending to your W. Somersetshire business as well as his own. He can't get Thynne, nor as yet a good substitute.
Yours ever,
W.C. Bridgeman

Wednesday 15 November   The Carlton meeting on Monday went off quite admirably. Harry Chaplin in the chair a very great success. A good many men came into the room by no means inclined to acquiesce in the proposed arrangement. Walter Long proposed Bonar Law. His speech was one of the best things I ever heard. Manly and rather touching. The country gentleman at his very best. He spoke and evidently felt strongly of the degradation that it would have been to the party to have elected a leader by secret ballot. Austen followed. Noticeable that he was very pale while Walter Long had been very red. He went more into the history of the thing and stated that they had met immediately after Balfour had determined to resign and had agreed that steps were to be taken to find out what the wishes of the party were. On the Friday morning he sent for Bal and asked for his impression. Bal said that if it came to a vote it would be a very close thing between the two. Austen on that said the only solution was for both to stand down and asked Bal to go to Walter Long. Walter Long said the same thing. And so it was arranged. Both paid a very high tribute to Bal's diplomacy. Bal says that as a matter of fact he merely acted as a messenger. The solution certainly was not what he wanted. When Austen sat down Chaplin suggested that he had better put the question at once and on getting an affirmative shout did so. A clever way of stifling discussion and few could have done it so well. Motion carried unanimously. Bonar Law then sent for. All got up to cheer him except Banbury who remained seated. His speech struck me as feeblest of the day. He was evidently moved and nervous. The meeting separated in great content with the Conservative party all round. The whole thing was certainly creditable. It was, however, a curious feature that while Walter Long was speaking of the decision as the Swan Song of the country gentleman, he and Chaplin, the two country gentlemen, cut the finest figures in the proceedings.

At the House Bonar Law got a great reception on entering, the Liberals joining in the cheering. He came into the Whips' room in the course of the afternoon, and seemed rather to be asking for orders from Austen. He struck me as rather shy and awkward. The Viscount was there and shook hands. He said afterwards that it was not so long ago that he had ordered Law out of the room. The old history was that the Viscount had abused him for refusing to go to a meeting and Law had asked him to apologise. Alick Hood put it right at the end. The feeling of the party all day was one of great satisfaction. The only dissentient note that I heard was one of regret that Austen had not retired in favour of Walter Long as being the older man. On the other hand I think the L.U. clique is a little sore. The victory at Oldham came as a good fillip in the evening.[19]

A comic little episode about South Somerset election. I asked F.E. to go down, so did Talbot. But he declined, on ground of being too busy. Doughty the same. I then suggested putting the Carnarvons on to F.E. This was quite effective. A countess on his door step brought F.E. in at once. He is to go down Monday next. Doughty on getting a letter from Carnarvon actually came and asked to go. But I don't think we shall want him.

Wednesday 6 December   We won the S.Somerset election by 148 votes. It was a great triumph as Lloyd George played every possible low down trick.

We rather outjockeyed him by casting doubt on all his promises. But the agricultural vote really turned the scales. Vivian the Radical candidate was quite ignorant and displayed his ignorance of farming matters. While the victory was very cheering it is not much evidence of a change of feeling in the country. I personally received many congratulations, that which pleased the most being a card from Elibank saying: 'Congratulats on success which is really your own.'

Third reading of Insurance Bill today. We have had a good deal of trouble in the party on the subject. Some of our people said they must vote against it. Others equally determined to vote for it. Harry Foster's 'reasoned amendment' has rather cleverly united the party. But it is not quite clear that all will abstain on third reading. There are signs that the Bill is by no means popular in the country; and the way it has been rushed through has caused even Radical papers to protest.

The biggest thing of the past few weeks has been the Foreign Debate. Grey's speech very good and clear, but by no means conciliatory to Germany. It seemed pretty clear that at one interview between him and Metternich[20] both lost their tempers. Another point that struck one was that probably some undisclosed pressure from France was the real motive of the Lloyd George speech. Bonar Law following Grey came out very well. The German papers commented on the fact that he was much more friendly to Germany than Grey. Mark Sykes made his reputation at once by a maiden speech dealing mainly with Eastern affairs.

It seems to be settled that the Lords will throw out the Naval Prize Bill but let the Insurance Bill through unaltered. If they once began altering it Lloyd George might drop it. Many of his party would be glad it he did.

Saturday 16 December House prorogued today. Rather a hard week to finish with. Committee report and third reading of budget taken in three nights. This due to an arrangement made between Bal and Elibank. Bonar Law knew about it, but Austen did not as he had been away. He was annoyed that the arrangement had been made. So were several of our people including Pretyman,[21] but the arrangement was really inevitable. Second foreign debate on last Thursday of session. Aubrey Herbert[22] made excellent maiden speech. On the whole our people wound up full of buck. Difference in feeling between now and what it was in August quite extraordinary. Bonar Law has done very well. His speech on third reading of Insurance Bill a masterpiece. Lloyd George's hold both on the House and in the country seems to be getting less. His speech at Bath in November to National Liberal Federation generally admitted to be a failure. And in the House our people stand up to him much better than they did a year ago. His attack on our ways of working the Insurance Bill at elections fell quite flat. Asquith also seems waning in power. He wound up debate on Insurance. Very good for about five minutes, then poor and dull. Our people spoilt his carefully prepared peroration by laughing at each sentence as it came out. We were discussing his speeches one day when Bonar Law remarked: 'Well whatever you say, he can speak better when he is drunk than the rest of us when we are sober.' It is rumoured that he is shortly to go to the Upper House. That would be rather an amusing finish to his Lords campaign.

CHAPTER 2 NOTES

1   1st Baron Rothschild, Liberal M.P. 1865–1885 and subsequently a Unionist. He was quite consistent in his attitude for, after Hood's retirement, Bonar Law was informed by his Party Chairman that Lord Rothschild had been '*very* generous'. (Steel-Maitland to Law, 5 November 1911, Steel-Maitland Papers, GD 193/108/3.)

2   J. Percival Hughes was the Principal Agent who had the misfortune to preside over the two Unionist Party defeats of 1910; he was widely criticised as being at least partly responsible for the disorganised state of the Party and was finally removed from office in 1912.

3   This was the Reciprocity Treaty, negotiated by Sir Wilfrid Laurier's Canadian Liberal Government, and which, by making a separate deal with the United States, seemed to deal a body-blow to all plans for Imperial Preference or Integration. The treaty was not, however, ratified by Canada, since Laurier was defeated at the general election of 1911 by the pro-Imperial Preference Conservatives, led by Sir Robert Borden.

4   William Redmond was a Nationalist M.P. and the younger brother of John Redmond, the leader of the Nationalist Party.

5   1st Earl Carrington was President of the Board of Agriculture from 1905 to 1911 and rather too moderate for the taste of most radicals.

6   It was a favourite and quite justified Radical complaint that they and their supporters were under-represented on the magistrates' benches. See J.M. Lee, **Parliament and the Appointment of Magistrates**, in *Parliamentary Affairs*, 1959–60.

7   Lord Balcarres was Chief Whip 1911 to 1913 before inheriting the Earldom of Crawford. Sir Arthur Steel-Maitland was the first Chairman of the Party Organisation. The division of responsibilities was recommended by the final report of the Unionist Organisation Committee, which had just been published, and followed widespread

and justified criticism of a system where one man was expected to do what amounted to three full-time jobs. In the end, Hood's pride was rather hurt by his apparent demotion and he refused to remain responsible for finance; the first Party Treasurer was therefore Lord Farquhar. In practice, the division of responsibility was very successful because Balcarres, Steel-Maitland and Farquhar worked well together as a team.

8   This is one of two mis-datings in the diary: it should clearly read Thursday 29 June, and was perhaps due to being written up after midnight.

9   1st Viscount Milner and 2nd Earl of Selborne were presumably thought to be good choices because of their experience as well as their opinions: both were diehard peers and both had considerable administrative experience as successive High Commissioners in South Africa. It illustrates neatly how Conservatives thought of Imperial politics and the Irish question in the same terms.

10   This was Henry Wilson, currently Director of Military Operations at the War Office and notoriously indiscreet in regard to the information that he passed on to members of the Opposition. His preference for Lloyd George is interesting for it was as L.G.'s favourite that he became C.I.G.S. in succession to Robertson in 1918.

11   This should be Thursday July 27th.

12   This showed great ingenuity on Steel-Maitland's part: if the party and its M.P.s were opposed to the payment of M.P.s, then they could hardly refuse to part with some at least of the £400 a year to party funds. He sent out letters to M.P.s making exactly this point but, although he was successful in raising money, there is no evidence that this specific appeal raised much money.

13   This is a very shrewd observation: as many as eight of the sixteen Unionist gains at by elections in the years 1911 to 1914 were attributable to the splitting of the Labour vote in the constituencies, but nothing like that ever happened in the House of Commons.

14   Sir E. Strachey, 1st Lord Strachey (1911) did in fact become Paymaster General in May 1912.

15   Viscount Valentia was an Irish peer and longstanding Unionist M.P.; he became 1st Lord Annesley in the U.K. peerage in 1917.

17   This view was substantiated by Arthur Henderson. See Peter Rowlands, *The Last Liberal Governments*, vol.II, p. 66.

17   The letter from Bridgeman is summarised in the diary. The full text is printed as the next item.

18   Goulding's change of heart was apparently due to his prolonged exposure to Max Aitken on a transatlantic crossing. Robert Blake, *The Unknown Prime Minister*, p. 74.

20 Count Paul Metternich had been German Ambassador in London since 1901.
21 E.G. Pretyman (*sic*) Conservative M.P. 1895–1906 and from 1910, a very influential back-bencher of moderate views.
22 Aubrey Herbert had been an M.P. since December 1910. For his maiden speech, see Peter Rowlands, *op.cit.*, II, p. 138.

Chapter 3   1912 'The Belfast men want a row at once'

Monday 19 February   House reassembled on Wednesday 14 February. The usual custom is to meet on a Tuesday. But report says the Irishmen objected to the Home Rule session starting on the 13th of the month. During the recess we won a bye election in Ayrshire, and in other elections got a big turn over our way. Bonar Law made a very strong speech in the Albert Hall. In it he accused the Government of wholesale corruption. After the moving and seconding of the address he made a general attack on the government, and in the course of it went for the Insurance Bill. In the course of his reply Asquith, in a sort of cross-examining manner, asked whether he would repeal the Act if and when he came in. Law said: 'Certainly.' This caused tremendous cheers on the Radical benches. House adjourned after Asquith's speech. In the lobbies the Rads were hilarious and our people much disturbed. The result was a letter from Bonar Law to *The Times* explaining away what he said. The fact was that he rather lost his head, and the word 'Certainly' slipped out. That was Bal's explanation next day. Certainly Asquith had the best of the opening round. My own experience, however, of the feeling about the Insurance Bill is that its repeal would be exceedingly popular. Bal predicts a very hard session and says we must keep on going for them, but he does not expect to beat them and thinks the very fact that the country is going against them will make them stick to office like limpets. His line is that we must rub in that Asquith is lazy and Lloyd George is corrupt. Our people hope to make a lot out of the charge of corruption. I rather doubt it myself. Bal's idea is to bring it up on the various estimates.

Sunday 25 February   Address finished. Nothing exciting happened but it has been rather a good week for us. Bonar Law made a first class speech on Tuesday on the official amendment. Ure who wound up for the Radicals was very feeble as they themselves admitted. At question time Masterman admitted that lecturers paid out of public money were addressing public meetings on the Insurance Act in Scotland and Wales. This knocked the bottom out of Asquith's denial of Bonar Law's statement on first night of the session. In the amendments about tariff reform and small holdings the Government majority went down to 65 and 56 respectively. No official news about the coal strike question. The general opinion seems to be that it will come off, and a large number of people say the sooner the better. Henderson told me the railway directors would make it an excuse for decreasing their staffs and getting rid of the most militant trades unionists.[1]

Monday 11 March   As far as Parliamentary business has been concerned it has been a dull fortnight. Financial business and private members resolutions. I spoke on one of the latter about small holdings last Tuesday. It is noticeable that the Government is in no hurry. Things are going quite slowly. The coal strike is the great topic of interest. Up to now the Government's intervention has been most futile – Asquith has delivered pompous platitudes both to the federation and to the House without much effect. It cannot be said that any one on our side has useful proposals to make. Meanwhile the strike goes on amid perfect quiet all over the country. The other excitement has been caused by the suffragettes breaking shop windows. Many supporters of the Conciliation Bill have now announced that they will vote against it. The position of the Government just now is very bad. The bye election in Manchester was an awful blow to them.[2] Percy Illingworth said when it began that they would get 1,000 majority. Lloyd George is said to be like a bear with a sore head and all the Radicals are rounding on him. There seems a general idea that they will very soon be out; but there is nothing tangible to go on and Bal's policy is not to be in any hurry to try and beat them. He even said before the Manchester result was announced that it would be better for the party that we should not win. He wants to work for getting them out about November. A very risky game as we don't know what may turn up by then. The Home Rule Bill is not to be introduced till after Easter. They have not yet finished drafting it as their time has been taken up over the coal negotiations. There are rumours that the question of customs is proving a great difficulty.

Tuesday 19 March   Asquith announced yesterday that he will introduce today a Bill establishing a minimum wage in coal trade. Its provisions have been kept quite dark; and throughout the strike the Government have had no communication on the subject with the Unionist leaders. Our people are very divided as to what we ought to do. On the whole the majority is against a minimum wage and several Liberals have announced their hostility to it. Churchill introduced Navy Estimates yesterday and his speech made a good impression on our side, but annoyed the extreme people on his own. He was rather unnecessarily provocative to Germany. Charlie Beresford on the other hand made a speech that was thought very foolish by people on our side. He laughed at Arthur Lee and attacked Churchill for his attitude to Germany in a way that the German papers are sure to rejoice over.

Wednesday 20 March   Asquith introduced his Minimum Wage Bill. The Bill itself merely says that if a man works underground he must be paid a minimum wage, such wage to be fixed by local boards who would also provide safeguards. Nothing in the Bill to compel owners to open or men to work. Asquith however said that if the Bill did not stop the strike the hands of the Government would be immensely strengthened for taking drastic measures. Bonar Law, while declining to commit himself till the bill was in print, crabbed it all round, but would not be drawn as to an alternative. I was not much impressed by his speech. St Audries thought it very good. All through the debate the trouble was that our people were afraid to announce an alternative policy. On the other hand Lloyd George, when challenged to say what was to be the next step if this fails, refused to do so. The owners say an enormous number of mines will be closed if the Bill passes. Beauchamp of Radstock told me that nine-tenths of the Somerset pits could not pay the minimum asked by the miners. Balfour, Austen Chamberlain and Selborne discussed the situation in the Whips' room afterwards. All agreed it was a very bad Bill. Selborne contended that the Lords might be right in throwing it out. Both Balfour and Austen were very strong against that course on the ground that the Lords could not carry on the Government if Asquith resigned in consequence of their action. Lord Lansdowne told Bal that if our party took a strong line against the Bill in the Commons he was not sure how far he could restrain his men in the Lords. He is evidently afraid the Bill may be thrown out in spite of anything he can say. One result of the crisis is that the Conciliation Bill is postponed from Friday.

Thursday 21 March   Yesterday business in House was quite humdrum and everyone was talking about the Mines Bill. Our leaders had a meeting and decided to oppose the second reading from the front bench. Balfour rose to move rejection. At the same time representatives of the owners' federation met and passed resolutions that best course was to let second reading pass and move amendments in committee; but Harmood Banner[3] told me they could not agree as to what the amendment enforcing decisions of arbitration should be. In the afternoon we got the news that the Miners' conference had decided that the Bill was not acceptable unless their own schedule were put on it. If they stick to that of course the Bill is quite useless. But there seems a general idea that it is a bit of bluff. Personally I don't think so. Another rumour is that Government will accept some of their proposals and put them in. A few of our men don't like opposing second reading and the *Morning Post* correspondent told me it was very dangerous for mining representatives to do so.

Sunday 24 March   Rejection of Mines Bill moved by Balfour on Thursday. He was in very good form. Laid it down that our party regarded it as an executive matter, that we opposed second reading and if we defeated it were ready to take office and rely on House of Commons to support us in dealing with crisis; but that having made that protest we should put no further difficulties in way of Government. Brace a Welsh miner made a very good speech. The line on our side was to talk about syndicalism, and on the other to taunt us with not proposing an alternative. Austen and Grey wound up except for Markham who insisted on talking for 50 minutes against the wish of the House. At last moment Banbury raised a point of order which would have upset the Bill. On the explanation of the Government the Speaker overruled it, but he acknowledged to Banbury the next day that the Government had misled him and that the objection was good. Had he upheld it he said he would either have appealed to Banbury to withdraw it, or have created a precedent by saying that in case of such importance the Bill must go on. The great subject of discussion in the evening was whether the Government would agree to put in the bill a clause fixing wages for day men and boys at 5/- and 2/- respectively. On Friday morning *The Times* said they would not, most of other papers that they would. House met at 12 and Asquith announced that we should sit Saturday for report and third reading. The 5/- and 2/-amendment came on very soon. Asquith quite firm against it and came out rather strong. Rather a thrilling debate followed. The Labour men announced that if Government would concede the 5/- and 2/- the men would give way as to the schedule and go back to work. Laurence Hardy declared that most of the owners had no objection to the 5/-and 2/-. At last Asquith, while adhering to refusal to put it in the Bill, hoped that before report stage an agreement might be reached on the subject by the opposing parties in conference. Later in day he announced that there would be no sitting on Saturday, but conference between owners and men on Monday morning and report stage after that. John Ward informed me in lobby that he had been acting as go-between and that if the 5/- and 2/- was arranged privately even with a clause authorising exceptions where necessary the men would go back at once. As to Hartshorn and Stanton, the leaders of the extremists among the men, he said: 'We will put the roller over them; we are quite as anxious to do that as you are.' On our side there seems a feeling that for the owners to compromise would be a mistake as the men are bound to come in anyhow and only want an excuse to save their faces. My own impression is that the point is so narrowed down that there will be a compromise, the withdrawal of the schedule by the men being the determining factor. But that is not the general opinion. Bal declared on Friday night that the Government were in a greater mess than ever. Many people on our side are surprised that they were firm about the 5/- and 2/- and it is very generally believed that

Lloyd George was anxious to give in on that point. But there was a very strong section of the Liberal rank and file against it and according to Austen the government was given a hint that the House of Lords would not have it. In the second reading division three of our men voted with Government and one Liberal (Clifford Cory) with us. Several of our people abstained and six Ulster men were absent.

Friday 29 March No settlement of mines job on Monday. Reported that Lloyd George and Buxton were only men in Cabinet who wanted to give in on the 5/- and 2/- question. Bill postponed till Tuesday. Asquith then stated at beginning of committee stage that there was no settlement, but Bill must go on. He broke down in course of his speech. Papers described it as a 'moving scene.' Bal said he was 'blubbing sherry.' Sat till 2:50 in morning. On third reading Ramsay Macdonald attacked Government and announced Labour party would vote against third reading. Lloyd George put up to answer him; very sour with Labour men. John Ward got up and rounded on Macdonald; there is a feud between them. Then O'Grady rounded on Ward. A few of our men voted for third reading; a few more against. Party as a whole abstained. I spoke again in House on Wednesday on small holdings matters.

Thursday, women's suffrage. Arnold Ward made quite good speech near end of debate. Bill defeated by 222 to 208 amid great excitement. The Irishmen opposed it, because Asquith had promised to give a week for committee stage and they thought time was all wanted for Home Rule. Still Bill would have been carried if it had not been for the window breaking. I voted for it, but was not very sad when it was beaten. It shows that this form of hooliganism does not pay. Agg Gardener who moved second reading first got into House in 1874. This was his maiden speech, and a very poor effort. He was frightened out of his life all through.

I was speaking at Keynsham on Monday. A certain amount of opposition in room. When I talked Coal Mines and Insurance there was some interruption. When I came to Home Rule they were all quiet and evidently all with me.

Wednesday 17 April Home Rule Bill introduced last Thursday. Opening day rather disappointing. No very great crowd. Asquith rather apologetic all through. Only warmed up when he attacked Bonar Law's Belfast speech.[4] He seems to have a good deal of personal animosity against him. In the course of the three days debate Balfour, Hugh Cecil, Tim Healy and Bonar Law made the best speeches. Bonar Law's about the best he ever made. A very fine attack on the Government. The division was a success from our point of view. The majority was 94. We brought up 268 men. That included tellers and one Rad – Clifford Cory. As the total strength of the party including Speaker and all dead men is 278 it was a very good performance. The Belfast demonstration on Easter Tuesday made an enormous impression on all who went there. Even an unemotional person like Finlay was quite excited about it. Carson says the feeling there is hotter than it has ever been before. It is the fact that there are hundreds there who are ready to be shot sooner than submit. The Bill is very cleverly drawn if its object is to make resistance to a Dublin Parliament difficult. Customs are to be collected by English officials and the constabulary is under English control. Another trouble is that the Bill cannot become law for over two years, and that the Belfast men want a row at once.

Friday 26 April   Stayed last week-end at Castle Hill, Haldane being one of the party. He told Lady Fortescue that the members of the Cabinet were quite worn out and that Lloyd George had become quite an old man.[5] The Nottingham election went much better than we expected. Morrison's was a false majority. *The Times* on the eve of poll said that 1,000 would be a great Unionist triumph; and we got 1,300. Welsh disestablishment this week. Opening day very tame. McKenna and Lyttleton not attractive speakers. But Lloyd George yesterday in great form; really eloquent at times. Billy Gore did very well too. Government majority 79. Our men turned up very well. Our people very pleased at Single Schools Areas Bill being dropped. Our men on the Standing Committee attended in force every day and prevented any progress being made, till Rads threw up the sponge.[6] The present plan of the Government is to have a longish holiday at Whitsuntide and then sit right on till their Bills are passed. We propose to request our men not to pair. Bonar Law is ready to have a party meeting and to tell them so. The idea is that if we hold out the Rads will funk when it comes to sitting through August and September. A mild sensation the other night on Malcolm's drawing attention to a speech in which Pointer, a Labour member, said he had seen the rival leaders in the House both drunk. Pointer merely said the report was inaccurate. His own people very angry with him.

Friday 10 May   Home Rule debate finished last night. Speeches throughout very long. Great difficulty and discontent on account of very large number of men who wanted to speak and had no chance of getting in. We could have kept the debate going for another week without difficulty. Austen made about the best speech on our side. Devlin was perhaps the best for the Government but he was violently hostile to Protestant Belfast. In the final division we were beaten by 101. Clifford Cory voted with us. Robartes and Kemp abstained.[7] There is no sign of any considerable feeling against the Bill in the country. Welsh disestablishment seems more unpopular. Such are the reports we get. My personal experience rather shows that there is a feeling against Home Rule. We badly want another bye election or two in which we have a chance. We tried for a snap division on Wednesday night on a motion by Grant urging the Government to make terms with the doctors over Insurance Bill. Our people rolled up all right and Government were so frightened that Lloyd George accepted the motion. Unfortunate that it was not drawn a little stronger. Grant submitted it to Finlay who was really responsible for whittling it down. We have decided to stop pairing in future. Holiday at Whitsuntide is to be just under a fortnight. After much hesitation Government have announced that the Welsh Bill is to go to Committee of Whole House. We cheered that as great triumph for us. As a matter of fact we might have better chance to beat it upstairs. But to get it and Home Rule through committee on floor of House will be an almost endless job.

Wednesday 19 June   During Whitsuntide holidays and since the House resumed, things seem to me to have been going a little better for the Government. The bye elections at Hackney and in Norfolk showed a gain for us but not at all on the same scale as before. Lloyd George is raising the land question again. He tacks it on to Welsh disestablishment on the ground of the confiscation of church lands by Henry VIII. Hemmerde fought the Norfolk election on the land taxing policy and was successful with it.[8] The feeling against Insurance seems to be rather diminishing and the country is lethargic about Home Rule and disestablishment. It is announced that we adjourn early in August till the beginning of October. In the House our party is doing well. Last night the Government majority was down to 69 on the motion to leave Ulster out of Home Rule. A strike of London Transport workers is going on. The Government intervened and got snubbed by the employers who seem to be winning on their own. One night Banbury gave notice that on the adjournment he would call attention to McKenna's refusal to send police to Purfleet.[9] Geoffrey Howard forgot to let McKenna know. When the adjournment came he was sent for and is said to have been interrupted in dressing for the 'Hundred Years Ago Ball' to which he was going in the part of Fouché. He came back in a hurry and gave himself away considerably in what he said. The result was a vote of censure. He then certainly showed that he had on the whole played the game in deeds, but did not withdraw his words. Last Friday afternoon we gave the Government a little trouble by flagrantly obstructing over a small Bill that came before the Plural Voting Bill and then defeating a motion for closure. We are doing all we can to stop our men pairing and have reduced it to a minimum much to the annoyance of the Radicals. The Government Franchise Bill was introduced on Monday. It is said that it is only to go on in order to fulfil Asquith's promise that a female suffrage amendment be put in.[10] The Speaker has told Banbury that

such an amendment would not be in order after the defeat of Agg
Gardener's Bill. No doubt Asquith knows this. It is pretty low down. The
Bill itself sounds very bad for our party.

Tuesday 25 June   Last night we very nearly beat the Government on one
of the budget resolutions. Bull had worked it all out for a division just after
11 p.m. For once the Government did not know of it. We got 177 to their
199 in the division but we did not bring up 18 men who were close at hand.
Hewins was sent to get them. As he crossed Palace Yard the division bell
rang. Instead of running to get his men, he ran back to the division.[11] Very
annoying. But they would just have had a majority even then. It is all
practice and each time we try it on things run a little easier.

Sunday 15 July   The Radical party is going hard for a vague land taxing
policy. They have just won Hanley on that after rather a bitter split with
the Labour party. The Ilkeston election where Seely's majority went down
by 2800 was a great blow to them.[12] In the House of Commons they are
thoroughly uncomfortable. They never know when we are going to turn
up. Last Thursday they telegraphed for men from all over the country
thinking we were going for a snap division. As a matter of fact we were not
whipping strongly for it at all. The Government announced at first that
they meant to adjourn on 2 or 3 August. We are driving them into staying
an extra week. Elibank has told Bal that his men are absolutely fagged out.
There is a sort of idea that we may beat them before the adjournment. Our
men are playing the game very well. The refusal to pair is doing us very
good service. The dock strike still lingers on and is causing great distress in
the East End. Lord Devonport who was made head of the Port Authority
by the present Government refuses all terms to the men, and the Trades
Unionists are furious with him. Probably he has gone a bit too far. The
Franchise Bill has been on this last week. Every one very languid and it has
not been easy to keep the debate going. Balfour made a very good speech
on the last day, but that was the only speech of any note. The Government
got a majority of 72.

Tuesday 29 July   Last week we got the Government majority down to
three on Friday at 12:15. We whipped for 12:15 and if our men had played
the game better we should have beaten them easily. The division was on a
question of procedure and they would not have gone out if they had been
beaten. The next day we won Crewe but on a split vote. The only
unfortunate business has been on the Navy Estimates. There is a good deal
of divergence as to the sufficiency of Churchill's programme. C.Beresford
says it is quite insufficient; but Balfour made it very difficult for the party to
take that line by commending the proposals in the speech in which he

followed Winston. My own impression is that we are all right for the present.

Sunday 11 August   House adjourned on the 7th. We ran the Government to 22 on one division and 29 on another during the last week. On both these occasions they had whipped their men as hard as they could. The Irish were there in force but the Radicals did not come. It is not quite clear whether this is due to mere slackness or to some extent to annoyance with the Government. Certainly the idea of a new land policy has upset the respectable sort of Radical. The only exciting debate in the latter part of the session took place on the Irish estimates. Bonar Law definitely reaffirmed what he had said at a public meeting at Blenheim that if Ulster resisted the sympathy of the whole Unionist party would be with her.[13] Asquith replied to him and the House for a bit was quite excited. The party as a whole quite agrees with Bonar Law that Ulster would be justified in any steps she might take, but I have not yet been able to find out who she is going to fight or what form resistance can take. A great Unionist victory took place at Manchester just after the House rose.[14] Looking back on the session, things at first seemed very gloomy for the Radicals, then about June they pulled together a bit, but lately their position has got steadily worse. The Insurance Act has been the most important factor against them in the country, and though it may be true that the country has now no great repugnance either to Home Rule or disestablishment, certainly there are no votes to be won by either measure. In the House our system as to pairs has had a most worrying effect on the Radicals. Several times they have come down in numbers when we have not taken a division at all. Elibank has just announced that he is taking a peerage and is going into partnership in Pearson's business. There is much speculation as to the reason. As far as I can make out it is mainly due to money causes. He finds the family estates in such a bad way that he wants to take the chance of making a bit of money. I doubt whether Percy Illingworth who succeeds is man enough for the job. The *Daily Chronicle* in commenting on the matter paid a most flattering tribute to our efficiency saying that the opposition whips were the most formidable team the party had had for ten years. Bal has certainly done very well; but it has been a hard time for him and he seems nearly done up.

Asquith has rather recovered himself this session. He has had a trying time but has been in quite good form latterly. The man who has really had the hardest time on their side is Masterman who has had to stand all the heckling about the Insurance Bill. He has really come out of it very well. Worthington-Evans has established a good position on our side and George Sandys made a very good speech in committee on Home Rule that attracted attention. On our front bench Bonar Law has done very well. He

is a little too easily drawn but he has now consolidated his position and got
the confidence of the party. F.E. has not been so good in his speeches in
the House as in previous sessions.

Sunday 13 October   House reassembled last Monday. Our victories at
Manchester and Midlothian during the recess very encouraging.[15] Rather a
rotten mess has been made of the 'Imperial Fund'. George Wyndham got
it up with the Duke of Westminster as a figure head. In September they
sent out a circular saying the Duke would ask anyone to dinner who gave
£1,000 to the fund! This the Radical papers got hold of and published. The
next thing was an invitation to dinner sent to many of us. That we declined
and then received a letter saying his Grace was sorry we could not come
but hoped never the less that our names might be announced as subscribers
of substantial sums. Many of our people are much annoyed over the whole
business. Sir A. Henderson who is Treasurer of the Tariff Reform League
has never been consulted about the matter, and threatens to resign. On the
Radical side there has been a lot of trouble over a threatened land
campaign by Lloyd George on the Wedgwood-Outhwaite[16] lines. Many
rich Rads are furious. Havelock Allen and Munro Ferguson were down
West and both very shy of it. Lloyd George's popularity with them is at a
very low ebb. At the present moment it seems as if things were to be
smoothed over by dropping the whole matter. Percy Illingworth, the new
Chief Whip, is said to be pressing strongly for that. Our 'social reformers'
have been thinking of outbidding the Rads. Sam Kidner came to me in a
great state of mind because he had been asked to appear before a
committee consisting of Peto, C. Bathurst and C. Mills and sitting at the
Central Office.[17] This committee suggested to him a policy that included a
tribunal to fix labourers' wages. Kidner much perturbed at such a
suggestion. St Audries actually wrote Bonar Law on the subject and got a
reply saying the policy was quite unauthorised.

The Ulster covenant business has certainly had a good deal of effect,
though the bye elections were won on the Insurance Act. An idea had got
about that there was to be a row in the House on Thursday last when the
guillotine motion was to be brought in. Our leaders and Bal were rather
anxious about it and wanted tactfully to keep our Ulster men quiet. But
when the Ulster men came we found that they were so impressed with the
gravity of the whole matter that they looked on a row as quite beneath
their dignity. John Lonsdale sat for a quarter of an hour in the Whip's
room and held forth about the Almighty, and the altar and the solemnity
of the whole affair.[18] In the actual debate our people were solemn and the
Radicals ribald. Lloyd George tried to draw Bonar Law as to whether he
would approve resistance if at a general election the country decided
against Home Rule. Law refused to be drawn. But as a matter of fact he

has said both publicly and privately that in that case he would not support resistance. There he differs from Carson. Austen wound up the debate with a very good speech.

The Balkan troubles seem to have caught our people napping. Grey is reported to have been fishing up to the last moment. Charlie Hunter declares that when Saxonoff came over Grey wrote to the King to say he did not propose to go to Balmoral but Sir Arthur Nicholson would do as well.[19] The King furious and commanded his attendance. Wilfrid Ashley, who through Cassel knows something of inner foreign affairs, takes a very serious view and thinks we are very likely to be dragged in.[20]

Sunday 20 October Rather a hard week in the House. On Monday we rose at 4 a.m.; then I caught 7:30 train from Paddington, went down to County Council at Wells and returned to House by 7 p.m. There was rather a row on the adjournment that night. Rawlinson and Mildmay raised question of Lloyd George's committee of inquiry about the land. George in a tight place, but our men made the mistake of constantly interrupting. At the end Austen Chamberlain asked an ill-timed question which enabled George to make a retort that raised tremendous cheers from his own side. He was actually hooted by our men as he went out behind the Speaker's chair. Quiet staid men like Bigland got absolutely wild. Monsell very nearly came to blows with Eustace Fiennes as they went out. The general opinion was that if only Lloyd George had been left alone he would have done us a lot more good. On Home Rule the debates have run very much in our favour, the divisions no better. The Radicals are all there now. There seems little chance at present of beating them on a division. So our tactics will be to send our men to speak in the country for the next six weeks with an occasional rush to London just to keep the Rads there.

War is now delared in the Balkans. The Buxton stamp of Radical is anxious to get up an anti-Turk agitation in the country. Masterman has just made a speech against the Turks. The feeling on our side of the House is certainly in favour of the Turks but against proclaiming our feelings in any way.

Sunday 17 November A very thrilling week just over. We at last succeeded in snapping the Government on Monday last. We had watched things carefully for weeks and found that early on a Monday afternoon was the only time the Radical members were short. Last Monday was report stage of finance resolution on Home Rule Bill. We arranged that Banbury should move without notice to limit the grant to the Irish Parliament, and that the debate should collapse as soon as possible. The idea was that Banbury would excite less suspicion than anyone else as he always moves to limit grants. We whipped our men to come at 4:15. Personally I thought the Rads were sure to smell a rat and talk on. However it all came off exactly as planned. When the division bell rang at 4:13 I thought we had got them. The numbers came out 228 for us against their 206. We were most of us hoarse for days afterwards with the shouting. There were no men hidden as suggested. They simply came to the House at just the time on the whip. House adjourned at once. Some of our people spent the evening searching for any way the Government could get out of it and came to the conclusion there was none. Tuesday we passed White Slave Bill, a good thing done.[21] On Wednesday Asquith moved to rescind resolution of Monday last and to repair his time table. The Speaker said the motion was without precedent but he could not rule it out of order, on the ground that the House had power to abrogate its own rules if it wished. It was quite evident that he gave his decision with much doubt and reluctance. Our tactics were to let Asquith speak and Bonar Law answer him. Then the adjournment was to be moved and after that our men were to howl down all the speakers. The plan very nearly went wrong. When the adjournment was to be moved, Asquith simply said he could not accept it, the Speaker put the question and we were beaten by 109. After that young Harcourt got up and was howled down; then no Radical would get up and we had to put up men to keep the debate going somehow and had great difficulty in doing it. All our people grumbled like fury and the whips had a really bad time. The tide turned soon after 7 o'clock when Rufus Isaacs got up. He was given no sort of hearing and the Speaker adjourned the House for an hour. During that hour it was arranged that Helmsley was to get up and be howled down by our own side. That came off and the Speaker adjourned the House. Charlie Helmsley did it very well. He looked as cool as could be, but when he came out the sweat was pouring off his face. The Speaker stated that as the cries were only 'Adjourn' and 'Divide' he could not drop on them. After the adjournment the McNiel incident took place. McNiel was in a furious temper. It would have taken very little to make a general fight. On Thursday the same sort of thing was to have continued. Then came the Speaker's intervention and the House adjourned till Monday. Our people are very triumphant and the Radicals very sick. Bal's last instruction on Thursday was that our future tactics were to be quite moderate.[22]

Our Eastern pundits have all been ridiculously wrong about the Turks. Mark Sykes and Aubrey Herbert etc. were all convinced that they would win easily in the end in spite of initial defeats. They were quite ignorant of the rot that seemed to have set in. The difficulties of the foreign situation are among the reasons given for the Government's clinging to office.

Taunton election was not so good as we hoped. Our majority only went up by 50. I made a speech which annoyed the Catholics and I believe actually lost us a few votes. The Radicals bribed like fun. They gave away half crowns wrapped up in Radical leaflets.

Monday 25 November A quiet week. Our people made no objection to Asquith's amended procedure. Objections of order might have been taken, but the desire was to make things as easy as possible for the Speaker. There was a fear that he might resign. The week has been devoted to criticism of Home Rule finance, but nothing has come of the renowned Radical cave. A deputation is to go to Bonar Law today to press for the dropping of payment of members if we come in. Arnold Ward has been collecting the names of those for and against payment. Only seven say they are for it. It is rather comic that one of the seven is Rothschild.

It is generally rumoured that Lloyd George was anxious for the Government to resign after their defeat last week. It is also very generally rumoured that the Government will drop Welsh disendowment. Bonar Law says 'If they do they will drop themselves; George can't go back to Wales without it.'

Sunday 8 December Our party is in a great state of mind on account of Lansdowne's speeches as to colonial preference and food taxatiion. The general view is that it was most unwise to bring that question to the front again when the party is making great headway on a platform of mere attack. Lansdowne undoubtedly spoke after consultation with the leaders and under pressure from Austen and the tariff reform stalwarts. In the South and West and Home Counties I don't think any harm will be done by it; but it is generally agreed that the effect will be very bad in the North. The agents there are a good deal troubled about it. The *Daily Mail* series of articles on the 'Trade Boom' also go against tariff reform. Fletcher the S.Somerset agent tells me that in the last fortnight Vivian, the Radical candidate, has addressed his speeches entirely to the old dear food cry. I had a long talk to Austen on the subject. He maintains that if candidates would only tackle the question instead of funking it they would have nothing to fear from it. He confirmed a rumour that I had already heard. When the Canadian Ministers were over in the summer Bonar Law sounded them about dropping the idea of taxing corn. They assured him that the effect of doing so would be extremely bad in Canada especially after the victory of Imperial ideas on the reciprocity question.

Things have been quiet in the House. Moore, the Ulsterman made a very good speech the other night on the subject of the appointment of judges by a Home Rule ministry. There are now strong rumours that the Government mean to adjourn early in February.

Sunday 15 December   Our people still much troubled over the 'food tax' business. In Scotland and the North of England effect said to be particularly bad. In the House much talk as to Churchill turning out Sir F. Bridgeman, the First Sea Lord. Under pressure he owned that he told Bridgeman he must resign. Churchill denies that there was any difference of policy. Gossip says there was acute difference on the subject of men's pay, and that there has been friction all along because Churchill tried to treat Lords of the Admiralty like clerks at the Board of Trade; on one occasion he had to apologise for a letter he wrote to Bridgeman. According to C. Beresford (a prejudicial witness) Battenburg has all along toadied Winston and intrigued against Bridgeman. If Bridgeman cares to move in the matter no doubt he can make things awkward. But he is said to be an easy going fellow. His health was bad in the summer, but he declares he is all right now and he is hunting regularly with the Bramham.[24]

The Radicals were very nervous about the debate on Friday over the Welsh disendowment clauses. France moved to take tithe only. Young Gladstone seconded and made a very good speech, palpably nervous but very sincere. Ministers alternately tried to bully and cajole their dissentients. Eventually the numbers were 215 for the amendment and 265 against; 73 Nationalists in the majority. About a dozen Rads voted with us and many abstained. Home Rule is through committee after many divisions.[25]

Bal tells me that Bonar Law will eventually declare against payment of members. The Trades Union Bill rather complicates the matter as he does not want it said that we won't pay Labour members and won't let the Unions pay them.

I sat next a War Office man at lunch the other day who told me he was amazed at the want of anxiety on foreign affairs among politicians. He says it is not more than three to one against Austria and Servia going to war within three weeks. Aubrey declares that the Servians castrated the Austrian Consul at Prisrend. Probably untrue; but if true rather hard to see what reparations can be made.

Sunday 29 December   Just finished a brief holiday. Asquith announced that he expects to complete his business and adjourn early in February. Hard to see how he can get through the Franchise Bill in that case. But he states that the Government mean to pass their three Bills before that. On the day of the adjournment the Rads were afraid we were going to try a snap division. They called all their men up; some Irishmen were actually taken out of the train and brought down. Of course no division. We only had about 40 present. Only matter of interest was the Bridgeman business. Churchill made a very violent attack on C. Beresford; but he obviously lied when he said he could not remember if Sir F. Bridgeman had at one time threatened to resign. My impression is that there was a difference of opinion, that Sir F.B. got the best of it; that Churchill bided his time and then turned him out. In the actual debate Churchill scored on the whole.[26] The Welsh Radicals very fierce because the Government made some small concessions over the Church Bill. Towyn Jones said to one of the whips: 'You have betrayed a nation.' They talked rather big, but all came in to heel.

Our domestic troubles as bad as ever. About 70 per cent of our party in the House want to drop or postpone 'Food Taxes'. Even Harry Foster who has been a strong advocate of them all along says it must come to that. It really comes to the leaders going one way and the rank and file the other. There are no complaints personally against Bonar Law. The Harmsworth press is doing all the harm it can, no one quite knows why.

CHAPTER 3 NOTES

1 This was presumably Arthur Henderson, the future Labour Leader, evidence of Sanders' widening circle of contacts in the Commons.
2 Manchester South, was gained by the Unionists on March 5th on a swing of 10.8 per cent in a straight fight with the Liberals.
3 J.S. Harmood-Banner, Conservative M.P. and a prominent coal and railway director in the North West.
4 On 9 April, Law had addressed a rally of about 100,000 Unionists near Belfast and apparently condoned their treasonous plans. Asquith's continuing antipathy to Law was undoubted, as in his coining of the phrase 'the unknown Prime Minister' on Law's death in 1923. For a superb example of damning with faint praise, see Asquith's assessment of Law's abilities in 1916, quoted by Robert Donald in K.O. Morgan, *The Age of Lloyd George*, p. 181.
5 Castlehill was Earl Fortescue's country seat in North Devon; Lady F. was presumably the countess.
6 The Single Schools Areas Bill had been committed to Standing Committee after a hotly contested second reading on 8 March. It was a private member's bill, sponsored by Sir Croydon Marks, which provided for the transfer to local education authorities of denominational schools in areas where no other school existed. It was strongly supported by nonconformists on the Liberal side but equally strongly opposed by Anglican Conservatives under the leadership of Lord Hugh Cecil.
7 Cory, Robartes and Kemp were all Liberal M.P.s clearly being watched by the Conservative whips as possible defectors from the government side.

8 E.G. Hemmerde, Liberal M.P. 1906–1910 and 1912–1918, Labour M.P. 1922–4; Hackney and Norfolk, North-West, had both been held by the Liberals despite swings to the Conservatives.

9 On 6 June, Houlders Ltd. had asked for police protection for strikebreakers whom they had engaged to work at Purfleet during the Port of London strike. Banbury alleged in the House of Commons that McKenna, the Home Secretary, had refused to send the police. McKenna replied that in his view it was the strikebreakers and not the strikers who constituted a threat to public order.

10 Asquith had given a promise in 1910 that a Government Bill on women's suffrage would be introduced during the next parliament. See Peter Rowlands, *op.cit.* p. 38.

11 W.A.S. Hewins, Professor of Economics and the first Director of the London School of Economics, had been a Conservative M.P. only since March.

12 The by election at Hanley on 13 July was a Liberal gain from Labour, retaliation against Labour intervention in Liberal seats since 1910; Ilkeston, a very safe Liberal seat, was held by Seely on his appointment to the War Office.

13 Law's speech at the Blenheim Rally on 29 July had been his most outspoken so far. He described the government as 'a Revolutionary Committee which has seized upon despotic power by fraud', and which could therefore be legitimately opposed by similar unconstitutional means.

14 The by election victory at Manchester, North West, was more than usually exciting for the Conservatives since this was the same seat in which Churchill had been defeated in 1908 and Bonar Law in 1910.

15 Winning Gladstone's old seat at Midlothian on 10 September was a particulary good boost for Conservative morale.

16 Josiah Wedgwood was a keen land-taxer among radical M.P.s and R.L. Outhwaite had been the victorious Liberal candidate at Hanley, fighting on a platform of land taxes. See A.J. Morris *Edwardian Radicalism*, pp. 148–161.

17 This was clearly a sub-committee of the Unionist Social Reform Committee, a semi-official backbench pressure group of progressive M.P.s who had the facilities of Central Office placed at their disposal by a sympathetic Steel-Maitland.

18 J.B. Lonsdale had been a Unionist M.P. since 1900 and was Secretary of the Irish Unionist Party.

19 Sergei Sazonov, the Russian Foreign Minister, was in Britain for discussions during September 1912. Sir Arthur Nicholson was the Permanent Secretary at the Foreign Office from 1910 to 1916.

20 Sir Ernest Cassel, the international banker and industrialist, had been decorated by at least five foreign governments and was Wilfrid Ashley's father-in-law.

21 The Criminal Law Amendment Bill of 1912 increased the penalties under the Vagrancy and Immoral Traffic Act after a considerable agitation against slave-trafficking through London and prostitution in London itself.

22 Ronald McNeill (sic) had in fact thrown a copy of the Standing Orders of the House of Commons at Churchill, soon after the Speaker adjourned the House. His apology was accepted by Churchill on the following day. The Speaker suggested on Thursday 14 November that the temper of the House was such that it ought to be adjourned until the following Monday. See Peter Rowlands, *op.cit.*, II, p. 181.

23 Lord Lansdowne had, as leader of the Unionist Peers, announced a change in the party policy towards tariffs during his speech at the Albert Hall on November 14; this was confirmed in speeches by Bonar Law, repudiating Balfour's 1910 pledge to hold a referendum before introducing food taxes.

24 Prince Louis of Battenburg became First Sea Lord in succession to Bridgeman, only to be removed to make way for Admiral Fisher on the outbreak of war. Bridgeman did in fact decide to make things difficult for Churchill as the following entries show.

25 Gerald France and W.G.C. Gladstone (grandson of the Prime Minister) were the leading Liberal speakers against the provisions of the Welsh Disestablishment Bill. The Government's narrow margin of survival led to a watering down of the Bill. See Peter Rowlands, *op.cit.*, II, p. 183.

26 Bridgeman had certainly got the better of Churchill over several matters during 1912 and Churchill was doubtless glad to see him go, but it is by no means clear that Churchill engineered Bridgeman's departure. What is certain, as Sanders himself noted on December 15, is that Bridgeman had been ill and this provided Churchill with the excuse to prompt his resignation. What is still unclear is if that resignation was unwilling. See R.S. Churchill, *Winston S. Churchill*, vol. II, pp. 628–639.

Chapter 4   1913 'The chief excitement has been the Marconi business'

Sunday 5 January   'Food Tax' trouble more acute than ever. It has been a worrying week for the whips. I hear from Bal that the leaders agreed in March 1912 to drop the referendum on tariff reform. Balfour quite concurrred; said it was an election expedient and not a very good one at that. But Bonar Law wanted to postpone announcement on subject so that it might not appear that he was upsetting A.J.B.'s policy. Announcement came from Lansdowne at Albert Hall. Then came murmuring from the North. Ned Talbot said at the time it would cost us 50 seats at an election. Bonar Law's speech at Ashton made things worse instead of better, and he spoke so emphatically that it is very hard for him to climb down. His line now is that he thinks all he said then was perfectly right; but he does not regard the question of a second election before carrying food taxes as one of principle; only he does not see how he can give way on the point without enormous loss of prestige. Austen is for going full steam ahead and Bonar Law has a great feeling of loyalty for him. At an interview with the Lancashire Members, Bonar Law told them that at the coming meeting on 11 Jan. of the Lancashire Division of the National Union he expected them to pass a vote of confidence in him, and no vote condemning food taxes. He told them he would resign if they did otherwise. Meanwhile the party is becoming almost unanimous in favour of the policy advocated by the *Daily Telegraph*, viz. 'No food taxes until after a second election.' F.E. says it must be done. Even George Wyndham now concurs. Peto reluctantly agrees. Hewins, George Lloyd and a few others are strong the other way. There is a good deal of lobbying and chattering but everyone is perfectly good humoured and there is no ill feeling among members on the subject. The press continues atrocious. The *Morning Post* and *Express* make violent attacks on Lord Northcliffe and Garvin takes the same line in the *Pall Mall*. The real difficulty now is for Bonar Law to find a dignified line of retreat. It is rather ironical that for years the party jibed at Balfour for being nervous about this policy; now that the leader is a thorough whole-hogger it goes back on him at the first opportunity. The position is a surprise to me. I quite saw that there must be a conflict on the subject; but I thought the party would be 75 per cent for the full programme and that the rest would be brought into line.

Carson made a very good speech on moving the omission of Ulster from Home Rule. Bonar Law in course of debate said definitely that if at a general election the country concurred in Home Rule put as a clear issue before them, he would not countenance further Ulster resistance.

Sunday 12 January Things are now coming right. As far as I can gather the inner history is this. Last Monday Carson saw Bonar Law and Lord Lansdowne at the Duke of Abercorn's funeral. He learnt from them that they both intended to retire from leadership of the party. On that he went to Goulding and asked him to get together a few of the strongest tariff reformers and prepare a letter to Bonar asking him to postpone food taxes but retain the leadership. Goulding got a few together. Hewins, McNiel and Page Croft among others. Carson and F.E. Smith joined them later and the letter was drafted. Ronald McNiel, who had been chairman of the Confederates, was put in charge. The letter stated the adherence of the signatories to tariff reform and preference, advocated the postponement of taxes on food till after a second election on account of the other important issues before the country now, and asked Bonar Law not to think of resignation. Bal was consulted and the document was offered for signature on Thursday and Friday. Goulding is my informant as to its origin. Only eight of the party refused to sign; Amery, Archer Shee, George Lloyd, Winterton, Ben Bathurst, Charles Bathurst, Burdett Coutts and Touche.[1] Bonar Law is to give his answer on Tuesday probably by a letter to Bal. Austen does not like it, but he will play the game. The party as a whole is very pleased.

We ran the Government majority down to 40 on Friday afternoon over the Welsh Bill.

Sunday 19 January The party is satisfied with Bonar Law's letter though some remarked that there was no note of appreciation of the feelings of esteem for himself expressed in the memorial. He insisted on inserting the passage that said he thought a change of leaders would have been desirable.

Third reading of Home Rule Bill carried on Thursday by 110 (or rather 109 as there was a mistake in the counting). Several of our men were ill and unable to turn up. The Government people came up very well.

I have been rather busy over the Franchise Bill. The general idea is that it will have a most disastrous effect on our party if it goes through. I am trying hard to get our people to support the women's vote in some form; it seems to me if we get the two questions mixed up together there must be an appeal to the country before the Bill becomes law, but Banbury and Co. are all against any concession on the question. Gilmour is to be the new whip in place of Wilfrid Ashley; he is a very good fellow. There was some idea of having George Gibbs to please Walter Long.[2]

Sunday 26 January   Franchise Bill has begun. The Government moved a guillotine resolution on the Bill on Thursday. Before it began Bonar Law asked the Speaker whether the carrying of the Government amendments destroying the occupation franchise would so alter the Bill that it ought to be withdrawn and a new one introduced. The point had been discussed at a little meeting that we had in Bonar Law's room a few days before. He then spoke of it as a good debating point, but did not seem to rely on it for more than that. However, the Speaker while saying he must 'wait and see', stated that the rule was quite clear that if such alterations were made in committee as practically to make a Bill a different one to that which passed second reading the proper course was for the Government to withdraw the Bill and introduce a new one. He referred to the women's amendments, though B.L. had not raised that point, as other ways in which the Bill might be transformed. In the guillotine debate F.E. Smith made a very brilliant speech; Lloyd George in answering him was very conciliatory and clever. I made a short speech on one of the minor amendments about midnight trying to get Pease[3] to promise some discussion on the most important points. I was rather amused at being cheered a little by both sides when I got up, a tribute probably to my accustomed silence.

There is great excitement over the women's question, and it is agreed on all sides that the Government is in a great hole. The general opinion now is that they will drop the Bill and introduce Harold Baker's Plural Voting Bill which passed second reading as a Private Bill last March.

Sunday 16 February   Our holiday has begun at last after a very arduous finish. The Government dropped the Franchise Bill on Monday 27 January without taking a division on Grey's amendment. They did not take up Baker's Bill. So it is hard to see how they can pass any franchise measure under the Parliament Act. It will be a great gain for our party if they fail to do so. I had worked very hard on the case against the Franchise Bill, labour lost for the present. But it was a big score for us. Unfortunately the party sustained two blows just afterwards. First came the Derry election. That showed nothing really, the win being due to the Liberal candidate being a Protestant and a local employer; but it looked bad.[4] A much greater loss was Lord Crawford's death which transferred Balcarres to the Upper House. He was a very good Chief Whip. A wonderful worker, thoroughly up in procedure and a very clever man. He had a very difficult year and a half of office. First came the Die Hard trouble, then A.J.B.'s resignation and finally the free food difficulty. He got the party successfully through all these never turning a hair himself, but showing extraordinary tact on every occasion. He simply hated the Radicals, never having a good word to say for them; and he was fond of shouting offensive observations across the floor during debate. On the few occasions when he spoke in the House he took a curiously superior and detached line. I remember his being told once that the course he advocated was not legal. He dismissed that as a technicality and said he was arguing in broad principles. During the session he indulged in no amusements; his exercise was a walk round the park. He very rarely dined, but ate eggs in the tea room about 5 o'clock. The appended letter is characteristic. There has been a good deal of discussion as to a new Chief Whip. Edmund Talbot said at once he could not do it on account of ignorance of procedure and doubtful health. He wanted Harry Foster to come back. Other names mentioned were Hayes Fisher, Steel Maitland[5] and of course Pike Pease. Either of the first two would have been most unpopular, as numerous fellows made a point of telling us. Eventually Talbot agreed to take it on much to the satisfaction of the Whips' room.

The winding up stages have not been without interest. On the supplementaries the chief points were the insurance doctors and Irish foot and mouth disease. On the former a curious constitutional point arose as to the vote. After Lloyd George and Masterman had sworn the Government was strictly in the right and abused our people and Tim Healy for objecting, Asquith intervened and owned that our people were right and conceded what they asked for. I spoke on the foot and mouth question in absence of Walter Long to give a front bench blessing to Runciman for the way in which he has stood up to the Irishmen.[6]

On consideration of Lords' amendments to Scotch Temperance Bill there was an animated debate on 'disinterested management', and at one time it looked as if the Government would give in on account of the speeches from their own supporters.[7] McKinnon Wood was heard to threaten to resign if that was done. Lloyd George then faced the music and got a large majority, our people not being there in any numbers. There is considerable doubt as to what the Lords will do about this matter. The Duke of Devonshire told us in the Whips' room at the end of the session that they meant to adhere to all their important amendments. We tried to convince him that this would be a great mistake and he went off to Lord Lansdowne to report our views.

We had a scheme for taking a snap division on the last day but one on committee of Appropriation Bill. I rather think it would have come off. But unfortunately the Makse incident cropped up.[8] This meant that there was no chance of finishing questions early as we intended and the Radicals were likely to be down in force. So the whole thing was dropped.

On the whole we are not in such a good position as in October. We have had no triumphs at bye elections. The Radicals are pulling together. The land taxing campaign is shelved for the present. Since the snap division when we beat them their whips have insisted on 300 being always present and have got them. Though the strain must have been severe they have had less men sick than we have. While the free food trouble was on we were afraid to try to beat them and though that is over for the present the party is none the better for it.

I don't know that any reputations have been made in the autumn session. On the whole the best work on our side has been done by Mitchell Thompson who organised the opposition on the Home Rule Bill committee most admirably. On the other side Lloyd George's speech on the third reading of the Welsh Bill was about the best thing done.

Balcarres (Earl of Crawford) to Sanders – 3 February 1913

Peter,

Thank you for your letter. I am more upset than I can say, and my thoughts are with my friends and colleagues in the Room. Keep hard at it, I think we have laid the effective basis of cooperation in the House, tho' much still remains to accomplish.

You will not be able to guess with what deep interest I shall watch – from afar – your progress. Thank you, Peter, for all the readiness and zeal with which you have always helped me.

Bal.

Sunday 16 March   New session opened on Monday the 10th. Everything very slack. It was only by the greatest efforts that we could keep the debate on the front bench amendment for a whole day. Tariff matters not very smooth. A fiscal amendment to address was put down. After a good deal of bother it was arranged that it should come after dinner on Thursday, the Labour men agreeing to finish their amendment by dinner. Thursday morning a blocking motion put down by Sir Frederick Low, a Radical, appeared on the paper. That stopped the amendment and enabled us to blame the other side for preventing a discussion which they challenged. Chief trouble is about the candidature of Col Weston for Bagot's seat in Westmorland. When Bagot got ill it was arranged that a man called Aigle should be his understudy. When Bagot died the local association threw over Aigle and adopted Weston. The latter is said to be a very good fellow and a most popular local man but a free trader and rather a trimmer on other political matters. After many unsuccessful efforts to get him to meet us more or less he has been formally disavowed by the party headquarters. Local men say he will get in and no one else would. The division cares for persons not politics. But our tariff reformers are furious.[9]

George Stanley is the new whip. A very good thing.

Sunday 23 March The chief, in fact the only, excitement of the week has been the Marconi business. The press was got at two or three days beforehand and has been very feeble. But in the House every one on our side thinks very badly of Rufus and George's conduct. It remains to be seen what line the government will take. As far as I hear the Radicals are very sick about it. I have been surprised to find how little notice the matter has attracted in the country up to now.

Sunday 13 April On Wednesday March 26 we very nearly beat the Government on the committee stage of the Consolidated Fund Bill. Whitley actually put the question. Then Booth declared he had risen to speak and Whitley after saying he could not allow him eventually did so. We had a majority at the moment. It is generally acknowledged that Whitley's ruling was wrong. There was a good deal of row for the rest of the afternoon. Since then things have been very quiet, but the Government have got through their business much less quickly than they expected.

The Marconi business has now filtered down to the country. It is certainly having some effect. The Radicals are taking the line that Isaacs and George are much maligned innocents.

Sunday 27 April There is a vague but general feeling in the House that the Government is not going on much longer. I can find no ground for it. It is said that both the Cabinet and the Liberal party want to get rid of Lloyd George. The Marconi job has certainly done him a lot of harm. There is also a rumour that Asquith means to be L.C.J. when that office falls vacant. The budget showed a deficit of seven millions and Lloyd George budgeted to make it up without any fresh taxation. It is said that his estimate of the yield of the taxes was unduly sanguine, and that he means to leave a successor a deficit. There is not much in all this, but it is a good thing for us that such ideas should get about. The Radicals are as jumpy as can be about snap divisions. They and the Irish talked for hours on a Railway Bill last Thursday in order to avoid a division on the Post Office vote.

I spoke on Friday afternoon on a Bill that proposes to extend the hours of polling. We obstructed it to prevent anything else being taken.

Sunday 1 June Our party are in great spirits over the bye elections at Newmarket and Altrincham. In both cases we did better than either side expected.[10] The Insurance Act was a great factor in both cases. The Government now promise an amending Bill. But they have already got into a very congested state over their business. They are going on very slackly now; and it seems impossible for them to get through even the necessary work until late in August. Just before the Whitsuntide adjournment John Hills from our side introduced a Bill to establish minimum wage boards for agricultural labourers.[11] On reassembling a Labour member introduced another Bill on similar lines. Such a measure would have very few real supporters on our side at present. There is a good deal of feeling about Carson and F.E. appearing for Godfrey Isaacs in the Chesterton case.[12] I have tried to rub in that an explanation ought to be officially given in the press.

Tuesday 10 June   More Marconi excitements. The latest revelation is that Elibank bought American Marconis with Radical party funds. Elibank is in Ecuador and seems in no hurry to come back. His brother Capt. Murray told Illingworth about this. Illingworth knew nothing of it previously. No doubt this business was the reason for Elibank's resignation.[13] When Illingworth came to the House after the committee Ronald McNeil shouted 'The co-trustee.' Illingworth stood and glared for a bit then sat down looking very yellow. It was hard luck on him. There is a strong feeling on our side that this portends an early break up of the Government. Goulding told me that Lloyd George has more than once told him that they would never commit Balfour's mistake of hanging on when everything was going against them. I am sceptical. They cannot get in a much worse position, and something may turn up. Even before these last revelations they were wonderfully jumpy. On Monday 2 June the second reading of the budget was on. Snowden moved an amendment condemning food duties and advocating more income tax and death duties. We had whipped our people meaning to divide against second reading of the bill. George thought we meant to vote with Snowden, got very nervous and put Dalziel up to move the adjournment of the debate; now they must give another day to it. Second reading of Home Rule Bill yesterday. Balfour moved rejection in rather a feeble speech.

News came yesterday of George Wyndham's sudden death. He was an exceedingly attractive fellow. I stayed with him at Clouds just before Easter. He seemed so happy and full of spirits then, revelling in his new library that he had just built at Clouds and delighted over his son's engagement. In politics he just missed being in the first rank. His curious jumpy manner spoilt his speaking. When Chief Secretary he used to drink and had to give up on that account. It would have been difficult to know where he was to be put had we come into office.

Monday 22 June   Marconi debate of last Wednesday and Thursday overshadows all else in politics. The report of the committee overruling their own chairman did the Radicals no good.[14] Asquith announced that the two days should be given for the consideration of the report, but put down no motion. On Monday George Cave's motion was put down after a leaders' confab on our side. On Tuesday Talbot told Illingworth that he really must say what the attitude of the Government was to be. Illingworth then told him that after the speeches of the mover and seconder Rufus and George would appear in a white sheet. The idea was that Bonar Law should follow and say whether after that we should press our motion. When the debate came on George Cave made an excellent speech. Helmsley who seconded somehow failed. He was too long and did not go down. Rufus made a good advocate's speech and George attacked Walter Guinness fiercely for the *Outlook* articles.[15] They both expressed regret but it was mainly regret at being found out. Still their party gave them quite an ovation as they left the House. Their attitude being unsatisfactory, Bob Cecil was put up and the debate went on in the ordinary dinner hour way. On Thursday morning we did not look to have done much good by it. However, speaking after Asquith that afternoon Balfour made a speech that was on all hands pronounced first rate. He suggested the possibility of a resolution on which all could agree. The next few hours were spent in negotiations. They were, and were bound to be, fruitless; because Unionists insisted throughout that the House must express regret and Radicals would not have that because it would have involved the resignation of the two Ministers. But all our young bloods were in an awful stew lest we should agree to something less. In the end Ryland Adkins moved a resolution accepting Ministers' expression of regret. We adhered to Cave's motion after Bonar Law had stated the words we were ready to accept. Bonar made a fine fighting speech and put all the points very strongly. Grey replied, evidently not liking his job. They defeated Cave's motion by 78. Then we did not divide against Adkins'. My impression is that the debate will have done them harm. The whole Radical party is now in the position of condoning the transactions. The threats of raking up past sores have all fallen through. And the country may well get the impression that it is a dirty business that cannot be defended by any one. The fact that our side did not cheer at the diminution of the Government majority created a good impression.

Tuesday 8 July Alfred Lyttleton died last Friday night. One of the most attractive men in the House, he was universally popular. The only complaint against him was that he was too kind to the other side. He was not a great speaker either in the House or on the platform, but both on the Welsh Church Bill and on Marconi he had lately made quite good speeches. His extreme moderation gave extra effect to any attack that did come from him. Asquith's words about him at the beginning of yesterday's sitting were absolutely perfect. Nothing could have been more apt than saying that Alfred was exactly the man that every English father hoped his son would grow up to be.

I have been very busy lately over the Plural Voting Bill. The Government were very anxious to finish the third reading last Friday. They had an all night sitting on Wednesday and tried very hard to bully us into agreeing that they should get it by then. However, we eventually prevented that. Cassel's ingenuity in drafting a new clause just saved us. Whitley after consenting to a lot of gagging at last told Talbot he would not let them have it if we were not obstructive. Now they are in rather a difficulty about time.

George has been Limehousing.[16] Our people think his speeches will do us good. I am not very sure of that. I know Bonar Law is a little nervous of his land campaign whenever it does come off.

Tuesday 5 August   Things have been very dull. The Government have introduced a Revenue Bill and a new Insurance Bill, both full of concessions to us. They have cleverly left them to the end of the session, and tell us that we can take them or leave them, but if we delay them they will be lost. Consequence is that things are now going through at railroad speed and there seems every chance of our getting away on the 15th. We had another go last Wednesday on Seely's salary. Joynson Hicks and George Sandys had been down to look at the aeroplanes and clearly proved that Seely had lied as to their numbers.[17] Sandys made a very good speech on the subject. We had whipped vigorously and got the majority down to 33, but they knew what was up. The story of some of our men hiding in the bathroom was quite true.

Rather a remarkable feat was accomplished by Wedgwood on report of Mental Deficiency Bill. He obstructed for twelve hours almost singlehanded, was in the House the whole time and ate nothing but some chocolate and spoke something like 50 times.

Our side is slack and tired, but there is no grumbling or intriguing going on just now, and on the whole things look healthy.

House rose on 14 August.

Thursday 13 November   Since the House rose two things have happened. The Government have got frightened about Ulster, and George has started his land campaign. As to Ulster, Cave told me in August that Carson had consulted him as to whether a particular course of action amounted to high treason. Cave advised that it did. I asked him if he thought it more or less likely that Carson would adopt the course in question on account of that advice. Cave said: 'Really I don't know.' Most of the men I speak to on our side think there will be no compromise, but a great many expect a January election. Banbury quite expects one on the ground that the Radicals stand to lose less then than they would after there was fighting in Ulster. I saw Carson the other day. He said they had got

£850,000 for their guarantee fund and would get a million. He showed me a most gushing letter from Rufus Isaacs thanking him for his congratulation on the L.C.Justiceship,[18] also thanking him for his attitude in the summer and calling him 'the Bayard of the Bar'. Charlie Hunter told me that Carson had said: 'The whole thing is a matter of whose nerve lasts the longest, mine or Asquith's. My health may give way but my nerve will not.' Hunter also told me he had been in Paris with Henry Wilson who went to see the French C.S.O. The C.S.O. much perturbed about Ulster; said if you send your troops over there, the Germans will choose that time to make war on us.

As to George and the land his blunders about marigolds and deer forests have brought a good deal of ridicule on him; Talbot and Steel Maitland sent out a circular to Unionist candidates asking them to ridicule or pass over George in their speeches and concentrate on Home Rule. Of course this got about and George is making fun of it. In any case the advice is not very practicable in county divisions. I am trying hard to find out how the labourers regard it but get very contradictory information. There is no disguising the fact that in the West Country the most knowing people are uneasy about its effect. A certain number of our party go openly for wage boards. Men like St Audries and Banbury scout the idea and say: 'Stick to the farmer who is on our side and never mind the labourer whose vote you won't get anyhow.' Alex Thynne[19] is strong for wage boards, but when I got him to come to a meeting of the County Conservative Association, he would not speak out. I wrote to Talbot last week pointing out that the party must have a declared policy in the matter, or else all our candidates will take different lines. Even a Tory like Tom Calley[20] is inclined to advocate wage boards. Talbot says Bonar Law will speak about it at Norwich today. Steel Maitland was staying with me on Monday; he says he has tried hard to get some pronouncement on the matter, but Bonar Law has been so engrossed with Ireland that he cannot get any real attention given to the matter.

Sunday 7 December   The other day Steel Maitland wrote to ask me if I would take on the job of 'shepherding' the agricultural societies in the party interests. I told him I would do what I could, though not very sanguine as to being able to do much with them. I am to meet Trustram Eve and Prothero and talk matters over with them next week.[21] I went on to lunch with Bonar Law and had a very interesting talk with him. On the wages question he says he advocates local inquiries in each district and if conditions are very bad he is ready to go for some compulsory means of improving them. I said: 'How about Walter Long?' He said: 'Walter will come into line all right if he finds that it is the general feeling of the party.' Turning to other matters he told me that he thought it impossible the

Government could hold on long enough to carry the Plural Voting Bill. He told me Asquith had said this himself, so he was informed. I said: 'But what is to turn them out?' He replied: 'Ulster.' I asked him if he was sure that Carson's arrangements were complete and were sure to produce a crisis. He said yes. Ulster would refuse to obey judges and would turn out the R.I.C. and appoint their own police. No Government could stand that. I then sounded him as to the chances of compromising. He said if the Government would exclude six counties, would take away from the Home Rule Government post office and customs and would leave appointment of judges to the British Government, there could be a deal on those terms. He did not, however, think Redmond would consent to such terms. As to the army he said his information was that they would refuse to fight Ulster. On that point I myself get very contradictory reports. The fact is that I don't expect most officers have made up their minds on the subject.

CHAPTER 4 NOTES

1   This is a very specific list and, as a whip, Sanders certainly ought to have been in a position to know, but it does not tally with other accounts. There are eight M.P.s listed here instead of the usual six and most sources include Aitken as one of those who did not sign. (See A.J.P. Taylor, *Beaverbrook*, p. 77.) The discrepancy may be partially explained by the fact that the memorial was not finally presented to Law until the following day; some who refused at the week-end may have agreed by the Monday morning in view of the near-unanimity of the party. There remains doubt as to whether Aitken really did refuse to sign, as he later claimed. See also J.E. Amery, *The Life of Joseph Chamberlain*, vol.IV, p. 982, and A.M. Gollin, *The Observer and J.L. Garvin*, p. 366.

2   G.A. Gibbs, Conservative M.P. since 1906, was Walter Long's son-in-law and, as Long had been, he was a Bristol M.P. He became a Unionist whip in 1917.

3   This was J.A. ('Jack') Pease, Liberal M.P. since 1901, President of the Board of Education 1911–1915 and 1st Lord Gainford in 1917. Not to be confused with Pike Pease the Unionist Whip.

4   The Liberals had gained the by election at Londonderry on January 30.

5   W. Hayes Fisher, Conservative Whip for the London Area, and Steel-Maitland were both unpopular men throughout their careers and for reasons that must have had their origins in personalities rather than respective abilities.

6 The doctors were still in conflict with the Government over the implementation of the National Insurance Act. Runciman had placed the restriction of double inspection on imported Irish cattle because of an outbreak of foot and mouth disease in Ireland. He stuck to his decision despite great pressure from the Irish M.P.s.

7 'Disinterested management' was a favourite proposal of the temperance lobby, whereby the state would become involved in the drink trade as an alternative to prohibition, with decisions taken by local option. This would prevent the trade from being run by those with an interest in making money out of it.

8 L.J. Maxse, the Diehard editor of the *National Review*, had given evidence to the Select Committee on the Marconi scandal on 13 February and had made several allegations but had refused to name his sources. The Committee reported him to the House of Commons itself which, after debate, took no action. Frances Donaldson, *The Marconi Affair*, p. 88.

9 Weston duly held the seat at South Westmorland on 18 March.

10 Cambridgeshire, Newmarket, was won from the Liberals on 16 May and Cheshire, Altrincham, was held by the Conservatives on 28 May.

11 Major Jack Hills had been a Unionist M.P. since 1910 and was a leading member of the Unionist Social Reform Committee. See the diary entry for 13 October 1912 for the background to this Bill.

12 Cecil Chesterton was being sued for libel in connection with articles on the Marconi affair that had appeared in *Eye Witness*, a magazine that he edited. It was thought by Unionists, who wanted to make all possible political capital out of the affair, that Carson and Smith were obscuring the issues by appearing on the Liberal side. This was actually in the parallel libel action against *Le Matin*, not the case against Chesterton. Frances Donaldson, *The Marconi Affair*, p. 99.

13 See diary entry for 11 August 1912.

14 The attempt of the Chairman, Sir Albert Spicer, to draft a report that would be accepted by the entire Select Committee was perhaps doomed to failure in so highly charged a political atmosphere. It was however the Liberal majority on the Committee that voted it down and ensured that the majority report should completely exonerate Lloyd George and Isaacs. Frances Donaldson, *op.cit.*, p. 198.

15 Walter Guinness, Unionist M.P. since 1907, was the owner of *Outlook*, which had published some of the most outspoken revelations of the whole of the Marconi Affair.

16 Already a convenient short-hand for political vituperation, after Lloyd George's Limehouse speech of 30 July 1909.

17 Motions to reduce a Minister's salary were a convenient way of getting policy debates on supply days. For Joynson-Hicks' attempts to push

the Liberal government into a more active air policy, see H.A. Taylor, *Jix, Viscount Brentford*, p. 124.

18 Rufus Isaacs was appointed Lord Chief Justice on 19 October to howls of protest from the Opposition, which had just been accusing him of corruption over Marconi. Carson had of course represented him in that question too.

19 Lord Alexander Thynne, Conservative M.P. since 1910 and, as a son of the Marquess of Bath, an influential figure in the West Country.

20 Colonel Thomas Calley of Burderop had been Conservative M.P. for Cricklade between January and December 1910.

21 H. Trustram Eve and R.E. Prothero were both leaders of agricultural opinion and became respectively Chairman of the Forage Committee and President of the Board of Agriculture during World War I.

Chapter 5 1914–15 'Neither the Nationalists nor the Ulstermen want to compromise'

Sunday 8 February Bonar Law announced in his speech at Bristol that negotiations as to Home Rule had failed and that he saw no hope of their succeeding in the future. On the other hand Lady Ilchester told me last week that Carson believed the matter would eventually be squared by the omission of the six counties.

I spoke at Lincoln on January 30 at the dinner of the Lincolnshire Farmers Union. The chairman of that body and a member of it called Gilbert have been the leading spirits in a body called the Farmers' Tariff Union that is trying to make difficulties over tariff reform. Bonar Law sent me down to speak. I told them that of course they could vote Radical if they liked but that their agitation would not make us change our policy. I believe I did some good. The Farmers' Tariff Union is really a radical affair and a bit of plain speaking makes the Tory farmers see that they are being tricked. The other landed job on which I have been at work is to get the committee over which Lord Salisbury presided in July called together again to discuss the wages questiion. James Hope pressed for this. I have done all I could to forward it. Lord Lansdowne is very anxious to do nothing on the wages question. On the other hand I had a strong letter from Maurice Woods, the secretary of the Unionist Social Reform Committee protesting against the committee sitting again and saying that he and his friends were settling the whole business. Woods wrote later to apologise. I want the committee to meet and appoint a small sub-committee to devise a scheme and submit it to the leaders.

Wednesday 11 February New session opened yesterday. Went to Bonar Law's dinner on Monday night. All our people talking of possible ways of settling Home Rule. There have been altogether five interviews between Asquith, Bonar Law and Carson. The question of the exclusion of Ulster was evidently considered and Carson said he suggested that Ulster be excluded until Parliament otherwise determines. Carson struck me as rather pacific. But he said he would not recommend Ulster to accept anything short of exclusion. If other terms were proposed he would say:

71

'consult the Ulster people; I stand aside; but if they are satisfied, I am.'
Bonar Law and still more F.E. were apprehensive that any announcement
of concessions would put us in a bad position in the country. Balfour was
for challenging Asquith to put his proposals in writing. The Scotchmen
Clyde and Scott Dickson seemed rather against any sort of settlement. All
seemed agreed that in no case could the Rads pass a Bill, however much
amended. Any amendments would have to be put in a separate bill. F.E.
very full of buck later on. He has taken a huge house in Grosvenor
Gardens and describes his doing so as the greatest bit of bluff ever known.
He declares he has insured his life for £20,000 to maintain his family if he
gets shot in Ulster. He, Bonar, Harold Henderson and I played bridge
until 1 o'clock after the dinner.

Tuesday morning we had a whips' meeting at 11 a.m. I heard there that
Seely says in no circumstances is the army to be used against Ulster. An
officer sent in his papers and said he meant to fight for Ulster. French[1] said
he must be court martialled. The matter came before the Cabinet and
French was overruled.

It was at first intended that Bonar Law should speak after Asquith in
debate on Long's amendment to address. But Salter was to be ready if
required. The first part of Asquith's speech was very poor – just a lawyer's
bit of forensic argument. But his latter part and especially his references to
possible exclusion of Ulster made a great impression. Rumour was that the
Nationalists were very sick. They certainly looked it. Bonar Law offered to
bet five to one that the Home Rule Bill in its present form does not pass
third reading.

Friday 13 February   Carson's speech on the Home Rule amendment was
about the best thing I have heard in the House of Commons. It was really
moving. The division was good, better than we expected. It is surprising
how the Radicals have got their tails down. I expected to find them rather
full of themselves and our own people not too confident. But in the House
it is just the other way. And yet none of our people seem to think that we
should get a working majority as the result of a general election. Our old
hands all predict a spring election. St Audries puts it in May. H. Samuel[2] is
reported to have said that their best course might be to get defeated in a
snap division. Willoughby de Broke is investigating the question of
amending the Army Annual Bill. He told me Lord Halsbury and Bob Cecil
are looking it up. I tried to convince him that it would be unwise to try any
such game if it seemed likely that the Government would come to grief
without it.

Tuesday 24 February   Things have been very quiet lately. The bye
elections have been the only excitement. I never knew the Radicals so

ready and anxious to bet as they were about Bethnal Green.[3] Both Will Crooks and Dalziel declared that the Labour candidates both there and at Poplar would take votes from us, but none from the Radicals. In both divisions the Unionist poll was almost exactly 25 per cent below the promises – a very big percentage to deduct. On the whole the elections show a turn in our favour, but it cannot be called a great wave. Meanwhile no one knows anything about the Government's proposals. The prospects of exclusion seem rather going back. I got word the other day that the Under Sheriff's Council are considering a draft Referendum Bill. It is possible that the Government may adopt that course.

Thursday 5 March   The event of the week has been Asquith's announcement that he would announce his proposed alterations to the Home Rule Bill on Monday next. In answer to a question from James Hope on Monday last he promised to bring them very shortly if an arrangement as to business could be made between the whips. In the negotiations that followed Edmund stood out for Monday the 9th all through. Illingworth raised every possble objection but eventually gave in. Everyone is of course speculating as to the proposals but I don't think anything has leaked out. I think the general feeling in our party is that in any case they must not be rejected without careful consideration.

The Leith election was an immense surprise. Both George Younger and Boraston told me we had no chance. The result was caused by 600 to 800 Liberal abstentions.[4]

Thursday 12 March   Last Monday Asquith announced his proposals for modification of the Home Rule Bill. His speech was too long but dignified and earnest. Bonar Law was not so good. He had let us know beforehand that he would not accept a 'time limit' proposal. Carson made a very good speech though he was in great pain from neuralgia at the time. He threw the Bill back to them by his words about the time limit. F.E. Smith was standing by me at the time, and was rather nervous that he had gone too far. Mitchell Thomson and next day Carson himself both told me that there was absolutely no chance of the Nationalists allowing Asquith to accept Carson's proposal. The fact is neither the Nationalists nor the Ulstermen want to compromise. Dr Esmond said afterwards that now the plan would be 'Full Steam ahead' with the original Bill and an election after it was passed but before it came into operation. He said the Nationalists had an immense admiration for Carson. The feeling in our party now is stronger against compromise than it was.

On Tuesday we had the motion condemning Lloyd George's lies. We had a good division getting their majority down to 64. But we did not score much by the debate. The Radical game was to treat the whole thing as a joke and they were on the whole successful. George insisted on having an hour and a quarter for his speech. F.E. who wound up for us wanted three-quarters of an hour. Cassel the seconder spoke beyond his allotted time. F.E. was furious and his speech was not up to his usual form.

Thursday 19 March   Last Saturday Winston made a very truculent speech on Home Rule in Bradford. On Monday Asquith followed this up by refusing to give details of his proposals unless the principle was accepted. The Radicals cheered Winston very heartily when he came into the House. They are apparently well pleased with the new turn. Our people are not happy. My own opinion is that it would have been better to have welcomed Asquith's proposals as a step in the right direction. On the other hand some men have told me that any compromise would smash the party to atoms. The idea of the Lords amending the Army Annual Act is now being seriously considered. Edmund has told us to find out the views of our own people about it. Edmund himself rather favours it. Most of the whips are against it, and on the whole the feeling in the party is against it. The Scotchmen say it would be fatal to Unionist prospects in Scotland. Curiously enough Ronald McNiel says it would be most unpopular with the Orangemen who say they have no quarrel with the army. The one strong point is that it must force an election, and it is rather hard to see how to force one otherwise. At the present moment there are rumours that the Government mean to make arrests in Ulster. If they do there will be a row for certain. Mitchell Thomson attributes the Government's change of attitude to Devlin having put his foot down. Vote of censure today. I don't suppose we shall gain much by that.
Same evening The debate on the vote of censure was at a very high level. Bonar Law serious and moderate. Bar his reference to the army, a very statesmanlike speech. Asquith followed. His voice was bad from a cold but his tone was moderate, unlike Winston's Bradford speech. Carson was to have wound up, but there was a report that arrests were to take place in Ulster. So he spoke after Asquith. He made a strong attack on Winston. Then Devlin followed and introduced the old yarn about Carson having been a Liberal. Carson said it was an infamous lie and on the intervention of the Speaker changed his expression to 'wilful falsehood'. That passed muster. Carson then left for Ireland. There was a report that he was to be arrested at the station. So at Edmund's request I went with him to Euston to see what happened. Nothing happened. Carson is in good spirits. Borrowed a fiver from me to pay for his journey! Dillon and Hugh Cecil both made good speeches and Austen who wound up for us was also very good. They got a majority of 97. Most of the Ulstermen were away. On the whole the debate has made things look more peaceful. There was a report on the Stock Exchange in the afternoon that the Government had resigned

and stocks rose at once in consequence. Walter Long met Carson at the station to see him off. When I saw him later he told me that his information from a good source was that Carson's arrest was intended but his going by the early train defeated the intention. I don't myself believe it.

Thursday 26 March Things have been moving very fast this last week. The affair of the Curragh officers has created an enormous sensation. When Bonar Law spoke about it on Monday he made a reference to the right of soldiers under certain circumstances to disobey, which was not approved by our party and gave the other side an opening. Balfour made an extraordinarily fine speech. On Tuesday report of army estimates. Asquith promised to lay papers that night and suggested the debate on the subject should come next day on the Consolidated Fund Bill. This was generally agreed to, but Amery on his own account must needs make a speech about Gough, and that let feelings loose on the subject.[5] The debate showed the extraordinary hostility to the army felt by the Labour men and most of the Radicals. John Ward and Thomas both made very good speeches from their point of view, and Ward's attack on the King and army caused one of the greatest demonstrations from Labour and Radical members I ever saw in the House. Bob Cecil made an excellent sensible speech later on. On Wednesday morning we got the White Paper with the Gough correspondence. In the face of Seely's pledge to Gough it seemed certain that the Radicals must throw the Government over. The denouement by which the Government threw over the pledge yet did not accept Seely's resignation took us all by surprise. It has saved the Government for the time. But how either Gough or French will stand it remains to be seen. George Stanley declares that a large number of the officers at the War Office would go if Gough did. Austen made a very good speech rubbing in the points about Seely.

Wednesday 1 April Things are quiet again now. F.E. made a very good speech on Monday on the officers' question and Winston certainly got hold of a number of quotations rather damaging to our side. I knew Rowland Hunt had been writing foolish letters to NCOs and had wondered they have not been produced before. Now everyone is talking again about conciliation. It is said that Radicals are rather surprised how strong the feeling in the country in favour of the army seems to be. Asquith's move is generally approved. Strachie told me he did it quite on his own; very few of the Cabinet knew anything about it till the last moment.[6]

Tuesday 28 April The Ulster leaders manifesto as to the 'plot' raised the whole of that question again just when it seemed to be quieting down. Carson told me that the report was false that warrants were prepared for the arrest of leaders. The warrants were really search warrants. The Ulstermen's secret service was extraordinarily good. On one occasion Walter Long asked me to go out and see John Arkwright[7] in the middle of a debate. Arkwright told me that Birrell has removed his code book from his house and has locked it up in a safe at the Irish Office and that he had sent a letter to his wife under cover of one to the governess! Also that Paget had been asked for an answer Yes or No and has sent a long cypher telegram in reply. I reported to Long who said he knew what it all meant. Wilfrid Ashley told me that the contents of McKenna's telegrams about warrants were known to the Ulstermen before they were known in Dublin. He also told me that the Volunteers were short of arms having enough to arm only 25 per cent of their men. The Government proclamation had come at a very bad time for them. He blamed the leaders for enlisting so many more men than they could arm. Now the exploit of last Friday has put them all right. That exploit was run by James Craig and McCalmont.[8]

Rumours were strong yesterday that Government contemplated a dissolution at once as the only way out of the trouble. Bob Cecil and Pike were both of that opinion. The success of the gun running makes our position in today's debate somewhat difficult. The need for precautions is more manifest than it was before. If the Government had taken the bold line throughout they would be in a much stronger position.

Thursday 30 April The debate of the last two days was most curious. Austen began with a very able speech on the plot, a little too long. Churchill followed. Very violent to start with; F.E. said afterwards 'You can't blame him much; having scored all round in Ulster we can allow them to talk.' At the end of his speech he made his 'offer' to Carson. That knocked the stuffing out of the debate that evening while our leaders were talking the matter over. Next day Balfour began and made the most moving speech I have heard in the House. Carson also spoke and went very far towards conciliation. He only spoke for about a quarter of an hour. He said he left out all the first part of his speech as to the Ulster plot because Balfour had already said it all so well. Asquith wound up and was very non-committal. The result today is that a large section of the Radicals are furious and the Nationalists alarmed while there is serious discontent among a section of our own party. Bob Cecil told me that in the 'shadow cabinet' Balfour was strong for compromise and Bonar Law rather against it. Carson after his speech said that what weighed with him most was that if the Unionists got in they would find Ireland very difficult to govern. He said there would probably be a refusal to pay instalments on the lines of the old 'No Rent' business. The Duke of Devonshire agreed and also expressed the opinion that if Home Rule was carried with exclusion of

Ulster the Unionists of the South would not suffer, because the Home Rule Parliament would be on its good behaviour in order to induce Ulster to come in eventually. I took the chair tonight at the St Stephen's Club for an address by Maxse. He was very indignant at the speeches of the night before and held forth on thoroughly 'Die Hard' lines. The feeling of the members of the Club present was certainly with him. Things look difficult but I think the tendency is for peace on the whole.

Wednesday 6 May   Budget introduced on Monday. Lloyd George made a singularly ineffective speech. It was really impossible to understand at all what his proposals were as to local taxation. Burden thrown on direct tax payer very heavy. I was amused next day to find Howell Davies grumbling a great deal about it. Sam Hoare says it will be a vote catcher in London where the relief to rates will come to about 1/- in the pound. I doubt if it will help the rural districts much.

I took the chair at the Monday night dinner with Lord Halsbury as the guest. The old man was as lively as could be. We were a little afraid his speech would be very bitter about any idea of compromise on Home Rule. But he spoke mainly of the iniquities of the Reform Bill of 1832!

The party opposed to compromise on Home Rule is in the ascendant just now. Bob Cecil called a meeting at St Stephen's Club of about 100 private members to discuss the situation, and the Federal people were said to consist of the least experienced members of the party and to be in a hopeless minority. Bonar has expressed the hope that no memorials will be sent to him, but is ready to see people and discuss matter with them.

Friday 15 May   The only alteration in the situation is Asquith's definite announcement that the Government intends to introduce an amending Bill. One of the lobby correspondents told me that this course had the real approval of the Nationalists, but that they would certainly oppose it in the House to appease their own supporters in Ireland and America. This would explain Redmond's truculent speech which created rather a sensation at the time. We were a good deal relieved at the result of the Grimsby election. Most of our people expected to lose. The place is entirely non-political, and the Radical is very popular locally.

We tried to 'snap' yesterday. Our arrangements worked very well and the secret did not get out. We got 234, but they had 255 present. They were taken by surprise and very frightened. Gulland's face was a white as a sheet when he came to the table. They would not have gone out I suppose, but their time would have been put out.

Thursday 18 June   I went out with the Yeomanry on 19 May, and was not present on the occasion of the vote on th 21st. That row was not got up by the whips. Amery did more than anyone else to promote it. The two election successes that week were a great score for us.[9] Since the holidays things have been fairly quiet. On the whole things look less like a compromise, and our people are less confident about getting an election. I do not know whether our leaders have yet come to the conclusion that if we beat Home Rule we could not govern Ireland, but it is becoming more apparent every day. Hogg, M.P. for Derry is very ill. O'Neil tells me that in case of a bye election we should lose by more than before, and a row would be almost certain in the event of a contest.

I moved the rejection of the Plural Voting Bill on third reading last Monday. It is the first leading thing I have done. Was pleased to find that the papers took hold of the phrase 'low down trick' which I used about the Bill and put it in big letters.

Monday 6 July   Joe Chamberlain died suddenly last week. Austen was at the House the day before. One of his last sayings on politics was: 'They are on the run; we ought to increase our terms.' The reports now are that the Government mean to accept almost any terms the Ulstermen ask, and that they do not mean to have an election. If there is no election it looks as if the House will sit well into September. The budget proceedings have got into a great muddle and now the Government are moving a time table on the third day of committee. There is no precedent for a time table on a budget. We were finding very hard to keep the debate going, and they could probably have got it quicker without a special motion.

I was very anxious last week to try a snap division on the Foreign Office vote. I suggested to Pike and Edmund and got them with Steel-Maitland, Banbury and Baird to back up the idea. Baird went to Bonar Law about it. B.L. went to Lansdowne who vetoed it emphatically. He said it would be against all that he had advocated in public life. So nothing was done. I think it quite possible that we should have beaten them.

Lucy met Mrs James Craig about a fortnight ago. She is usually very calm about politics; but she took Lucy aside and told her that both James and Carson took a more serious view of things than they had ever done. Mrs Craig spoke as if she was saying a long farewell and said she had been seeing her boys before returning to Ireland as she did not know what might happen before she saw them again. Altogether she was quite tragic about it.

Wednesday 16 July   Things still drifting. Bonar Law does not seem very anxious to hurry the Government on the Amending Bill question. It looks to me as if they were playing for time. The feeling against compromise is certainly hardening in our party. It seems to be assumed that if there is no compromise there must be an election. I don't see the necessity unless the

King insists. I have been using what little influence I have in favour of our accepting exclusion of the six counties with no time limit. The latest rumour is that the Government will raise no objection to Carson's provisional government.

Saturday 19 July　Charles Beresford has a circumstantial story that the King insisted on a Conference on Ireland. Failing agreement by the conference he will not consent to the Bill without an appeal to 'my people'. Edmund has instructed us to tell our fellows that there will be no conference unless necessitated by pressure from the King. The Nationalists seem very depressed.[10]

Tuesday 21 July　Yesterday's announcement as to the Conference was received by all parties with disapproval. C. Beresford, Sir H. Samuel and Sir H. Craik are perhaps the most vehement against it on our side. They say they will not vote in the House against agreement embodied in a Bill. St Audries says the House of Lords will pass nothing less than total exclusion. The fear with our people is as to the effect on our supporters in the country of anything like abandonment of opposition to every sort of Home Rule. George Lane Fox told me he thought compromise would be acceptable in Yorkshire.[11] The Labour men are furious at being ignored. Hence their impertinent manifesto.

Friday 24 July　Asquith announced on motion for adjournment today that the conference had failed to come to an agreement on the area for exclusion. Amending Bill to be taken on Tuesday. Horner, the Tyrone M.P., was very gloomy the other day as to prospects. He looked on a collision in Tyrone as certain to take place soon. One of the lobby correspondents tells me the Liberals expect an early election. Most of our people expect it too. On the other hand Geoffrey Howard laid Harold Henderson five to one against an election within a month. Carson said that before the Conference the Speaker said an agreement was possible if only Carson was reasonable. C. much annoyed with Speaker in consequence.

　I saw Francis Acland today and spoke to him about the Austro-Servian trouble. He said our Government had pressed Germany to press for moderation and Germany 'had not played th game' at all.[12]

Tuesday 4 August　In the last ten days the war cloud has been growing closer. But till about Wednesday the man in the street took little if any notice.[13] The difficulty in getting gold brought it home to people more than anything else. Grey's speech yesterday was an historic performance. But many of our people think we have been too slow in mobilising the army. Churchill has come out very well. Duke of Devonshire told me he mobilised the Fleet off his own bat without consulting Asquith. While Grey was speaking he was crying with excitement and afterwards rushed up to Carson and insisted on shaking hands. They had not spoken to one another for six years. A good deal of regret was expressed on our side that Carson did not speak after Redmond's speech. The latter was eloquent though it did not amount to much. Carson says if he offered the Ulster Volunteers to the War Office he would only get snubbed for his pains. He evidently does not like things and expects the Ulstermen to be left in the lurch. We do not know yet if the expeditionary force is to be sent abroad. Charlie Hunter on Wilson's authority says the French expect it and we ought to send it at once. On the other hand Pole Carew says it would be a great mistake to send it at all, and Claude Willoughby declares the great thing is to let the recruits have a week to settle down. Our party is quite anxious to support the Government. The anti-war party was vocal yesterday, but it is not numerous or influential.

Tuesday 25 August House met again today after adjournment of a fortnight. Came up from camp at Tendring. To London in uniform and changed at the flat but a lot of fellows were in khaki. The fall of Namur and retirement of our armies took place yesterday. Talbot told me he heard the French on our right gave way during a night attack and rather put us in the cart. Reports of recruiting for the new army not very satisfactory. George Stanley says Kitchener is going for compulsion. Another piece of gossip is that the Belgians gave up Namur as part of a deal. On the other hand both Balfour and Talbot have an idea that the Namur forts are still holding out. As to Home Rule no proposal of any sort has been made by the Government. Nor have they said whether they mean to adjourn or prorogue. The Nationalist Volunteers refuse to sign any allegiance paper or to serve under the Union Jack. Ulster Volunteers both in Ulster, Liverpool and Glasgow would be ready to volunteer for foreign service in large numbers if they could be assured Home Rule would not be carried in their absence. The Yeomanry officers that I saw do not report very well as to number of Yeomen ready to go abroad. The North Devons come out better than any I heard of.[14]

Edmund Talbot to Sanders – 11 June 1915

My dear Peter,

I have been meaning to write to you for ages, though I know you did not expect any answer to your letter.

I know also you will realise that in your position as C.O. it was impossible to bring you back, though I don't suppose you would have

10 The King had certainly urged a conference on Asquith for several months but it is unlikely that any threat was needed to convince Asquith that it was the only option left at this stage. It was not announced until the following day. Harold Nicolson, *King George V*, pp. 321 ff.
11 George Lane Fox had been a Unionist M.P. since 1906 and was Chairman of the Yorkshire Division of the National Union.
12 F.D. Acland was a Liberal M.P. and Under-Secretary at the Foreign Office, 1911–15.
13 War was declared on Germany on 4 August. The previous entry in the diary shows how suddenly the prospect of war had broken in on Sanders himself. This entry conveys some of the strangeness and unexpectedness of the first few days of actual war.
14 The Yeomanry enlisted only for service in Britain and so in 1914 they were invited to volunteer for service abroad. There was of course no means of compelling them until conscription was introduced in 1916.
15 The last part of this letter is cut off, perhaps by the military censor since it begins: 'Bobby is home for a few days; thinks he is going to command one of the new . . .

Chapter 6 1917 'The Franchise Bill has been making steady progress'

Edmund Talbot to Sanders 2 March 1917

My dear Peter,

I am told your second-in-command is good and competent and this being so I do not hesitate to write and ask you to consider whether you will not come for duty in the House.

I cannot offer you any definite employment, but things often turn up where an able man is wanted to help in some department or office and I have a feeling that as things now are in the near East you would probably be of more use at home.

I have had this idea in mind for some time but felt it was asking a lot of a C.O. and might be wrong for the Regiment. But if I am correctly informed as to your second-in-command I hesitate no longer. Of course I imagine it would mean that in the event of your wanting ro rejoin for service the War Office would not guarantee your going back to the same regiment.

But you have done your share at the Front and I believe now you would be of more value at home. So if you can see your way to telling the authorities that you have been asked to return for work in the House I hope you will do so.

Yours ever,
Edmund Talbot.

Sunday 27 May I arrived in London on 2 May after soldiering in Gallipoli, Egypt and Palestine. Edmund Talbot had written to ask me back. He told me he could not offer me a job at present, but said something was sure to turn up before long. There was a chance that Charles Bathurst would give up his job and he promised to run me for that,[1] but Bathurst made it up with Devonport and went on, rather to my relief. The trouble was about the meatless day. Bathurst got his way and it was dropped. I was present at the secret session of 10 and 11 May. W. Churchill made a very good speech arguing that we would do no real good at present on the West Front in view of the Russian trouble and that our sound policy was to wait till next year when the U.S. could give really effective help on land. Lloyd George made a most optimistic speech going out of his way to say that we must retain all we had won. He was very sanguine about the food position quoting figures to show that with reasonable care we were in no real danger. Later in the debate he was asked to explain why he said on the same subject in February that the country was in deadly peril. He replied: 'Oh, then I wanted to get the land cultivated.' Curiously characteristic. R. Cecil hinted at the possibility of separate terms with Bulgaria and Austria. Carson made a long defence of the Admiralty that was well received.

On the 22nd the Franchise Bill came on for second reading. There was very strong feeling among the party organisations in the country about it. It was said that Simon was much too clever for Harry Samuel, Bull and other Unionist members of the Speaker's Conference. However, when the report of the Conference came before the House, the Unionist M.P.s funked voting against it. After consultation with C. Hamilton, Banbury and H. Cecil, I undertook to move the amendment against the bill. My speech was very well received but we got only 40 in the lobby. The division was a good illustration of the difficulty of getting a decent vote without a party whip. H. Cecil made a most able and amusing speech against the Bill.

I had a talk one evening to T.P. O'Connor about the Irish convention. He said the great thing was to 'sit on the forces of disorder'. He also said they must have an Irish chairman.

My brother was over on the 22nd from France. He is usually very sanguine, but this time he said that owing to Russia letting us down the Germans on the West Front are just as strong as we are. He told me that some of our divisions were at half strength owing to want of drafts.

On hearing Lloyd George's speeches again after three years away, it struck me he had lost much of his old fire. Physically he has grown fat. His speeches while still forcible have become somewhat bombastic, sometimes even pompous.

Sunday 10 June On the last day of the Whitsuntide recess St Audries died. He gave me my start politically and had always been a really good friend to me. In Somerset he had an extraordinary influence with the farmers and did a great deal of good by it. He had worked very hard on the county agriculture war committee and broke down at it. As chief whip he was not popular. His manner appeared surly and 'stand-offish'. This was, I always thought, largely shyness. But it did harm. With his intimates he was the very best of companions.

During the recess the first notices of the divisions of the counties by the Boundary Commissioners appeared. Somerset stands to lose two county seats besides Taunton and one of the Bath seats. The committee stage of the Bill began on Wednesday. Since the second reading agriculture has woken up. The Central Chamber passed a strong resolution urging that area as well as population should be taken into account. At the beginning of committee stage I spoke on an instruction and again pressed the claims of agriculture and urged that we ought at least to have a chance of discussing the instructions to the Commissioners. Cave then got up and promised that an opportunity should be given on Monday 11. Walter Long then signalled me to come out. He told me the action of the Commissioners in rushing things had taken the Government entirely by surprise. He suggested that I should put down an amendment to Cave's motion and should consult with Cave as to the wording. The Government would not consent to putting in figures but he intimated that they were prepared to accept the principle of area. I saw Cave and did as W.L. suggested. I had written privately to George Lambert asking him if he would back up the agricultural cause.[2] He replied that he was in a difficult position as he had been on the Conference and there they paid no attention to him. But when I saw him in the House he told me that he and some of his friends would back me up. The feature of the proceedings in committee on the first two days was the way in which the Radicals persisted in obstructing the Bill. They were most easily drawn.

Rumour is very rife as to the activity of the pacifists and extreme socialists in the country. Page Croft told me they are working Lancashire systematically and spending a lot of money there. Pike told me the same thing with regard to Durham. He expects a very strong Labour Party in the next House. I had a talk with Hayes Fisher on the same subject. He thinks the inevitable split in the trades unions will paralyse them for some time. The recent strike on the Clyde was organised by a returned soldier, a very bad sign.

I have heard nothing from inside as to the reshuffling of places in the Government. The National Union on Friday passed a resolution that to give office to Winston would be an insult to the army and navy.

Friday 15 June   Debated the instructions to Boundary Commissioners on Monday last. I moved an amendment that the Commissioners were to take account of area as well as population. George Lambert seconded, but the Radicals began to kick at once. Eventually Cave threw my amendment over and accepted one by James Mason in rather vaguer terms. Hayes Fisher told me afterwards that the Commissioners would be told to stretch a point in favour of agriculture, but I don't trust him much. However, I got the promise that the inquiries in the various counties would be held up if an adjournment was applied for. A discussion on proportional representation followed and P.R. was defeated by eight in a dinner hour division. The Speaker was very angry as P.R. was an integral part of the recommendations of the Conference but was left by Lloyd George as an open question. The debate on the instructions was not completed at the end of two days and was talked out by a Radical.

There is a scheme on foot for holding a series of meetings in the country to counteract the pacifist and syndicalist propaganda. Edmund wants me to represent the party on the executive committee. Freddy Guest is very keen. I have had two very long talks with him about it. In the course of the first he told me that the pacifist meeting at Leeds cost £7,500 and that the Labour people believed the Liberal Central Office had a finger in it. Gulland however has said he will be ready to assist in the suggested campaign.[3]

Bonar Law has got news that his boy is safe though a prisoner. He is a different man since the news came. It is now eight weeks since the boy was reported missing and he has been fearfully upset all the latter part of the time, so much so that he had to knock off work for about a week.

Friday 6 July Franchise Bill has been making steady progress. After a good deal of excitement proportional representation was definitely beaten by 32 votes. There was a rumour that the Nationalists were going to support it in force in the hope of carrying English seats under its provisions. However, all went well and even the promise to exclude London was insufficient.

Had an interesting little discussion in a committee room with several military members on the subject of the chance of a separate peace with Turkey. The object was mainly to enable us to bring more troops to the West Front where the want of men is so badly felt. Lloyd George has promised Italy that in event of complete victory she is to have Smyrna and Konia. A protest against that has been numerously signed and sent to him.[4] On the larger question the balance of opinion was not hopeful. At present we do not seem to be able to do anything effective anywhere. L.A. scouted the idea of Turkey making terms unless we can advance to Damascus or Aleppo. At the time of Kut we tried hard to bribe them to let Townsend's army out and they laughed at us. M.S. reported the U.S. ambassador as saying that victory in the West was no good unless we could block the Berlin and Bagdad scheme.[5]

I heard Lord Hardinge's apologia in House of Lords. The general opinion was that he had not done himself much good.[6]

Thursday 12 July Air raid last Saturday gave occasion for a secret session on Monday afternoon. George gave an account of the enormous progress in aeroplane construction, but said the West Front must come first, and at present there are not enough for that and London defence. The House on the whole was satisfied.

Gulland has been making difficulties as to joining the propaganda campaign now being organised. His reasons are somewhat petty. It looks rather as if his party is now out for blood. A good many things are making the Government unpopular, and Asquith & Co. may think they see their chance. They voted against the Government on Corn Production Bill on Tuesday night and got 100 in the lobby. Prothero has not shone in his conduct of the Bill.

George Younger told me the other night that Lloyd George had actually offered Winston the Air Board a month or six weeks ago and that he withdrew the offer next day owing to Younger's letter stating that the Conservative party would not have it.[7]

Friday 20 July The Mesopotamia debate revealed House of Commons at its worst. Ministers, especially F.E. and Balfour, made a mistake in attacking the commission and the feeling of the House throughout was against them all except Austen, who is the one man generally considered to have come out of it well. The attacks on Hardinge are doing much harm in India where he had a tremendous reputation with the natives.[8]

The redistribution proposals lately announced have more than fulfilled my expectations as regards agriculture. Cave told me that he promised to back the Speaker if he gave more seats to agricultural counties even if the limit was exceeded. Cave and Hayes Fisher tell me that they mean to go for proxies for soldiers, a thing they have been fighting for all through.

After a good deal of hesitation by the Government and pressure by agricultural members it is now announced that Corn Bill is to go through before the recess. But the Radicals are obstructing and progress is slow.[9]

Our party is sullen and annoyed over the appointments of Montagu and Winston, especially the latter. Walter Long, Cave and Edmund knew nothing till they saw it in the papers. It is probably all part of a deal. Gulland is now quite friendly as regards our speaking committee. J. Craig tells me Carson approves of Churchill. McCaw, an Irish Unionist member, told me last night that another Irish rebellion in a few months is probable. Sinn Fein is getting arms and ammunition quietly.

Sunday 29 July There was an idea that the Government might get beaten over the Radical proposal to raise the minimum wage in the Corn Bill from 25 to 30 shillings. F.E. and Freddy Guest spent the week-end trying to square it, but it ought to have been obvious that it could not be squared. Prothero stood to his guns; there was an urgent whip, soldiers brought from France, etc. and the Government won by 300 to 100. Rest of week spent on vote of credit and Consolidated Fund Bill. Pacifists well sat on. The week has strengthened the Government. But on Friday feeling was all against their Bill for creating a Ministry of Reconstructiion. It is really just a job to pension off Addison who has been a hopeless failure at Munitions. The Executive Committee of the National Union met the same day. They are very angry over Churchill and want to get a conference called. Archer-Shee, Billing and Ginnell have enlivened the proceedings of the week.[10]

Saturday 4 August   The chief excitement this week has been over Henderson's visit to Paris.[11] His explanation in the House was badly received but Lloyd George got him out of it in a very adroit speech. The Labour party is now in a state of chaos. Blumenfeld who is a knowing person declares that Ramsay Macdonald is a Government agent whose mission is to keep in order the pacifists of this and other countries.[12] Freddy Guest tells me the Radicals are furious over the appointment of Churchill and Montagu, as taking away men useful to them. He says Haig was anxious that Winston should be in the Government. He also says Winston is a very different man to what he was two years ago, and quite realises that he has to make a fresh start.

Friday 31 August   The House adjourned without any great flare-up. Henderson was very weak in explaining his resignation. But George Younger tells me that the telegram from the Russian government was sent in answer to a request. The Labour men in the Government seem quite happy over the situation.[13]

The War Aims Committee started off well with L. George at the Queen's Hall. I had to move the resolution and got on all right by saying I used to think there was not much to choose between L.G. and the Devil. L.G. quite liked it. Since the House rose preparations are being made to carry on the work on a large scale. Carson has now come to look after us and is going to try to get public money for the work. Asquith and Gulland have stopped that up to now. We are exploiting the Americans in England.

G.Y. told me last night that when the Ulster question was so strenuous the Unionist party funds provided £115,000 to the Ulstermen.

Gossip says Germans will insist on peace in the autumn and offer terms we can't refuse; also that they are going to bomb London at night; also that L.G. cannot last and that Balfour and Asquith will coalesce.

Wednesday 3 October   War Aims work has been going on steadily though the question of finance is still undecided. All our reports show that on the whole feeling in the country is sound. In some places there is difficulty in getting the official cooperation of the Labour party, but the rank and file of Labour seems much less pacifist than the delegates. Bonar Law has another boy missing and is very upset. There is a good deal of grumbling against him in the Unionist party on the ground that he lets L.G. have things all his own way. The 'National Party' has been received with derision. They started earlier than intended owing to the rumour that L.G. meant to start a party under that name. One of them told me that of course they wanted a leader, but they counted on some leading Conservative falling out with the party and coming to them. Walter Morrison's money is their chief asset.[14]

I am on the House of Lords Conference which held its first meeting yesterday. We had a preliminary meeting of Unionists at Lansdowne House in the morning and agreed to try to get the question of powers considered first, and also to try to hurry things on as much as possible.[15]

Friday 5 October   House of Lords Conference held second meeting today. There was a general discussion. Lord Loreburn expressed strong opinion in favour a 'House of Notables' to whose powers of resistance he attached little value. The main point from the Conservative speakers was the unsatisfactory state of things present. Selborne emphasised the fact that the Conservatives were not against democracy. Then Hobhouse and Whittaker spoke strongly in favouur of an elected second chamber. The latter went for direct election by large constituencies, small numbers, election for long period, age limit for election, and referendum. Crewe was against these proposals, so was Archbishop of Canterbury on ground that an elected second chamber would be a rival to the House of Commons. Hudson the Labour man said he was for abolition, but if there must be a second chamber he wanted it to be merely helpful to the first.

Saturday 20 October   House of Lords Conference has gone on steadily. We have been discussing the question of composition. Most of the Liberals have been pressing for elected members solely. Lord Lansdowne wants one-third to be peers elected by the peers. Crewe also wants a large element of peers but suggests that they should be elected by House of Commons. C. Hobhouse came to me on Thursday and asked what I thought was the minimum number of peers that our party would accept. I suggested one-sixth. Austen has now been put in place of Salter who was made a judge.

House of Commons reassembled on Tuesday. There seemed the makings of a row over the question of Irish redistribution. Ulster presses for it. The Nationalists protested vehemently, but Cave said either they must have it or Ireland must be left out of the Bill entirely. They still protested, but do not really much object.[16]

Frank Mildmay told me that the last push in Flanders would have come off two months earlier if it had not been for the French who insisted in having a hand in it and could not get their men there before.

Monday 5 November   In House of Lords Conference written schemes have been submitted by most of the members. Indirect election finds most favour. Hobhouse is still strongly against it. I have been advocating election by territorial panels of House of Commons, with hereditary peers coopted by elected members. Robertson and Murray Macdonald seem the most unlikely men to come into line as they are evidently against a second chamber altogether. Lord Lansdowne on our side is rather difficult in the other direction.

Franchise Bill is through committee. A proxy clause has been put in but at present its operation is limited to duration of the war. Still it is a great thing to have got the principle recognised in spite of the steady opposition of the official Liberal party. Younger and I had a very hard time during the discussion of the schedules, as so few of our people turned up to move the amendments put down in their names and we kept on moving and very often got them accepted. George Cave's handling of the Bill throughout has been very skilful.

George Fox came to me a fortnight ago and asked me to join a little group to lunch together once a week and try to act together. Their members at present are G.L. Fox, E. Wood, Astor, Hills, H. Bentinck, C. Bathurst, P. Harris and self.[17]

War Aims is now definitely a public charge. We organised a great campaign in South Wales on account of the miners' threat to strike if 'combing out' was allowed. The result seems to have been very good.[18]

Saturday 17 November Some sensation has been caused by Lloyd George's speech in Paris. Aubrey Herbert says it is part of a regular intrigue by L.G. against Haig and Robertson.[19] It certainly is the fact that George wanted in the summer to send British troops to Italy, and that Haig protested and got his way. Henry Bentinck told me he had breakfast with L.G. a fortnight ago and that he then poured out to him very much what he said in his speech. Henry Wilson is said to be very jealous of Haig. The debate on the speech is fixed for Monday. The prevalent idea now is that it will fizzle out.

In the House of Lords Conference things are going slow. It has become evident that Robertson and Murray Macdonald are impossible, but the attitude of the other Liberals is fairly promising.

There was a debate on Tuesday on the token vote for War Aims Committee. A lot of opposition was shown. F. Guest was not very strong as mover, but Carson intervened after a bit and eventually only 22 voted against it.

Wednesday 22 November Lloyd George scored a big personal success on Monday when Asquith attacked his Paris speech. His defence of the speech was characteristic. He did not attempt to substantiate what he had said, but maintained that he knew something of 'political strategy', that he wanted to get a particular result, and that he had got it. The speech was of the 'platform' type but it produced a great effect on the House and has raised L.G.'s stock enormously.[20]

Yesterday over the Franchise Bill was satisfactory from the party point of view. The Radicals pressed that an amendment with regard to the local government vote for women should be left to the House. Cave agreed but also left the House the question of the vote for soldiers at age of nineteen and the C.O. amendment.[21] On an important question of the plural vote in towns he opposed the Radicals firmly. They divided and the Government majority was nineteen only. The Government have been very wobbly on the subject and their attitude was due to strong pressure from our party which I had a considerable share in engineering. The point was rather technical, but the result is to give a plural vote in places like Bristol where it did not previously exist.[22]

Saturday 1 December　The proceedings about the alternative vote in committee on the Franchise Bill have been of the farcical order. On Thursday the alternative vote was carried shortly before the adjournment. Dr Chappell, a Radical, had an amendment down making the method of exercising it dependent on two schedules that he had tabled. George Younger seconded this amendment and sent out wires for our party to turn up at 5 p.m. on Monday. We then carried the amendment much to the annoyance of the Rads. The next move was Wednesday when the Rads appeared in force and defeated the schedule. So the Bill now provides for carrying out the alternative vote under a schedule that does not exist. There is to be a motion to recommit which will probably be carried. The proxy vote has gone through finally without opposition. It has been a pet child of mine and I am very glad.

Lord Lansdowne's letter on Thursday came as a bombshell. That it should appear at the moment of the Russian request for an armistice and of the Allied Conference in Paris seemed more than a coincidence. The pacifists of course are delighted. The decent Liberals say that it will have an enormous effect in the country. Among our party the dominant note is indignation, but several men have told me they were really in agreement with the letter on the ground that we could not win and had better make the best terms possible. Craik and Banbury hold that view. So does Walter Guinness who says it is largely the feeling of officers at the Front, G.H.Q. excepted. Talbot told me Lansdowne submitted a similar memorandum to the Cabinet eighteen months ago and said he was getting old and had lost his nerve. He certainly has not lost his mental vigour as one sees at the Lords Conference.[23]

Yesterday there was a conference of the National Union to hear Bonar Law.[24] The conference was the result of a lot of grumbling and was rather a touchy affair. Bonar was quite admirable. He took the meeting into his confidence and as reporters were not present spoke quite openly on one subject after another. The effect was excellent. Some points of the speech were:

1 He and the Unionists threatened resignation if compulsory service was not brought in.
2 After Asquith's resignation L.G. offered to serve as chairman of a War Council under Bonar as P.M. Bonar declined on the ground that the best chance of unity was a non-Unionist government supported by the Unionist party.
3 As an instance of L.G.'s energy: directly after the first attack on Gaza, L.G. said: 'We must have a change here.'
4 B.L. promised to do his utmost to get reform of second chamber if there should be anything like agreement in the Conference.
5 No change in tariff reform policy.
6 Advocated alliance with Imperialist section of Labour party.
7 Absolutely disagreed with whole tone of Lansdowne's letter.
8 As to Winston's appointment: L.G. left Bonar a free hand as to choice of Unionist members of Cabinet and claimed same right for himself.

I am staying the week-end with Godfrey Locker Lampson at Rowfant – Caves also here. Godfrey says Winston is most anxious to go on a special mission to Russia and Oliver L.L. would go with him.

Sunday 9 December   The Lansdowne letter seems to have fallen quite flat after all. The fact that the Russian collapse has put us in such a tight place makes ideas of negotiation less likely than before. Cave told me that he had a feeling that if we made a patched up peace we should find both Germany and Austria were at their last gasp.

In Parliament there has been during the week a rather poor Irish farce. The Nationalists for two or three days spent hours in the most wild denunciation of everyone and everything because an Irish redistribution scheme was introduced. The scheme has the effect of giving Ulster Unionists four or five more seats. On Thursday night an agreement was come to by which two Unionists and two Nationalists were to consider the scheme with the Speaker and arrive at an agreement. A separate Bill then to be carried and receive royal assent at same time as the Franchise Bill. On this the Nationalists declared that the last thing they wanted was to take from the Ulstermen anything unfair, in fact that they were only too anxious to give them their rights and even more. It is unlikely that any substantial alteration will be made.

At the House of Lords Conference we are getting nearer business. On Thursday Charles Hobhouse said that the Liberal party would never agree to indirect election by local authorities because of the preponderance of Conservatives on those bodies. At a subsequent meeting of the Unionist members of the Conference, Chamberlain pressed strongly for a democratic House of Lords with full powers and it was eventually agreed, Lansdowne and Balfour of Burleigh dissenting, that Chamberlain should approach Sir T. Whittaker with the suggestion that we should try to agree on the lines of a scheme that I formulated two months ago. Its features are election by territorial panels of the House of Commons of 200 members without qualification, and then cooption of 40 hereditary peers by the elected members; all elections to be by proportional representation.

Thursday 20 December Rather a curious sequel to the Lansdowne letter came to my notice. The War Cabinet instructed Guest to find out through the War Aims Committee what effect it was having in the country. The Secretaries were told to circularise our local agents.[25] But Carter, the chief Liberal agent, refused to do so till the next meeting, and when that meeting came actually told Guest he must withdraw from the committee if it was insisted on. The fact was that Asquith was strongly pressed by his colleagues to take the Lansdowne line in his Birmingham speech. But he stood firm.

In Second Chamber Conference, as a result of Austen's move, Crewe submitted to us a scheme that claimed support from nine of his party. The points are:– election by territorial groups of House of Commons, (but peers to be elected by peers instead of being coopted); payment of members of second chamber; and retirement in two lots instead of three. We shall probably accept it in the main.

On the occasion of the last air raid the House of Commons adjourned at 7 o'clock till the raid was over. Whitley who was in the chair announced that it was done at the request of the police and after consultation with Mr Speaker. One or two men protested. Orders were given that the press were not to mention it.

CHAPTER 6 NOTES

1   Charles Bathurst, later 1st Viscount Bledisloe, was then Parliamentary Secretary for Food Control, representing the department in the Commons. The 'meatless day' dispute concerned the beginnings of food control and rationing.
2   The redistribution of seats was intended to transfer a number of county seats to expanding boroughs and to merge small boroughs in their

surrounding county areas, both of which would reduce the number of specifically agricultural constituencies. As finally arranged, a number of boundaries were changed to retain the agricultural influence, as in Cheshire and in Kent.

3 F.E. Guest, Liberal M.P. from 1911 and Coalition Liberal Chief Whip 1917–21, later a Conservative M.P. The scheme mentioned was the War Aims movement, the progress of which Sanders describes below.

4 This interestingly foreshadows the events of 1921–2 when Lloyd George's instinctive anti-Turkish feeling led him into more serious difficulties with the Conservatives, in part because of promises made during the War.

5 'L.A.' is presumably Leo Amery and 'M.S.' Mark Sykes, both Members with keen military interests.

6 1st Lord Hardinge of Penshurst, Viceroy of India 1910–1916, had been held responsible for the failures and lack of preparation of the Indian forces in the Mesopotamian campaign. He had returned to London to his previous post as Permanent Secretary at the Foreign Office.

7 There had been widespread Conservative complaints when Lloyd George's intention to appoint Churchill to the Air Board was reported by the *Sunday Times* on 3 June. These complaints merely kept Churchill out of the Government for a few more weeks but their reactions to his actual appointment were even more violent. Martin Gilbert, *Winston S. Churchill*, IV, p. 23.

8 The House of Commons debated the failure of the Mesopotamia campaign on 12–13 July, following the report (CD 8610) of the Royal Commission, chaired by Lord Hamilton, which had been presented in May. The report criticised the Government of India in general and singled out Austen Chamberlain, Hardinge, Sir Beauchamp Duff and General Nixon for especial blame. Though not personally involved, Chamberlain accepted ministerial responsibility and resigned as Secretary of State. See Sir L. Woodward, *Great Britain and the War of 1914–1918*, p. 112.

9 The Corn Production Bill gave very wide powers to the Board of Agriculture to provide funds for the encouragement of production. It was defended as necessary in time of war but attacked by the radicals as a disguised subsidy for farmers.

10 L. Ginnell, Independent Nationalist M.P., had been suspended from the House of Commons on 26 July for persistently challenging the authority of the Chair and was then removed by force by the Serjeant at Arms. On 25 July, Pemberton Billing and Colonel Archer-Shee had, while abusing each other, combined to make bitter criticisms of the way in which the War was being run.

11   Arthur Henderson had visited Paris with Ramsay MacDonald to discuss the proposed Stockholm Conference which he wished to attend. This finally led to Henderson's dismissal from the Government a week later.

12   R.D. Blumenfeld, editor of the *Daily Express* 1902–1932.

13   This was the telegram supposedly sent by the Kerensky Government to Albert Thomas, the French Socialist leader, asking that the Stockholm Conference should not be held. It seems to have been prompted by a request from Nabokoff, Russian *Chargé d'Affaires* in London but by this time Kerensky had denied that he supported it anyway.

14   The National Party was a group of Conservatives on the extreme right, led by Henry Page Croft. Their call was for a more strenuous war effort and for a more overtly Imperial policy for Britain after the war. Most of them rejoined the Conservative Party at or after the general election of 1918. Walter Morrison (b.1836) had been a Conservative M.P. 1861–74, 1886–92 and 1895–1900 and was a wealthy land-owner in the North Riding.

15   Part of the price of Conservative support for a coalition, right up to 1922, was that it should reform (that is strengthen) the House of Lords, in accord with the pledge in the preamble of the 1911 Act that a reform would follow the reduction of powers. This Conference, like many more between 1918 and 1929, could not reach agreement between Conservatives who would not accept changes in the composition of the Upper House unless its powers were extended again, and Liberals and Labour M.P.s who would really have liked to abolish it altogether.

16   Ireland still had 100 seats allocated on a population basis in 1801; on the same basis in 1914, Ireland was due 53 seats. There was also a great inequality between the representation of the urban and rural areas, to the obvious disadvantage of Ulster.

17   All of these M.P.s (except Sanders himself) had been closely concerned with the Unionist Social Reform Committee before the war and all were to be involved in the making of social policy after 1918; their meetings provide an element of continuity in the planning and execution of social policy by the Conservative party before and after the War.

18   Combing out was the process of re-examining the categories of reserved occupations to release more men for military service.

19   In Paris on 12 November, Lloyd George had made a speech that denounced the strategy of mass offensives on the Western Front. His proposal of an Inter-Allied War Council was widely seen, as it was intended to be, as a criticism of Sir Douglas Haig (British Commander in France) and Sir William Robertson (C.I.G.S).

20   On 19 November, Asquith attacked Lloyd George's Paris speech as being unfair to the army and as an evasion of responsibility by the

Government. Lloyd George denied that there was any personal attack but claimed that there was a need for petter permanent co-ordination. No vote was taken as the support for Lloyd George in the House was so strong.

21   The Central Office amendment was proposed by Younger after it had been approved by the National Union Executive Committee. It proposed to disfranchise conscientious objectors and deserters for the rest of their lives; on a free vote it was carried by 209 to 171 with almost all the Unionist members of the government voting for it.

22   It was always illegal to cast two votes in the same constituency, but qualification for second votes in different constituencies was possible. Previously, boroughs had been treated as single registration areas for the purpose of this qualification but this was now changed. Henceforth, a man could, for example, vote in Bristol East as a resident and in Bristol Central by virtue of a business qualification there. This led to a great increase in the number of business votes in provincial boroughs where businessmen would normally live within the borough but away from their place of work. By 1929, some 400,000 electors were qualified under this clause and it resulted in a net bonus of about four seats to the Conservatives in each election.

23   Lord Lansdowne had written to the press to suggest that negotiations should be opened for a compromise peace with Germany, for which he was vigorously denounced.

24   This unofficial party conference was called after pressure on Law from the National Union to answer questions about the future. The transcript of proceedings, now at Conservative Central Office, bears out Sanders' impression of Law's masterly handling of an extremely difficult audience. It was perhaps unique as a conference at which the party Leader has been cross-examined by constituency delegates.

25   Liberal and Conservative agents, having worked on recruiting in 1914 and 1915, were fully occupied with War Savings and War Aims by this stage of the war.

Chapter 7   1918 Negotiations for a party agreement

Sunday 20 January   The House met last Monday after the Xmas holidays. L.G.'s War Aims speech to the Labour members had produced a good effect.[1] Auckland Geddes introduced his Man Power Bill in a maiden speech. He read it all from manuscript. It lasted over an hour. He had a full and attentive House to start with, but members gradually melted away and he finished with the House nearly empty.[2] On Thursday at the dinner hour during debate on second reading of Man Power Bill, Hogge moved for a secret session and the House was cleared. At 10 p.m. L.G. got up and made a really great speech. He quoted figures to show that we had and would retain a preponderance in numbers on the Western Front and stated that Austria and Turkey were in a very bad way. But the inner meaning of the speech seemed to me to point to peace through the exhaustion of the Central Powers not to the 'knockout blow'. He gave the numbers of American troops now in France. He had an ovation when he sat down.

After the sitting of the Second Chamber Conference on Tuesday had spent a whole morning discussing a scheme of Lansdowne's that no one approved, I suggested that on Thursday we should go on to a scheme drafted by Bryce on lines of Crewe's memorandum and divide on it clause by clause. This was accepted and on Thursday we really made great progress.

A letter signed by our 'luncheon club' on the establishment of a Ministry of Health was printed in *The Times* the first week in January. I think it is generally approved but unfortunately not by Hayes Fisher. The proposal is to hand over all health functions to the L.G.B. and then gradually take other work away from that department.[3]

At Carson's request I have undertaken the chairmanship of a committee to arrange sending parties of trades unionists on trips to the French Front. We are going to send from 150 to 300 a week.

There has been a good deal of trouble in the Conservative party over Bonar's statement as to conscription of wealth. George Younger tells me that he admits he had not thought it out; but he is obstinate about it and told a Conservative deputation that his plan held the field till they proposed something better.

Barnes' recantation of his Glasgow speech was the most humiliating performance that I ever heard from a Minister. Winston was standing behind the Speaker's chair to hear it.[4]

Saturday 2 February The question of my helping at Central Office is standing over till redistribution scheme is finally settled. I had a talk with Bonar Law who is anxious for me to take it on and thinks I should find it more interesting than work in the House. George Younger would propose to leave all the settling of candidates to me except in Scotland.

The P.R. people got me to speak first on their Lords' Amendment. I spoke for about half an hour and think I did fairly well. I dwelt mainly on the practical consequences to the House and to individuals. The provisional schedule and Asquith's opposition spoilt whatever chance we had and the majority was larger than ever against P.R. I dined with Selborne and R. Cecil that night, and discussed the next step. Selborne very keen to get any experiment in P.R., not so keen about stopping the alternative vote. Cecil and I rubbed in the importance of the latter. Lloyd George is anxious for some P.R. according to Cecil. The idea was to get him to take part in the negotiations and urge the Commons to agree to the resulting scheme. Today there was a lot of talk about the matter at the Carlton. Stuart of Wortley told me it was proposed to apply alternative vote to single member boroughs and P.R. on some modified scale. George Younger all against this. He insists on no alternative vote and suggests P.R. for boroughs of three to five members only.

At House of Lords Conference on Thursday the question of bishops came up and it was decided to include five. Whittaker really flared up about it and wanted to break up the whole thing. That subsided and we laughed him out of it afterwards. But his feeling against the Church is very real and bitter. Austen said he was brought up with just the same feeling, due to petty slights caused by stupidity and want of tact on part of parsons and other strong churchmen.

There is much annoyance among farmers who came to town in great numbers on Friday for a meeting at Caxton Hall where Prothero and Rhondda spoke. There was to have been a discussion but none was allowed and all they got was two rather feeble speeches. Rhondda's was very poor stuff.

The attacks on Haig are annoying the soldiers. Both Bertie and Reggie Home have written to me about it. Haig has talked rather too much to those who have been over to France as to what he was going to do. When his plans did not come off of course that told against him.[5]

Wednesday 23 January Carson's resignation was announced yesterday morning. I saw Jerry MacVeagh in the morning. He believed Carson was anxious to push Ulster into an agreement. He declared that the convention had come to agreement on every point except customs and excise, that the Southern Unionists and Nationalists agreed on that, but Belfast was against them. Edmund Talbot later gave me the true history: Midleton produced a scheme which got the agreement of Southern Unionists, Nationalists and priests;⁶ Ulster objected but it seemed likely that she might come in; suddenly the priests joined in the objection. As Edmund says they funk Home Rule. So at present it is priests and Orangemen against rest of Ireland. Carson and Craig resign in order to try to get a settlement. Either that or chaos must come soon. Their places are not to be filled as they are expected to come back soon. Edmund further told me that Cave would refuse P.R. and put on the whips against it on account of the difficulty as to the new schedule. Savile Crossley was a good deal bothered about the subject.⁷ He wanted me to arrange that either Edmund or George Younger should attend party meetings in the Lords, which he says get no guidance at all as to Unionist policy. Edmund asked me if I would be ready to help George Younger at the Central Office. I suggested that if I did it was to be understood that if a job in the House turned up for me I was to be free to take it.

At our luncheon yesterday we discussed next step about Health Ministry. Hayes Fisher's attitude seemed doubtful. He had written a very angry letter to Astor who replied in the same vein. I undertook to see Hayes and got hold of him in course of the afternoon. He told me he favoured our proposal but objected to Astor whom he described as a cheeky young dog!

Sunday 10 February The last days of the Franchise Bill caused some excitement. The Lords were very much keener on getting P.R. than on stopping the alternative vote. It needed strong pressure from Younger to keep them up to the scratch about the latter. In the Commons the debates showed the House at its worst, moody and intolerant. A curious feature was Austen's bitterness against the Lords for interfering over P.R. The alternative vote was carried by one on Tuesday. Then the Lords rejected it again, and another version was proposed on Wednesday. That was rejected by sixteen owing to abstention of Liberal members of the Government. After that the P.R. 'camouflage' went through very easily. I have now taken the job of organising the new constituencies.

In House of Lords Conference things have been going slow as the Chairman insists on raising numberless minute points that all lead to talk.

Wednesday 13 February Shaw, the Secretary of the Irish Convention, attended our Tuesday lunch.⁸ He said the Convention had agreed on composition of an Irish Parliament, the Unionists getting 40 per cent of the lower House and preponderance in the upper secured to them; no Ulster measures to be passed without concurrence of an Ulster committee. The trouble has come owing to the Nationalists and Catholic bishops insisting on control of customs which Ulster will not have at any price. Unless a compromise can be made in England the Convention will break up. Shaw thought such compromise possible if England supported the 'middle' party.

L.G.'s speech on the Address was a deplorable fiasco. He had a bad cold and looked and spoke like a beaten man. The feeling of the House was evidently against him. Rumour says that Repington and McKenna have been seen together. Certainly L.G. spoke as if Asquith and Repington were playing the same game. The Government is thought weak for not prosecuting the *Morning Post*. Repington goes over to Paris in uniform and noses out all the information he can get and is somewhat reckless in what he publishes.[9]

Sunday 3 March I had to go down to Devonshire last week for Jack Bayly's funeral. He died after an operation for appendicitis. Of the five senior officers of the North Devons who went to Gallipoli together, I am now the only one left.

L.G. recovered his position in the House by his speech on the Vote of Account. Asquith did as badly that day as L.G. did the week before. Austen made a very good speech attacking them both. Every one down on the press men who have been given places in the Government. Unionists are very angry at Beaverbrook's appointment.[10] Davidson, Bonar Law's secretary, told me it was impossible for Robertson to have taken on the Versailles job.[11] He says he has no use for the French; every time he makes a plan with them they let him down, etc. The fuss about his departure has quieted down now. L.G. was in a particularly difficult position on the Address because Derby[12] would not make up his mind whether to stand by Robertson or the Government.

In connection with the arrangement of seats I have had curious work about the British Workers League. Milner is very keen about it and thinks we should work with them in every possible way. The men who are running it are merely political adventurers, but they declare they are making a lot of headway in Northumberland and Durham particularly. The question is now getting urgent as to what seats we leave to them. Neville Chamberlain does not like them in the Midlands. Younger and I had a long interview with four of their men the other day and eventually asked them to draw up a list of seats to be submitted to Bonar Law, who is to decide whether we leave them a free hand in those places.

George Younger told me yesterday that he attended a meeting of the Unionist leaders to consider the question of an alliance with L.G. and his friends. Bob Cecil and Curzon against touching him on the ground that he is such a dirty little rogue. Balfour remarked that Bob wanted a small exclusive Unionist party. Eventually a committee consisting of Bonar, Clyde, Walter Long and Younger was appointed to draw a manifesto of policy for the party.

I went to Plymouth for Milner's War Aims meeting on 22 February. At the conference I was struck by the absence of complaints. The meeting was a very good one. Lloyd George's name was cheered when he was mentioned more than once.

Sunday 10 March   A quiet week in House of Commons. Some attacks on the Government for getting rid of Jellicoe. The real reason was that Jellicoe could not be got to consent to any change either of policy or personnel. He wanted to stick even to Bacon.[13]

On Tuesday last at the meeting of the Second Chamber Conference I protested strongly against leaving method of adjusting differences an open question and suggested a deal on lines of giving up some hereditary peers if the Radicals would agree to an appeal to the country in case of difference. The debate that followed showed hopeless diversity of opinion, but later Whittaker, Hobhouse and Davies had a confab with Chamberlain, Younger and myself and propounded a scheme for a sliding scale of representation of peerage and settlement by a majority of five in free conference.

Sunday 24 March   Our deal in the Second Chamber Conference has come off and a scheme has been agreed and is now adopted by a large majority. We ought to have finished the whole thing by now, but there has been a long discussion as to the exact form in which the dissent of dissentients should be made known. Loreburn and Balfour of Burleigh very insistent on that point. Still we shall produce a plan which is a good achievement considering everything. The Chairman has been very dilatory.[14]

I have been engaged in various confabs lately as to a working agreement with British Workers League, and with the Lloyd George Liberals. I had a long talk with Bonar Law about it at Downing Street yesterday. He is all for alliance with both lots. The point of difference with Guest is whether they should follow the Lib.Un. precedent and start a separate organisation, or as he prefers have a new joint party. The latter will never do. Guest reckons on about 10 per cent of Liberals following L.G.

The bad news from the Front is received with wonderful equanimity. Bonar told me he felt sure we should have to give way in places. Amery said the same two days earlier when the attack was just beginning.

Sunday 7 April   Spent Easter at Minehead. Returned to town last Tuesday. Exactly what happened about Gough is still a mystery. Certainly he was superseded very hurriedly. It is generally said that one division at St

Quentin bolted. I hear the rumour that Gough made no provision for evacuating his doctors and so on, and that the mistake was made of not blowing up the roads during the retreat; the Germans rushed their men on in motor lorries.[15]

With regard to inclusion of Ireland in new military service bill, before Easter Younger told me it was to be included. On Wednesday Dudley Ward told me the same. Next day I saw Queensborough who told me Midleton had just told him the Cabinet had funked it and decided to leave Ireland out; the *Morning Post* had an article on that assumption. On Friday I saw Hayes Fisher and tried to pump him about it. He said the Cabinet had to decide it on advice of the military authorities. On Saturday George Younger declared Ireland was to be included and that had been the intention all along.

Sunday 14 April   A strenuous week in House. Edmund Talbot asked me to assist in the whips' work as they were short handed. So I have been in the House pretty continuously. L.G.'s opening speech was not a good effort. He read most of it and got confused and involved when he came to figures. The Irish resistance has not really been very fierce. James Craig says that if carefully administered conscription will go all right in Ireland. Goulding tells me the Irish complaints as to the tactlessness of recruiting officers in Ireland at the beginning of the war are quite well founded.

The feeling as to the situation in France is very gloomy. Sam Scott says we have no strategic reserve. The French have a very large one, but it is difficult to move it so far north as Armentières.[16] The account given by Repington in the *Morning Post* of the 11th as to the Fifth Army came from Gough himself. It looks as if he had been rather too kind in taking over frontline from the French.[17]

Last sitting of Second Chamber Conference on Thursday. Report went through all right. It is at all events much more satisfactory than that of the Irish Convention.

Wednesday 17 April   There was a meeting of the Unionist War Committee yesterday to discuss the Government Home Rule proposals. Carson opened with a speech in which he said frankly he did not know what to do. The general tone of the meeting was distinctly adverse to Home Rule; but it was not a helpful meeting. The speeches too much on the abstract question, few dealing with the question what was to be done now that the Government are introducing the Bill.[18]

The talk in the House last night was of the most gloomy description relative to the War. One man solemnly assured me we were about to abandon the channel ports and hold a line further south.

Monday 29 April George Younger told me today that the Irish Secret-aryship was offered to Clyde a fortnight ago. Bonar put it to him as a duty, but he declined after consulting G.Y. and on his advice. Bonar asked G.Y. if he could suggest anyone. They both agreed Mark Sykes was too excitable. G.Y. suggested my name and Edward Wood's. It seems certain they will have Shortt. A dark horse. He started life in Boraston's Office as a L.U.[19] Devlin told G.Y. that the Irish were out for all sorts of sabotage such as destroying railways and poisoning water if we try to enforce conscription.

From the Central Office we are asking District Agents to tell us the feeling in the country about Home Rule. There is likely to be a party meeting in London before the Bill is introduced. Norman Craig who has been at work at the Air Ministry told me the reason Trenchard left was this. It has always been the custom to replenish a squadron immediately there are casualties and this has a wonderful effect on morale. Rothermere wanted to start a lot of new squadrons and the effect of this would be that the numbers of men would not be sufficient to continue the system of immediate replenishment. Trenchard objected and left in consequence.[20]

Sunday 5 May George Cave asked me if the Irish Secretaryship had been offered to me. He said my name was put forward to L.G. for consideration. If it had been offered to me I should have felt bound not to shirk it, but I am well out of it. The Irish difficulty in Parliament is increasing. Feeling in our party is hardening against Home Rule. George Younger and I sent out a memo to the Unionist district agents asking them to try to find out the state of opinion of Unionists in the country. Reports vary very much. Opposition strongest in the West. Safeguards for Ulster universally considered necessary. Edmund Talbot had a whips' meeting to discuss the matter the other day. He is very worried about it. He considers L.G. necessary to the cause of the alliance, and it is hard to see how L.G. can emerge from the difficulty. The one consolatory thing that Edmund said was: 'You know I have a feeling that all the time these Nationalists are in just as great a funk as we are.'

I spoke for nearly half an hour on Thursday on the subject of the registration urging that there ought not to be an election in wartime and that more time must be given for getting the register ready. Hayes Fisher told me afterwards that he was pressing for more time, but L.G. is very anxious to have a register ready at the earliest possible date, as he thinks he may want an election in October.

I met Cook of the Ministry of Shipping at lunch yesterday with Morley Knight.[21] He had a yarn that after the St Quentin break Petain lost his head altogether and came to Paris to say Paris would be in German hands in five days. Ministers wanted to clear out. Clemenceau said anyone who leaves Paris must first leave the Ministry.

Friday 10 May Maurice's letter has been the excitement of the week.[22] George Younger tells me that Asquith met Maurice at dinner a week ago and that Robertson was sounded but refused to have anything to do with it. Maurice is known to be a friend of Repington, and Repington has a personal grudge against Henry Wilson as the latter made him leave his regiment on account of the Lady Garstin business.[23] The affair turned out well for L.G. who had an unusually good answer. The real reason that the British line was extended was that Clemenceau said he would resign if it was not done.

The Irish difficulty gets worse. James Craig and Lindsay, a Belfast member, both assure me conscription cannot be enforced in Ireland. John Hills and Charles Bathurst both say now they would go against Home Rule on account of the action of the priests against conscription. The feeling in the party against it is distinctly getting stronger. B.L. has promised to have a party meeting before it is introduced.

Sunday 9 June Politics since Whitsuntide have been quiet. Not much heard about Ireland, and Education Bill the business in the House. During the last push there has not been the same excitement as on the two former occasions. Charlie Bean told me that before sending tired divisions to the Chemin des Dames Haig told Foch that his intelligence told him the attack would be there.[24] Foch declared it would not be. The French divisions there ran like hares and up to the Marne the German advance was little more than a route march. Bean says in three months we shall again have superiority in numbers.

I met old Lady Londonderry at dinner at the House with James Craig the other day. She is a most remarkable woman. There were five men dining and she was the only lady. She monopolised the conversation and kept us going the whole time; anything from high politics to improper stories.

The Central Office has been much occupied with the Honours List. That I have nothing to do with. One or two humorous incidents over it. The vacant Thistle was promised to a certain peer, but Tullibardine got it from the King. H.M. consulted L.G., who said it was all right quite casually, much to the annoyance of our office. George Faber's peerage was also quaint. He was told a stop gap must be found for the Clapham seat and produced his brother David who is ready to stand as a great favour. Now Clapham does not want David Faber a bit and another stop gap has to be found. David Faber much annoyed. The agreement with the British Workers' League is very difficult. In one division after another our party shies at them; in none more than Stourbridge where Victor Fisher is standing.[24]

The great topic lately has been the Billing case. Lonsdale, the theatrical librettist whom I meet at the Garrick, was in court almost all the time. He says Billing dominated the whole thing, never lost his head or got excited; he compared him to a boxer who could knock his opponent out at any time. Darling came out of it badly. Effect in the country must be bad.[26] Hickman went to Bonar to suggest that a commission of judges should be appointed to inquire into the 'Black Book' charges. Bonar told him the whole matter was being considered.

Monday 10 June   I am appointed Treasurer of the Household. The job has been vacant since James Craig resigned in January, but has not been filled up in case a settlement of the Irish question enabled him to return.

Sunday 23 June   Was returned unopposed at Bridgwater last Tuesday. The Labour party in the division talked about running a candidate but thought better of it. Took my seat Wednesday. A Lloyd George breakfast at St Stephen's Club Thursday. These are an institution of L.G.'s. He meets the Liberal members of the Government one day and the Unionists another. The breakfasts used to be at Lord Derby's but are now at St Stephen's. The Central Office pays for them. L.G. gives his views on the situation after breakfast. He told us everyone was puzzled at the delay in the German attack on the West front. It is all in our favour. He looked on the situation there as still very anxious. Said America would not allow Japanese intervention in Siberia. Thought a very awkward situation would arise if Germany offered good terms on West front as the French would not then want to fight on, but indicated no way out.

Curzon announced in the Lords the Government climb down on the Irish question. Next Tuesday is allotted for discussions of subject in House of Commons. James Craig prophesies that Curzon will then be explained away.[27]

My boy Arthur got his flannels the same day I was returned unopposed. He has been batting very well for Harrow.

Sunday 14 July   Lull on West front still continues. Godfrey Locker Lampson told me Sir H. Wilson was absolutely puzzled about it. At L.G. breakfast a fortnight ago the question of a coalition election was raised. L.G. quite confident that we could frame a joint programme. As a matter of fact we have been trying ever since March to get the Conservative leaders to announce a programme that L.G. might accept, but it has hung fire. Meanwhile Guest and Dudley Ward have been arranging with me about the distribution of seats, and have got a good way towards agreement. Agreement with British Workers' League is getting more and more difficult. Our people won't have them in many places and Victor Fisher is a very difficult man to deal with.

Sunday 21 July Bryce asked me to come and see him the other day and consider how to press forward the subject of reform of Second Chamber. Whittaker was also there. They agreed that the real difficulty was with the Liberal party in the Commons and proposed to attempt some press propaganda on the subject. Last Wednesday a deputation from the Executive Committee of our National Union waited on L.G. and Bonar on the subject. L.G. expressed sympathy, was evidently anxious to postpone but promised to put the matter on his programme and deal with it early in a new parliament. His mind is going strong for an election now. He seems to me to be on the look out for some sensational cry. He says it is 'the sauce' that makes a programme digestible. At the breakfast on Thursday he said Foch has moved some of our divisions to assist against the German push at the Marne and that he had protested against this being too far removed from our line. The bed of a Generalissimo can't be one of roses. L.G. apparently knew nothing of the counter attack which had actually begun at that time. He told us that America had agreed with Japan that each should send 7,000 men into Siberia, other powers contributing a smaller number.

Sunday 28 July The House has been engaged all the week on a lot of small Bills. It has meant hard work for the whips but nothing exciting. John Burns intervened one day with quite a violent speech and came into collision with the Speaker.

Our Shadow Cabinet of the Unionists met on Friday to consider plans for an election. Clyde told me that Bob Cecil is still strong against a 'deal' with Lloyd George. Curzon now assents and the others favour it. Guest told me that his people trust and like Bonar, Austen and Cave, but not Balfour and Walter Long.

Derby was at the breakfast on Thursday. He said on 14 July in Paris the greatest applause was given to the English troops. L.G. predicts another big attack on our line by Rupprecht's army. Charles Hunter told me that a week before the last German attack Foch said the Germans were going to make a very big blunder. Henry Wilson was his informant.

Friday 9 August Adjournment yesterday. Pressure was high during the last part of the session. No declaration of policy has yet been made. But L.G. let it be seen quite plainly at the last breakfast we had that he was all for an early election. Yesterday Guest spoke to me about Tariff Reform. He evidently funks it and wants L.G. to avoid declaring for it. I

told him that unless L.G. declares for preference and tariff against
dumping, it would be no good to ask Conservatives to back his candidates.

The news from the Front made a good finish. The Government comes
out at least as strong as it started. Things looked very gloomy for it about
Whitsuntide, but the stand up fight over the Maurice episode was really the
turning point of the session.

Cellulose will now be sub-judice. To all appearance it is a very bad
business. Grant Morden is a Conservative candidate but the Central Office
had nothing to do with him.[28]

I had a talk with Buckmaster the other day about Kitchener. He said K.
would sometimes be surly and shut up in his shell so that you could get
nothing out of him; at other times he would come out with remarks
showing extraordinary insight into the War. He said K. was very anxious
for an expedition to Alexandretta but he did not propose it till we were
already engaged at Gallipoli.

I stayed a Sunday night at Chorleywood with Willie Peel and met Milner
there. He said he always worked till two in the morning, then slept like a
top for six hours. He described Smuts as a man without great initiative but
wonderfully good at getting up and condensing a difficult subject if it was
referred to him.

Friday 30 August Have spent a week in town after a fortnight at
Minehead. Stayed a night with George Cave at Burnham last week. He
told me he considered an election necessary on account of legal and
constitutional considerations. George Younger and Edmund have been in
London. They think an election is coming.

I gather that the extent of our success in France has surprised our own
people. At the beginning of the push Macpherson said it was not to be a
big thing. Henry Wilson now says that it is going on so fast that he does not
know what to expect next.

L.G. has sent in his alternatives to the scheme of policy submitted to him
by the Unionists. It has been sent on to Clyde for his comments. There
should be no great difficulty about agreement. But L.G. goes for devolu-
tion all round. George Younger is going to speak at Newcastle next week
on policy and has told Bonar that he will go for no Home Rule while the
war lasts. Bonar consented to his doing so.

Sunday 29 September Have been in town a good part of the month. Work
at Central Office has been very heavy. The difficulties of convincing
Unionists that they ought not to fight L.G. Liberals get greater and
greater. Bonar and Balfour went down the night before last to stay with
L.G. Younger and I saw Bonar before he went. He said they were not
going to discuss the subject of an election. But Guest told me the day

before that L.G. meant to do so. Guest and Younger have both submitted schemes for settling who is to stand in the various divisions. I had a talk with Walter Long. He confirmed what I had heard, that our great success on the Western Front was a complete surprise to our Army Chiefs. Have seen Hayes Fisher several times lately. He says L.G. had a talk with him the other day about the register. L.G. quite offensive; accused Fisher of putting unnecessary difficulties in the way; said our candidates were a rotten lot. The Lancashire visit was meant to be a sort of Midlothian campaign, but the 'flu' stopped that; and it really was a very bad attack of flu.[29]

Sunday 13 October   From September 30 to October 8 I had a series of meetings in my division. I addressed fourteen meetings, attended the County Council and had two days staghunting. I found the meetings poorly attended at first, but getting better as I went on - no heckling or opposition. Lloyd George's name always well received; no rise for that of any Conservative leader. All keen to have no peace without victory.

On getting back to town found things no forrader about an election. L.George says he is too busy about the war and the peace offer to think of other things. Younger told Bonar that he really must know if there is to be a Coalition party as the practical difficulties of uncertainty are getting too great.

Edmund Talbot is in bed. I shall have to carry on at the start of the session. A lot of talk about friction between L.G. and Haig. In the despatch that has not been published Haig is supposed to have spoken strongly about units not being kept up to strength. The complaints as to L.G.'s wire to Haig saying 'I have heard from Marshal Foch' are absurd. L.G. was in Paris with Foch at the time so naturally heard through him. The wire was sent by a secretary.[30]

It looks as if we may have to make peace very soon, but the general feeling is that we ought not to.

Sunday 20 October   The best week we have had during the war. The excitement over that has been the feature of the House. I have been doing Chief Whip in Talbot's absence. Business has gone through much more quickly than was expected. The Scotch Education Bill is now disposed of. The question of feeding and selling cattle was raised by Spear on Wednesday both at questions and on the adjournment. Astor tackled the questions very well, but on the adjournment his explanation and defence was very weak.

Breakfast with L.G. on Thursday. He said our victories had taken everyone by surprise. They would have been even more complete but for the inefficiency of the American armies. At St Mihiel the staff work was done by the French and all went well.[31] Since then the Yanks have insisted on running their own show and have got on very slowly and with heavy losses, when British and French have gone quickly and cheaply. L.G. was in Paris at the time when the German request for an armistice was sent to Wilson.[32] Wilson answered without consulting the allies. Then L.G. and Clemenceau wired him to say that any armistice terms must be settled by the military authorities. Clemenceau said: 'Fourteen Points! Why the Bon Dieu himself could only think of ten commandments.' A captured note to a German attaché explains the peace offer as being caused by anxiety as to the Eastern Front, now that Bulgaria has collapsed and Turkey and Austria are likely to follow. L.G. has great ideas of advances on Austria by the Slav peoples from the Danube and by us on Constantinople. He insisted that the latter must be done by the British as we had done all the fighting against the Turks. The trouble in Bohemia might well frighten the Germans.[33] 'Side shows' had really been decisive. The Salonica force was one claw of the pincers. Allenby's victory was one of the best things ever done in the history of war. With regard to peace terms, we could never allow Freedom of the Seas as proposed by Wilson.

On the question of an election L.G. said if we put it off till some time after peace the inevitable discontent that would arise during the period of settling down might lead to a regular Bolshevic Government. Younger has not been able to get anything definite out of Bonar as to agreement on policy. L.G. told him that Bonar put up a real ultra-Tory programme, said he could not have that and hinted that he was being approached by the Asquith people. Now L.G. will draw a programme of his own and see if we cannot agree on it.

Sunday 27 October   L.G. was not nearly so full of buck at the breakfast last Thursday. He has seen Haig who says the Germans are fighting very well and making quite an orderly retreat. They have given up doing wanton damage to the country they evacuate. He was very strong about the failure of the Americans; said their staff work is so bad they can only put one division in the line at a time; and no one will tell Wilson about it. Foch is now being urged to do so. Turkey has released Townsend and sent him to approach us on the subject of peace.[34] Venizelos has been in London.[35] Foch said to him: 'There is no better general than Haig not excepting myself.'

Negotiations for a party agreement are getting a little forrader. L.G. very shy of the word tariff. He told Bonar he could arrange a policy with any member of the party except him. Bonar arranged on Friday that he should interview half a dozen members of our party and see how they took to his views. He is ready to promise colonial preference and protection of key industries, but does not want to mention the word tariff. That will probably be accepted. Carson and F.S. Oliver[36] have drafted a memorandum on the subject but L.G. says it is much too long. On Thursday the *Daily Chronicle* announced that a Manchester Liberal deputation was coming to London to interview first L.G. and then Asquith with a view to reuniting the party. L.G. showed this at the Thursday breakfast and said he did not know what he was going to say to them. That afternoon Bonar told me it was off as Asquith had refused to see them. Next day I saw Buckmaster at the Garrick. He tried to pump me about it. I said I heard Asquith declined to see them. He said that was quite wrong. Asquith had told him he was ready to see them at any time; the hitch came at the other end. Bonar asked me what our party would say if Asquith and a few of his friends were put in the Government. I said they would not like it at all. It would be very hard to get our candidates to stand down for them. Altogether L.G.'s position has been strengthened and it is possible that his satellites worked the Manchester affair.

Bonar is trying to square the National Party. Isabel Law saw Carnegie who may be left in the cold at Winchester. Then Bonar interviewed him and Paddy Goulding saw Page Croft with the result that Bonar is tomorrow to see Page Croft and a few of his friends.[37]

Sunday 3 November   Nothing came of the interview with Page Croft and Co., though Bonar said he thought it did good to have a talk with them. Later in the week I met at lunch a fellow called Benett Dampier who appears to run the National Party office. He said the N.P. could get on all right with the Conservatives but could not stick the Coalition. I said Page Croft professed to support the coalition. He said the National Party was sick of Page Croft and hoped to get rid of him.

Last Sunday a Cabinet meeting was held at which the arrangements for an election were reviewed. Auckland Geddes was told to report on it and had no good things to say of the English L.G.B. As a result of this L.G. wrote to tell Hayes Fisher he must resign. Bonar stopped the letter going but told Hayes of its contents. L.G. went off to Paris and it was settled to leave the matter over till his return. Hayes poured all this out to me on Thursday. I knew it before; he was much upset, said it was all part of an intrique against the Conservatives in the Cabinet and that if he were turned out Cave aand Walter Long would soon follow. Edmund Talbot says he told Bonar at the time of the appointment that Hayes was not man enough to be a Cabinet Minister, but that having put him in Bonar was bound to stand by him.

When L.G. left on Sunday night he took with him a draft of a letter he is to send Bonar as to a joint policy. He agreed to the principle but said he would make a few verbal changes and send it back from Folkestone. He did not do so. But he left word with Guest that an agreement was settled and that he was to take orders from Bonar during L.G.'s absence. As to seats, it was proposed that counting sitting members the L.G. party should run 150 candidates, the list of places to be settled between us and it looks as if we are very near a settlement already.

The announcement of the Turkish surrender was made by Cave on Thursday, Bonar having flown to France that day. It was loudly cheered but there was no great scene. I have known more noise over the result of a bye election in the old days.

Sunday 10 November   A wonderful week. Austria's surrender definitely announced in the House on Tuesday. Abdication of Kaiser and Crown Prince announced at the Lord Mayor's banquet last night. Strong as the armistice terms are known to be, everyone believes Germany must accept them. Her military position is now desperate. When one remembers last March it seems too wonderful.

As to domestic affairs: Hayes Fisher is consoled with the Duchy and a peerage and though rather bitter about it will not give trouble. We have been getting on with the work of trying to find 150 seats for the L.G. Liberals. Our difficulties are great, especially in London where in every seat there is a Unionist candidate with a vested interest. I have got Hayes Fisher to be responsible for all of them now. On Friday Freddy gave a luncheon at the Ritz to meet some newspaper men. He wanted to get them to work for the Coalition. That was a failure. Rothermere, Riddell and H. Dalziel were there. Henry Norman and Amery completed the party.[38] The dominant note of the conversation was the insistence by all these Liberals of the danger of the Tory dominance in the Coalition. Our people insist so constantly that we are being sold to L.G. that it was rather refreshing to hear the other side. Rothermere struck me as rather more of a bounder than I imagined. He was very emphatic that the Coalition would soon be considered a Junker affair and wanted more Liberals put in the Government. The same afternoon I went on to the Conservative Shadow Cabinet where Bonar read out the L.G. letter that has now been secured. It is most satisfactory. As Bonar said it is hard to see how L.G. will get his Liberal and Labour colleagues to agree to it. R. Cecil carped a little at the phrasing of a sentence about Welsh Church funds, but the reception of the whole thing was very favourable. Austen made an interesting statement, namely that at the Conference held after King Edward's death about the House of Lords L.G. suggested the formation of a Coalition party, saying among other things that such a party could deal properly with the question of National defence.[39] I took the opportunity of saying to Bonar that a vote of confidence in him should be moved at the meeting of the Unionist party. He said he would like Balfour to move it. Balfour agreed to do so.

I attended the Lord Mayor's banquet. The fault was the length of the speeches - Balfour and Eric Geddes both good but too long. L.G. did not rise till after ten but did very well.

Dined with Evelyn Cecil on Thursday. The Henry Wilsons there. He took L. in to dinner. She was struck by his immense admiration of the Germans as soldiers.

The business of the House has got rather into difficulties. Dillon moved the adjournment on Thursday just when I meant to get a lot of little Bills through and the Speaker allowed it. Both the Irish and the Labour party bitterly resent an election and are anxious to make themselves objectionable.

Saturday 16 November We got news about 10:30 on Monday of the signing of the armistice. When the House met the P.M. moved directly after prayers to adjourn the House and go to St Margaret's. The service was short and most admirably done. The singing of the hymn reminded one of Harrow chapel. There was a bit of 'mafficking' in the streets but rain came on in the afternoon and the crowd was not what I remember for instance at the Jubilee time. A certain amount has been going on all the week, mainly in Piccadilly Circus and Trafalgar Square. Flappers very much to the fore. The best thing has been the tremendous reception given to the King on every possible occasion.

There were meetings on Tuesday 12 November of L.G.'s followers at Downing Street and of our party at the Connaught Rooms. The latter went off very well. Bonar read the letter from L.G. on future policy. The meeting was well satisfied and the vote of confidence proposed by Balfour was unanimously passed. A short summary only not including the letter was sent to the press. On getting to the House I soon heard that L.G.'s speech to his own followers had been on different lines altogether. He told them very little of his letter to us but laid stress on his Liberalism and carried them all with him. Our people became suspicious at once. I spoke to Guest about it and urged the publication of the letter. On Wednesday afternoon Bonar sent me word to come to Downing Street where I found L.G., Balfour, Bonar and Auckland Geddes. Meanwhile there had appeared in *The Times* a fairly full report of L.G.'s speech to his own followers. L.G. said it must have been sent by someone in the audience who could write shorthand. He spoke impromptu and said that he had a difficult job and was anxious to make things easy for his Liberal supporters. It was agreed that a joint meeting should be held shortly at which he, Bonar and Barnes should speak. I pressed for the publication of the letter. L.G. rather deprecated that, saying he was not in love with it. As a matter of fact Bonar had written it and put it up to him to sign. I got no promise of its publication. On Thursday we had the usual breakfast. L.G. asked that

Auckland Geddes and I should sit on each side of him. After a lot of discussion about the date of election he asked Younger, W. Evans and myself to come to Downing Street. There we met Bonar, Dudley Ward and E. Cornwall. It was decided to announce election at once, to have the poll on 14 December and to arrange the joint meeting for today. Younger declares that the speech of Tuesday that appeared in *The Times* was given by Sutherland to Jones of the *Daily Chronicle* and sold by him to *The Times*. The meeting duly came off this morning. All went well. The speeches were vague but good; but the famous letter was printed and circulated.

On Wednesday the Liberals gave Asquith a dinner. The note there was to support the Coalition. And on Thursday Asquith had a long interview with L.G. but got nothing out of it. Also on Thursday the Labour party had a conference and decided by a large majority to call on the Labour members of the Government to resign. I don't think any of them mean to do so, but it means a split in the ranks.

I have had considerable difficulty in getting on with the business in the House. It has meant sitting up till two on Wednesday and three on Thursday, but it is now pretty well finished. It has been a strenuous week.

Copy of letter from Lloyd George to Bonar Law.[40] *2 November 1918.*

My Dear Bonar Law,

The more I think of it the more convinced I become that there ought to be a General Election, and that the sooner it can be arranged, subject to the exigencies of the military position, the better. We have discussed this so often that I need not go at length into my reasons for this view. My principal reason is that I believe it is essential that there should be a fresh Parliament, possessed of the authority which a General Election alone can give it, to deal with the difficult transitional period which will follow the cessation of hostilities.

If there is to be an Election I think it would be right that it should be a Coalition Election, that is to say, that the country should be definitely invited to return candidates who undertake to support the present Government not only to prosecute the War to its final end and negotiate the peace, but to deal with the problems of reconstruction which must immediately arise directly an armistice is signed. In other words, the test which in future must decide whether individual candidates will be sustained at the polls by your supporters and mine must be not, as in the past, a pledge to support the Government in the prosecution of the war but a definite pledge to support this Government. I should myself desire to see this arrangement carried through on personal grounds, for during the last two years I recognise that I have received the whole-hearted support of your Party, and that the Government has had a unity both in aims and in action which has been very remarkable in a Coalition Government. I am convinced also that such an arrangement will be the best for the Country. The problems with which we shall be faced immediately on the cessation of hostilities will be hardly less pressing and will require hardly less drastic action than those of the war itself. They cannot, in my opinion, be dealt with without disaster on party lines. It is vital that the national unity which has made possible victory in the war should be maintained until at least the main foundations of national and international reconstruction have been securely laid. A Parliament returned to support a Government constituted as is the present Coalition Government, would fulfil, I believe, this essential condition, and would also be possessed both of the necessary authority and unity of purpose alike as to principles and methods, to enable it to deal effectively with the grave problems which will confront it.

If an election on these lines is to take place I recognise that there must be a statement of policy of such a nature as will retain to the greatest extent possible the support of your followers and of mine. My fundamental object will be to promote the unity and development of the British Empire and of the nations of which it is composed, to preserve for them the position of influence and authority in the conduct of the world's affairs which they have gained by their sacrifices and efforts in the cause of human liberty and progress, and to bring into being such conditions of living for the inhabitants of the British Isles was will secure plenty and opportunity to all.

I do not think it necessary to discuss in detail how this programme is to be carried out. I said something on the subject at Manchester in September last, especially in regard to the imperative need of improving the physical conditions of the citizens of this country through better housing, better wages and better working conditions. I lay emphasis on this because the well-being of all the people is the foundation upon which alone can be built the prosperity, the security, and the greatness both of the United Kingdom and of the Empire. But there are some matters about which you, as leader of the Unionist party, will wish me to say something more definite.

In the first place in regard to economic policy. I have already accepted the policy of Imperial preference as defined in the Resolutions of the Imperial Conference, to the effect that a preference will be given on existing duties and on any duties which may subsequently be imposed. On this subject I think there is no difference of opinion between us. I have at the same time stated that our policy does not include a tax on food, but that does not of course interfere with the granting of a preference on any article, as for example, tea or coffee, on which for our own purposes we have imposed a duty. That question has, I think, been largely settled by the

Corn Production Bill, but, of course, one of the great objects which must be aimed at in the future is to maintain the improved agricultural position which has now been reached; and for this purpose a great deal can be and ought to be done in many directions, including, for instance, an improvement and, indeed, a complete change of the transport situation. As regards other aspects of this problem, I am prepared to say that the key industries on which the life of the nation depends must be preserved. I am prepared to say also that in order to keep up the present standard of production and develop it to the utmost extent possible, it is necessary that security should be given against the unfair competition to which our industries have been in the past subjected by the dumping of goods below the actual cost of production. Beyond this I should say that we must face all these questions with new eyes, without regard to pre-war views or to pre-war speeches. The object which we have in view is to increase to the greatest possible extent production in this country so that no man or woman may want, and that all who do an honest day's work may have comfort for themselves and for their children. In order to secure better production and better distribution, I shall look at every problem simply from the point of view of what is the best method of securing the objects at which we are aiming without any regard to theoretical opinions about Free Trade or Tariff Reform.

The second question is Home Rule. There will be no political peace either in the United Kingdom or the Empire so long as the present state of affairs continues. The situation in regard to Ireland is governed by two fundamental facts: the first, that the Home Rule Act of 1914 is upon the Statute book; the second that, in accordance with the pledge which has been given by me in the past, and indeed by all Party leaders, I can support no settlement which would involve the forcible coercion of Ulster. Eighteen months ago the Government made alternative proposals for the settlement of the Irish problem. It offered either to bring Home Rule into immediate effect while excluding the six Northern counties of Ulster from its operation, but setting up at the same time a joint council which would be empowered to extend the legislation of the Irish Parliament to Ulster, or to set up a convention of representative Irishmen to endeavour to find a settlement for themselves. The second alternative was adopted, but unfortunately after nearly a year's earnest deliberation the Convention found themselves unable to arrive at anything like agreement. In these circumstances I claim the right to bring a settlement into effect based on the first of these alternatives. I recognise, however, that in the present condition of Ireland such an attempt could not succeed and that it must be postponed until the condition of Ireland makes it possible. As to this last point, the Government will be chiefly guided by the advice it may receive from the Lord Lieutenant and the Irish Government.

Finally there is the question of Welsh Disestablishment. I am certain that nobody wishes to re-open religious controversy at this time. The Welsh Church Act is on the Statute Book, and I do not think that there is any desire, even on the part of the Welsh Church itself, that the Act should be repealed. But I recognise that the long continuance of the war has created financial problems which must be taken into account. I cannot make any definite proposals at the present moment, but I do not believe that once the question of principle no longer arises, it will be found impossible to arrive at a solution of these financial difficulties.

It is necessary that the question of whether the next election is to be fought by the existing administration as a coalition should be settled at once, otherwise the difficulties in connection with candidates, both of your Party and of my supporters, will become intolerable. I am prepared at once to agree that the Election should be contested on the basis of this letter, and after you have consulted your colleagues I should be glad to know definitely whether we may consider an arrangement on these lines as concluded.

Ever sincerely,
(Signed) D. LLOYD GEORGE.

Wednesday 27 November   Parliament was dissolved on Monday. The business of arranging candidates with the L.G. whips has been very difficult. Bonar and Winston arbitrated on the cases where we could not agree, but their decisions have not been kindly received, and in a good many cases Unionists are fighting in spite of them. The press is attacking all caucus arrangements, and the Liberal portion of it is trying to make out the Unionists have got the better of the deal. In Scotland there seems a good deal of resentment about it. L.G. sent for me on Monday and wanted to know what reports we had. I told him no one could judge yet what would happen. He is evidently a little uneasy. He was anxious to know if anyone could get at Northcliffe.[41] I was afraid not. There was a lot of clamouring for the letter signed by the leaders. But the Liberal Chairman in Scotland told me that there he thought it would do more harm than good.

CHAPTER 7 NOTES

1   On 5 January, Lloyd George had addressed the T.U.C. and laid down the War Aims of the Empire, much along the lines of President Wilson's Fourteen Points which were outlined three days later.

2   Auckland Geddes had been a Unionist M.P. only since 1917 and was Minister of National Service. As Sanders recounts, Lloyd George's

experiment in bringing businessmen into government was not entirely
successful in the House of Commons and subsequent governments
have got a similar result from the same experiment.

3 The letter to *The Times* was printed on 10 January and signed by
Waldorf Astor, Charles Bathurst, Henry Bentinck, Percy Harris, Jack
Hills, George Lane-Fox, Sanders, A.E. Weigall, and Edward Wood.
Hayes Fisher was President of the Local Government Board until
November 1918.

4 George Barnes, Henderson's replacement as Labour representative in
the War Cabinet, had made a speech in Glasgow on 15 January which
had been treated by the press as an attack on Churchill's involvement
in a wage claim for munitions workers in Glasgow. In the Commons
on 16 January, Barnes claimed that he had been misreported but that
he had in any case been wrong in what he had said.

5 For this see Nancy Maurice (ed.) *The Maurice Case*, p. 31.

6 1st Earl of Midleton, who had been a Cabinet Minister 1900–1905,
was a leading Unionist and owner of 5,000 acres of Southern Ireland.

7 Sir Savile Crossley had in fact been the 1st Lord Somerleyton since
1916 and was a Unionist Whip in the House of Lords. As the last
Chairman of the Liberal Unionists before their merging with the
Conservatives in 1912 he was still a figure of some influence although
his highest post was Paymaster General, 1902–5.

8 R.J.H. Shaw had been Secretary of the Irish Unionist Alliance,
1913–14 and was Assistant Press Censor for Ireland and Assistant
Secretary of the Irish Convention in 1917 and 1918.

9 Colonel Charles Repington was military correspondent of the *Morning Post*, previously of *The Times*. He had apparently met the
McKennas socially three times during January, prior to his publishing
a series of articles in the *Morning Post* attacking government policy on
the war. (Charles Repington, *The First World War*, vol. II, p. 177 ff.)
This surprising collaboration of military critics of the government with
Asquithean Liberals had begun with Asquith's denunciation of Lloyd
George's Paris speech in November and reached its height with the
Maurice Debate in May.

10 Lord Beaverbrook became Chancellor of the Duchy and Minister of
Information on 10 February, with Lord Northcliffe as Director of
Propaganda.

11 Robertson was removed by the obvious tactic of offering him the post
of British representative at the Allied War Council at Versailles. The
very establishment of the Council was a criticism of his work as
C.I.G.S.

12 A graphic account of Derby's hesitation over whether to resign in
support of Robertson is given by Sir Edward Spears in N. Maurice,

op.cit., p. 16. Derby eventually left the War Office to be Ambassaador to France in April.

13   Admiral Sir John Jellicoe had resigned as First Sea Lord in December 1917. Admiral Sir Reginald Bacon, an unsuccessful C. in C. Dover Patrol Area was 'promoted' to be Controller of Munitions Inventions in January 1918.

14   The Chairman of the Second Chamber Conference was the 1st Viscount Bryce, previously a Liberal Minister and Ambassador in Washington and a noted constitutional expert.

15   The heavy defeat of General Gough's Fifth Army on the Somme began on 21 March but was not at first recognised as a disaster that might even lose the war for the Allies. Gough was certainly ill-prepared to meet an attack, but part at least of the blame must fall on his political and military superiors, who had extended the Front held by his forces while their numbers fell. The attack had been halted by this stage, but was resumed further north on 9 April.

16   Sir Samuel Scott, Unionist M.P. since 1898 and a Major in the Royal Horse Guards.

17   Gough had in fact taken over an additional 25 miles of Front during January 1918, but only under protest and after much pressure from the government, who were themselves under pressure from the French, N. Maurice, *op.cit.*, p. 36.

18   The Unionist War Committee was a backbench ginger group that had been formed in January 1916, after Carson's resignation from Asquith's government. It had taken the lead in demanding conscription and the replacement of Asquith. Carson had resigned from the Lloyd George Government over its Irish policy in January 1918 and was now again using the U.W.C. as a means to exercise his influence. By this stage however, the U.W.C. had been widened to include almost all Unionist M.P.s; on 8 May, about 230 Unionist M.P.s attended its meeting on the Maurice Affair and it was by then more a precursor of the later 1922 Committee. See D.H. Close, The Growth of Backbench Organisation in the Conservative Party, in *Parliamentary Affairs*, 1974.

19   Edward Shortt (sic) had been a Liberal M.P. since 1910 and was appointed Chief Secretary for Ireland on 5 May; subsequently Home Secretary 1919–1922. Sir John Boraston was Principal Agent of the Unionist Party 1912–1920 and had been Organising Secretary of the Liberal Unionists 1895–1912.

20   Sir Hugh Trenchard resigned as Chief of the Air Staff but was reappointed in 1919. Lord Rothermere, President of the Air Council from 1917, had also resigned on 26 April.

21   Basil Cook was Director of Naval Sea Transport at the Ministry of Shipping.

22 Major-General Sir Frederick Maurice, lately Director of Military Operations at the War Office, had written a letter to *The Times*, published on 7 May, in which he accused the government of misleading the House of Commons about the number of men available for the Western Front.

23 There seems to be no truth in the persistent story that Wilson was responsible for Repington's disgrace and cashiering over the Garstin Divorce. However, there seems to be no reason to doubt that Repington himself did hold Wilson at least partly responsible. (Bernard Ash, *The Lost Dictator*, p. 34.) In any case, Maurice had not been conspiring with Repington or anyone else before sending his letter.

24 Charles Bean was the official War Correspondent with the Australian forces in Europe.

25 The British Workers' League was a government front organisation intended to appeal to 'patriotic labour' and Victor Fisher was its leader. See p. 101.

26 Sanders' informant was Frederick Lonsdale, whose work included 'The Maid of the Mountains'. Pemberton Billing, who was being tried for libel before Mr Justice Darling, was making great play out of his claim to know of a Black Book compiled in Germany which he said included the names of large numbers of homosexuals in high places in Britain. The discomfiture of the judge was increased by Billing's clear allegations that he was one of the people whose name was in the supposed Black Book.

27 Instead of trading off Home Rule (wanted by Liberals and Nationalists) against Irish conscription (wanted by Unionists) the government decided to shelve both plans, a decision that antagonised almost everyone.

28 Lt.Col. Grant Morden was proprietor of the British Cellulose Company, which had been the subject of press criticism and was also criticised for profiteering in the Report of the Committee on National Expenditure. A special enquiry was appointed and this announcement in the House of Commons took the heat out of the issue on 9 August. Grant Morden, perhaps appropriately, joined the Parliament of 1918–22 as a Conservative M.P.

29 Lloyd George spent most of his visit to Lancashire in bed with influenza in Manchester, where he was seen by C.P. Scott. (Trevor Wilson, ed., *The Political Diaries of C.P. Scott*, p. 356.)

30 This story is told from Haig's viewpoint in Robert Blake (ed.), *The Private Papers of Douglas Haig*, p. 331.

31 St Mihiel was a Franco-American victory near Verdun, 12–15 September 1918.

32 This was President Woodrow Wilson, not Sir Henry Wilson, usually referred to in the diary as 'Wilson'.

33 This was the outbreak of revolution in Prague that began the final disintegration of the Austro-Hungarian Empire.

34 General Townshend had been captured by the Turks after the disastrous failure at Kut during the Mesopotamian offensive of 1916.

35 Eleutherios Venizelos was Prime Minister of Greece, 1910–15, 1917–20, and 1928–32.

36 Frederick S. Oliver, journalist and confidant of several leading Conservatives.

37 Isabel Law was Bonar Law's daughter and Lt.Col. Carnegie was Unionist M.P. for Winchester 1916–1918. For the relation of the Unionists and the National Party in 1918, see W.D. Rubinstein, Henry Page Croft and the National Party, in the *Journal of Contemporary History*, 1974.

38 Lord Rothermere owned the *Daily Mirror*, Sir Henry Dalziel owned the *Pall Mall Gazette* and *Reynolds' News*, and Lord Riddell owned the *News of the World* but all had much wider newspaper interests too. Sir Henry Norman and Amery had both worked as journalists before becoming M.P.s.

39 This is a reference to the general package of proposals submitted to both Liberals and Conservatives as the basis for a Coalition Government in the summer of 1910. That whole episode in 1910 remained shrouded in secrecy until politicians in 1918 needed to point to respectable peacetime precedents for coalition government. See G.R. Searle, *The Quest for National Efficiency*, p. 181.

40 The Sanders Papers include this letter from Lloyd George to Law in its printed form, as it was polished up for circulation as an election leaflet.

41 See the diary entry for 8 May 1919.

Chapter 8 1919 'Labour matters look pretty bad'

Sunday 5 January   I went down to my election campaign on 28 November. I had a contest with Plummer, the Bridgwater Trades Union Secretary. His supporters said he had got wages raised and would get the agricultural labourers 40/- a week. My supporters said: 'Sanders went to fight and Plummer did not.' On such issues are the fates of Empires determined! All over the country there was a demand for punishing the Kaiser and getting an indemnity from Germany. Exclusion of aliens was another cry. All this fitted Tory politics well. The register was very badly done all over the country. My contest was not particularly strenuous. The result was

Sanders	12,587
Plummer	5,771
	6,816

Somerset returned seven solid Unionists, the first time the county has been solid. The Conservatives got about 50 more seats than I expected, the Liberal Coalitionists just what I thought they would. The victory was partly for L.G. and quite as much for the Conservative party. In Manchester the Conservatives refused to have anything to do with Coalition. They did not contest Hodge and Clynes but fought and won all the other seats. In Cardiff they won two seats out of three under the same conditions. In Central Wandsworth where Henry Guest stood as official candidate, Norton Griffiths beat him by over 4,000. The British Workers League won 11 seats and beat Henderson and Ramsay Macdonald.

Younger has seen Bonar about the Government shuffle. Walter Long may go to Admiralty and Shortt to Home Office. I pressed the claim of Harry Foster to have the W.O. if Milner resigns. I may be Secretary to Board of Agriculture with Prothero in the Lords as my chief. Henry Craik told me the other day that a good many of the *viri pietate graves* of the House of Commons had marked down either Pike Pease or me as the next Speaker. *The Times* announced that Lowther is resigning at once. He told me it was the first he had heard of it.

Sunday 9 February House met last Tuesday to elect the Speaker. The opening by the King will be next Tuesday. It cannot be said that the new Ministerial appointments have been generally approved. The greatest outcry has been over F.E.'s appointment as Chancellor. The Bar is furious. It is said that he is constantly drunk which is untrue; no doubt he does himself a bit too well. Of course the Conservatives are very angry about Winston, while the Northcliffe press is making a dead set at Austen. Balfour is over in France. Henry Wilson told him he had to go back to see Winston: 'Why what has he got to do with you?' asked Balfour. H.W. explained that Winston was his chief. 'Really,' said Balfour, 'and what has become of poor Milner?'

I did not get an Under Secretary's job but after being appointed to my old place am now a Junior Lord of the Treasury. I am relieved to get out of a court appointment without having to buy the uniform. Edmund told me he looked on me as likely to succeed him. It was suggested I should be Deputy Chairman of Committees, but I got out of that. Lady Edmund hinted that Edmund would like to be put in another office. The fact of his being such a good whip stands in the way of his preferment.

The strikes are the chief subject of interest just now. They are having the effect of setting the general public against trade union pretensions which may be all to the good.

President Wilson is now most unpopular in England.

Sunday 23 February The House has got through a fair amount of work in the first fortnight. After disposing of the address it has passed the new rules of procedure and the Re-election of Ministers Bill. Bonar handled them very skilfully. The House has been crowded most days. Bottomley made a very effective speech on the address. Bonar describes him as having a great gift of interpreting the thoughts of the man in the street.[1] Many new members have spoken. On the whole Moore Brabazon was the most effective that I have heard. In spite of all L.G.'s expedients it looks as if a coal strike will come off.

Friday 5 March L.G.'s handling of the Miners was a model of tact and dexterity. It now looks as if a strike will be avoided. Hickman, a very strong Tory and coal owner, told me that after getting out all the figures for his mine he thought the miners have a very good case for increase of wages. L.G. has now gone back to Paris.

A lot of new members have spoken in the House. They have generally been short and to the point. Whitley says he has been much impressed by the way one after another has spoken on something on which he had special knowledge. Winston Churchill has done very well both on the army estimates and on his bill for extension of compulsory service. The latter has been the only occasion of a fierce party debate. The Labour people and the 'Wee Frees' made a great point about breach of election pledges on conscription. Attempts made to unite the two sections of the Liberals have definitely broken down on the question of bye elections. The test case was Leyton where James Mason has stood against a Liberal, the vacancy owing to the death of a Conservative member. I had some difficulty in getting a letter from L.G. to support him and Bonar's aid had to be invoked. Eventually it was sent. Talbot says L.G. has refused to be proclaimed leader of the Liberal party, on the ground of the bad effect likely to be produced on Unionists.

Sunday 16 March   Opposition to the Ministry of Ways Bill is very considerable.[2] It comes mainly from Unionists. The chief point chosen is the question of roads. That has been engineered by the motor people and is not really a very serious matter. But the vital point is really Clause 4 which gives the Minister power to take over almost anything by Order in Council. John Baird told me yesterday that it rests with L.G. whether we stick to that or not. If we do there is sure to be trouble. Bonar is now in Paris consulting L.G.

Mason's defeat at Leyton is a blow. I was largely responsible for his going there. I thought the seat was safe and we want him back in the House. There was complete apathy during the contest. It was hard to get a decent meeting on either side. The Liberal promised to get railway fares reduced and as more than half the inhabitants go to London every day that was a big bribe and Mason's being a railway director did him harm.

Labour matters look pretty bad again.

Friday 21 March   The Ministry of Ways Bill went through triumphantly. Clause 4 was dropped. Geddes and Bonar made excellent speeches. There was a good deal of pressure from many of our own side to refer the Bill to Committee of the Whole House, and the Unionist War Committee unanimously passed a resolution to that effect and sent a deputation to Bonar. Bonar turned them down very firmly and eventually there was no division.

Last night the report of the coal commission was announced. Bonar at the end of his speech said if the Government's offer was not accepted all the resources of the state would be used against the strike. The Unionists cheered this and that much annoyed the Labour men. Tyson Wilson, Sexton and Walsh say there will not be a strike. It is generally admitted that before the commission Labour had the best of it all through. Their evidence was well put and their representatives much cleverer than the masters in cross examination.

Sunday 13 April   Business in the House has been going on very well. The Standing Committee scheme is entirely a success at present. The Liberals and Labour men obstructed the Military Service Bill for electioneering reasons. All other work has gone through quickly and smoothly so far. The delay in settling peace terms is rather getting on men's nerves. That is really the reason for the telegram to Paris.

The Hull election is bad again. I went down there. Eustace Percy was an excellent candidate. But the organisation was rotten. Seymour King got his followers into the way of doing nothing unless they were paid for it. Mark Sykes got in on his personality. The Military Service Bill was the cause of defeat.[3]

Thursday 8 May   I did not hear L.G.'s speech on the adjournment for Easter. I heard beforehand that he was going to disclose nothing and to attack Northcliffe. Part of his code is that when a newspaper goes for you persistently it pays to attack it in public. Then anything it says in the future is discounted. The Northcliffe story is pretty dirty. N. Approached L.G. in November and asked to be one of the British delegates at the Peace Conference. L.G. refused. Two days later the *Daily Mail* gave a free column to the Labour party for election purposes and Northclifffe's press has attacked the Government ever since. Alec Hood once told me that when Northcliffe was made a peer he offered a very large cheque to the Conservative party. Alec refused it.

Aberdeen election as bad as the others. At one of the L.G. breakfasts when we were discussing the best time for an election, L.G. prophesied great unpopularity for the Government during the period of demobilisation and said if we had an election in the spring we might get a Bolshevik Government. I always held that view and did all I could to press for an election before Xmas in order that we might get a majority large enough to stand the racket.

The budget is well received and every one considers that Austen has done very well over it. A few of the Coalition Liberals are inclined to kick about colonial preference; but that has its advantages as it enables us to mark them down.

Edmund Talbot and George Younger put my name forward for a baronetcy in the last Honours List, but both L.G. and Bonar refused to get anything for members of the Government. I have never asked for anything of the sort.

Thursday 15 May   Edmund told me L.G. was badly let down by Wilson over the American delegates to Ireland.[4] Wilson asked for passports for them without disclosing the sort of men they were. L.G. thought it would be good for them to go to Ireland and see what the conditions were there.

Bonar says L.G. has had a very hard time in France and is likely to be there for a month more. Meanwhile Bonar does not find the Cabinet easy to manage. He says if they were all like Winston it would be impossible. He will not stand the least interference with his department. Auckland Geddes tells me that trade is being held up by rings of employers who are out for enormous profits. They have cornered all building materials; but the biggest ramp is over wool.

Tuesday 17 June House rose for Whitsuntide recess on 6 June. Things went pretty quietly up to the finish. I went on the 7th for a trip to France with Sir H. Nield and Charles Craig. The War Office supplied us with cars and we went round the battlefields. The desolation of the whole place is extraordinary. In the Somme area villages have so entirely disappeared that you cannot see where they have been. The land looks impossible for any agricultural purpose. German prisoners are being employed to clear up in the towns but their work seems leisurely. On the other hand the special companies employed about the graves seem doing good work.

Guest went over to see L.G. about three weeks ago. He says he seems very fit and is full of ardour for a political campaign when he comes back. Lord Derby wrote to George Stanley that L.G. has done extraordinary work at the Conference, both in upholding British interests and getting the others to agree in cases of dispute. Peace terms are still in the balance and Bonar seems to think the Germans will not sign.

Malcolm Fraser[5] told me there is difficulty about Beatty. He wants to be First Sea Lord and Geddes practically promised him the position. Wemyss was to have Malta but that did not come off and now Beatty is making trouble.[6] Fraser is trying to square the press not to take the matter up.

Thursday 26 June House opened on Tuesday last. Edmund away. Bonar went over to Paris on Tuesday so business had to be rearranged at very short notice. It is assumed that Germans will sign the treaty, but there is no great excitement about it in this country. The two matters on which some trouble was expected were the scuttling of the German fleet and the big sale of linen.[7] In both cases the ministerial statement was well received. The real trouble ahead now is over nationalisation of mines. Sankey's report has upset most Conservatives. And it has increased the opposition to the Transport Bill.[8] Trouble looks likely. The absence of L.G. and Bonar makes things more difficult.

There were rumours yesterday of serious trouble in Ireland. Samuels the Irish Attorney General wired to the Castle for information. Answer came: 'Nothing unusual here, but Loch Lomond has beaten Panther in Irish Derby.'

Tuesday 1 July   L.G. and Bonar returned on Sunday. Great scene in the
House yesterday. Quite unorganised enthusiasm. Rounds of cheering,
then *God Save the King* started by Will Crooks. Neil Mclean and another
Labour man remained sitting while it was sung.[9]

Bonar seems to have reassured the deputation on the Transport Bill.
He assured them that the Government had not decided for nationalisation, and at a subsequent confab promised to meet the malcontents on
many points. Edmund told me that in the morning L.G. said with
reference to the coal business that nationalisation was a most dangerous
idea! He did not know what it might not lead to if a Labour Government
came in.

Guest told me that ten days ago Hindenburg advised the Germans to
sign as he had no chance of successful armed resistance on the West
Front.

Wednesday 9 July   The Government was defeated last Friday on third
reading of the Women's Emancipation Bill. Addison had muddled the
matter all through. He actually sent Kingsley Wood to represent him in
the Standing Committee and the Committee ignored him altogether.
Then Astor was put up to move the rejection of the third reading and we
got beaten by 100 to 85. No one seemed to mind much and we went on
with business as usual. On the day before L.G. made his peace speech. It
was considered a great performance. Personally I was not greatly
imprssed. He is at his best when he is attacked or attacking. On the
Friday night he gave a dinner to the Government. It went off very well –
L.G. made a happy speech, very warm towards Bonar. Curzon later on
was excellent. Many functions at week-end. St Paul's service on Sunday
most impressive. I had a talk with Horne the Labour Minister yesterday.
He is gloomy about the outlook. He thinks the trades unions will have a
general strike if they don't get nationalisation and that it is quite hopeless
to carry nationalisation in the present House of Commons. He attaches
great importance to the bye elections now in progress in Wales and
Scotland on the ground of the effect they are likely to have on L.G.

Saturday 19 July   A good deal of excitement over the announcement of
increase in price of coal. The Labour men in the House were thoroughly
taken aback. Debate on subject last Monday. Auckland Geddes put his
case clearly and well. The Labour men had no answer and were really
crying 'Kamerad' all the time. Bonar's offer to them at the end was an
inspiration that came to him just before he rose. It was recognised even
by old Chaplin as a most astute move. But it has not yet come off and
things look pretty gloomy in the Labour world. Carson's 12 July speech
came at a very unfortunate time. Of course Labour is making the most of

it. Every Conservative to whom I have spoken thinks it most ill judged. Bonar asked me what would have been thought if he had condemned it in his speech. I hedged over it.[10]

There has been some newspaper excitement over a body calling itself the Centre Party. It consists of new members from both sides of the Coalition. They held a dinner the other day and got Winston to speak. He made an exceedingly good speech, all for continued Coalition. George Younger and Guest both blessed it also. The older Conservatives are rather up in arms. The fact is that undue importance has been attached to the whole thing. I told a lobby correspondent that it was not a party but a dining club, a phrase that he promptly reproduced.

Peace celebration today. Everything upset in consequence. During the first three days of the week Falcon, a Norfolk M.P., played for Gentlemen versus Players all day and came down to dine and vote at the House in the evening. Probably unique.

Thursday 24 July   The labour situation is very bad. By all accounts L.G. is prepared to fight it out with labour which must mean great trouble in the immediate future. As to the rights of the Yorkshire dispute it is hard to get at the truth. Box, our Central Office Agent in Yorkshire, writes that it is all the fault of the owners. The newspapers put it on the coal controllers. L.G. and Bonar are to see the miners' leaders in London today.

L.G. was at the House on Monday for the debate on the peace treaties. In the course of the debate he spoke strongly in favour of Ulster's case against Home Rule. Unionists were delighted, but Devlin & Co. kept us up till four in the morning in consequence. The declaration means in my judgement the severance of L.G. from the Left.

Monday 4 August   There threatened to be trouble in the Lords last week. Salisbury moved to divide the Transport Bill into two parts. He has been harrying and constantly beating the Government all the session. Our whipping in the Lords seems rotten. However, this time a special wire was sent out in Curzon's name and though Willoughby de Broke told me they were going to beat the Government, the latter got a handsome majority. In our House we have got through a lot of business. I attended the Guildhall functions for the King and Foch, both worth seeing. The King's speech is to be produced on the cinema by the efforts of the Labour Ministry.

Robert Horne tells me we may safely issue propaganda against nationalisation. As he has lately been with L.G. that is a pretty good tip. The agricultural members interviewed L.G. the other day; they came away well satisfied, but *The Times* crabbed L.G.'s speech as being too vague. Fitzroy who introduced the deputation is issuing a full account that may put a different complexion on the matter. I had a long talk with Bal yesterday.

He is kept very hard at work by the Wheat Commission. He says there will be plenty of wheat at a price and that by Xmas there will be more shipping in the world than before the war. He believes that in five years we shall regain our shipping supremacy. The Americans build faster but their ships are shoddy!

Tuesday 19 August   We have finished at last after a very strenuous time. We have had one all night sitting and have been very late on several occasions. The Government introduced a Profiteering Bill at the last moment and in spite of much criticism carried it quickly through all stages. The promised deal on the Welsh Church has also come off and seems to satisfy everyone except the Cecil clique. They are furious with the Bishops for accepting it. Bob has been quite troublesome lately, and rumours are going about that he wants to form a Government himself. The Government has suddenly woken up in public to the need for economy. Freddie Guest tells me that at the present moment L.G. and Bonar have said that the estimates for the services must be cut down to 120 millions and a great fight is going on about it in the Cabinet. L.G.'s speech with announcement of future policy came off last night. He spoke for three hours but a lot might have been cut out. He was quite distinct against nationalisation and his trade policy is clear, though it may not satisfy either side. I have been engaged all today on the question of making propaganda out of the pronouncement.[11]

Lee's appointment to Board of Agriculture is not popular. Strutt pressed it strongly on L.G. He is expected to clear out a lot of the old staff at the Board.

Thursday 9 October   Returned to town on 3 October after spending holidays at Wellfield. Motored up on account of the strike.[12] I spoke on that subject at several meetings in my division. The feeling was certainly strong against the strikers there. F.Guest tells me that the Government are absolutely satisfied with the settlement. He said that when the trades union representatives came to Downing Street they absolutely refused to confer with anyone but L.G. and Bonar. Other Ministers sat in a separate room. On the Sunday at one time the T.U. leaders presented an ultimatum to L.G. who was quite firm in refusing their demands.

The Coalition is not running smoothly in the constituencies. Reports of ill feeling are constant. Guest does not want to hurry things but thinks a formal amalgamation will ultimately be the only possible solution.

Sunday 26 October   The Government was beaten on Thursday 23 October on an amendment to the Aliens Bill. It was quite evident on that and the proceeding day that there would be trouble. A little group with J.G.

Butcher and Nield at the head of them were very keen on making the Bill as strong as possible. Shortt was in charge of the Bill and his method of handling it put their backs up. We whips kept on warning him and B.L. that there would be trouble. On the actual amendment on which the defeat occurred the Government were absolutely in the right, but both Shortt and A. Geddes, whose department was affected, stated a good case badly. When the figures were announced there was almost absolute silence. B.L. moved the adjournment saying he did consider the situation serious. He then phoned L.G. saying he had announced they would resign. L.G. in a great stew till he found his leg was being pulled. The matter was squared during the week-end. It ought to have been squared before defeat not after.

On the opening day of the session I was called on to draw up a programme for a Ministers' speaking campaign in the country; and on 27 October a committee was appointed consisting of F.E., W.Evans, Horne, Winston, Addison and Munro to go into the whole question of propaganda. Guest and I attended and our scheme was adopted. We had a programme of nearly 80 meetings. Cox had all the skeletons ready, and one day's hard work filled in the details.[13]

Sunday 30 November   In spite of several small crises the position of the Government is much stronger than it was before the session resumed. The finance debate that was to be a great blow turned out a great triumph. Austen came out very strong. The attempt of the Labour men to carry a proposal for a levy on capital united the rest of the House against them and the Government lobby was the biggest I have ever seen. Soon after we came back L.G. gave orders for Ministers to speak all over the country. The arrangements were entrusted to Guest and myself and up to date nearly 60 meetings have been arranged before Xmas. In connection with this campaign a small committee has been set up consisting of F.E., Worthington Evans, Horne, Munro, W. Churchill and Addison to run arrangements for Coalition propaganda. Guest and I attended as assessors. Winston is very sanguine about Coalition prospects but anxious to avoid speaking at present. He has done very well, but his Russian policy has been unpopular in the country and rather to my surprise he funks facing the music. I think on the whole the tendency towards Coalition fusion is increasing. Bonar made a most useful speech at the Unionist conference; but it was noticeable there how coldly L.G.'s name was received. The bye elections have been a bit better. We actually held three Unionist seats running though with reduced majorities. Lady Astor's return has upset some of our people a good deal. Old Sir Henry Craik was quite livid about it.[14] The next trouble for the Government is the Bill to limit coal owners' profits. The halfpenny limit was recommended by the

Sankey commission and agreed to by Bonar Law six months ago without protest. The coal owners made no protest till within the last month. Now they are all up in arms. Bonar is in difficulties. The way out will probably be found in making the profit net.

Boxing Day   The session ended on 23 December. The last three weeks were very arduous. The Labour party got us out of the Coal Bill trouble by declaring against it. B.L. thereupon adjourned the debate. Some arrangement for pooling profits is now being made with the coal owners and should settle the difficulty for the time. The papers have jeered at the Government for dropping Home Rule and the Imports and Exports Bill. The latter has no friends. Free traders and tariff reformers both dislike it. Anyhow the idea of settling two such questions at the end of an autumn session was a bit too much. L.G. foreshadowed his Home Rule scheme at the sitting of last Monday. It struck me as much too small for any Home Ruler to accept; the Nationalists stayed away, but Carson gave the Bill a half-hearted blessing and the reception both in the House and the press was quite favourable. Meanwhile the state of Ireland is worse than ever.

Our speaking campaign has done well on the whole. There have been some rowdy meetings notably at Reading and Newport. Edmund thought that trouble was being systematically organiseed from London; but I can find no evidence of that and most of the meetings have been very successful. L.G. spoke to the Liberal Club at Manchester and said he approved the programme at the recent Liberal Federation meeting. This has caused much trouble among Conservatives, and the Executive of the National Union passed a resolution on the subject at the instance of Steel-Maitland. As a matter of fact L.G. quoted a speech made by Horne in Scotland. Horne spoke after the first day of the Liberal Federationg meeting when the resolutions passed were platitudes. L.G. copied him without looking at them. There is however considerable discontent among old Conservatives. I was asked to speak at a dinner and discussion at the Junior Constitutional and found the feeling against the Coalition running quite high there.

The Spen Valley election has split the Liberal Party more than ever. The local association adopted Simon by a large majority and though a few members split off, the running of a candidate against him is being done by the Conservative Association. I was sent up there to look into things. Saw L.G. before I went. He was mad keen to beat simon. 'I don't care who wins if that blighter is last,' he said to me. The result is likely to be close. On the eve of the poll Clynes said the Labour man had lost ground lately and he expected our man to win. Jamers Parker prophesies that there will not be 1,000 votes between first and last.

CHAPTER 8 NOTES

1 Horatio Bottomley, who had been a Liberal M.P. from 1906 until expelled for bankruptcy in 1912, had had his reputation revived by World War I. As a recruiting speaker, as a ceaseless campaigner for a better prosecution of the war and as proprietor of *John Bull*, he had acquired a great influence on popular opinion. He had been an independent M.P. since 1916 but was to be expelled for fraud in 1922.

2 The Ways and Communications Bill set up a Ministry of Transport with extremely wide powers, including the power to control or nationalise industries by Order in Council. Opposition from Conservatives continued, as Sanders notes later, and the Government eventually abandoned many of the new Ministry's proposed powers. See C.L. Mowat, *Britain Between the Wars*, p. 29.

3 Hull Central was won by the Liberals from Coalition Unionist on 29 March; Sir Henry Seymour King had represented the constituency from its creation in 1885 to 1911 while living in Kensington, and Mark Sykes had died soon after he had been re-elected in 1918. Under the Naval, Military and Air Service Act of 1919, the Secretary of State for War retained wide powers to recall demobilised soldiers from Class Z, up to a million men. Liberal and Labour critics surmised that the powers had been retained with possible labour disputes in mind.

4 These were the delegates sent by the Irish Race Convention of America to lobby President Wilson on behalf of the right of Ireland (but presumably not Ulster) to self-determination. They attempted to press the peace conference to discuss Ireland, visited Ireland to see conditions for themselves, and discussed the question of an American loan to the Dail. See Lord Longford and T.P. O'Neill, *De Valera*, p. 93.

5 Sir Malcolm Fraser was an ex-newspaperman and Press Adviser to the Unionist Party before becoming its Principal Agent in 1920. He was Deputy Director of Airship Production at the Admiralty, 1918–1919.

6 Admiral Sir Rosslyn Wemyss had succeeded Jellicoe as First Sea Lord in 1917 and Admiral Earl Beatty was to succeed him later in 1919. Sir Eric Geddes was First Lord of the Admiralty from January 1919.

7 The captured German High Seas Fleet was scuttled at Scapa Flow on 21 June. The dispute about linen was one of the most contentious of the problems caused by the decontrol of industry and the disposal of

factories and stockpiles after the war. Labour M.P.s alleged that stocks and factories were being sold off to private buyers at much less than market prices. C.L. Mowat, *op.cit*, p. 29.

8 Sankey had declared for the nationalisation of coal and this had made the theoretical powers in the Ways and Communications Bill seem more of a threat.

9 The Treaty of Versailles and the League of Nations Covenant had been signed at Versailles on 28 June, thus formally ending the war.

10 Carson had made a most inflammatory speech at the annual celebrations in Belfast on 12 July, in which he threatened to call the U.V.F. to arms if necessary to defend the rights of Ulster. It is a good indication of how feelings had changed on the subject that Bonar Law should consider condemning such a speech; one Unionist M.P. was so appalled by the speech that he apologised for ever having supported Ulster even before 1914. Patrick Buckland, *Irish Unionism*, vol. II, p. 116.

11 Sanders' special responsibilities at Central Office, as Deputy Chairman of the Party, were in the placing of parliamentary candidates and the organisation of literature.

12 There had been a national rail strike from 26 September to 5 October with a strong public relations campaign being mounted by the Government against the railwaymen. Mowat, *op.cit.*, p. 40.

13 Thomas Cox was Secretary of the National Union and in charge of the Speakers' Department at Unionist Central Office.

14 Nancy, Lady Astor, was elected M.P. for Plymouth Sutton after her husband inherited a viscountcy. She was the first woman elected to the House of Commons, presumably the grounds for Craik's outrage.

Chapter 9   1920 'Five-eighths for the coalition, the rest against'

Tuesday 6 January   I was made a baronet in the New Years honours. My constituents seem much pleased.

Coalitionists seem satisfied at the Spen Valley result because Simon did not get in. But the increase in the Labour vote at recent elections is ominous. I am afraid there will be trouble in many seats held by Coalition Liberals. The Asssociation in the division will go for the Asquith section, the L.G. Liberals have no organisation of their own, and in such seats our organisation is bound to go to pieces. There may be trouble over the Wrekin Division of Shropshire, and at Dartford, where Rowland is seriously ill.

I had a talk yesterday with Croydon Marks, a typical old Nonconformist Liberal but a Coalitionist. He told me Churchill was very much distrusted by his friends. They think a lot of Bonar and Austen, but can't do with Walter Long.

Thursday 8 January   Attended a dinner last night at F.E.'s house. Present F.E., the P.M., Salvidge, Horne, Macnamara, Winston, Edmund, Kellaway, Addison, Guest, Bonar and self. The discussion was fusion in order to strengthen resistance to Labour. Everyone thought it advisable in the course of the next few months. But several thought that a good excuse such as a big strike ought to be awaited. Bonar's attitude was the most hesitant. He considers we must fuse, but thinks that on doing so we must have an early election and does not want to hurry things. L.G. was anxious to state a programme that would last us for five or ten years. Winston also wanted a programme. Bonar deprecated programmes. All were pledged to secrecy.

Sunday 15 February   F.E.'s letters to a Sunday paper have not helped fusion.[1] He got £100 apiece for them. There has been a good deal of excitement over the Paisley election. Both George Younger and I were against opposing Asquith. For him to have been returned by the Tory vote would have been rather a good thing. The P.M. and Guest were all for fighting him and keeping him out on the ground that his presence would attract wobbly Liberals in the House to his side. However the matter was decided by the local people who insisted on running a Conservative. There is a very strong feeling against Asquith among Scotch Unionists. The session opened last Tuesday. L.G.'s speeches on the first two days have been the feature of the proceedings so far. They will do a lot of good in the way of rallying the discontented in our own party. His strong declaration against nationalisation means that he has burnt his boats; it should convince our people that he cannot go to the Labour party now even if he wants to. I am doing what I can to urge on the Second Chamber question. Selborne and his friends complain that everything Unionists dislike is in the front of the programme and what they want is held over till the end. Sutherland is appointed Scottish whip. I rather expect to see him in Guest's place before long.

Friday 20 February The Labour party in the House have got their tails down very noticeably. Last Wednesday Angus Hambro had a private member's motion. I suggested to him the question of the boycott by certain trades unions of discharged servicemen. He and George Hamilton brought it forward most successfully. The Labour men looked very sheepish and their attempt at defence was quite childish. For once the press have played the game and *The Times* this morning had an excellent leader on the subject. The result of the Wrekin election came out today. The explanation is that a lot of Conservatives would not support an unpopular local Liberal. I had warned Guest that Bailey was disliked but he had no one else to run.[2]

Sunday 29 February The Government was beaten on Wednesday on a private member's motion as to police pensions. Bonar took no notice. He asked me to look up the precedents for him next morning. They show not only that a Government need not resign, but that it may ignore the vote altogether.

Lady Astor made her maiden speech on Tuesday on a drink motion. Quite a good performance. Style rather 'street corner' but delivery good and points made well. Very few new members could have done so well. The Government have a Licensing Bill in hand. The draft was entrusted to Fisher and Shortt and the work done by the former. Result is a devil of a Bill, with a modified local option and all sorts of things. B.L. consulted George Younger. He was horrified at the proposals. He has impressed on B.L. that it won't do. So has Edmund. I rubbed it into Guest that he must let the P.M. know that such proposals would mean the revolt of more than half the Tory party from the Coalition. I think that is pretty well scotched now.

Much excitement over Asquith's return.[3] Clearly many Tories voted for him to keep the Labour man out. The coalition at the poll against Labour seems the feature of the moment. There is now a vacancy at Stockport, and a troublesome situation may arise. Guest's information supported by ours was that the Liberal Association was strongly for Asquith. Guest told the P.M. and B.L. so, and they said the Unionists had better run a candidate as 'Coalition'. This was duly communicated to the Unionist Association. Who set to work on getting a candidate. Then the secretary of the Liberal Association appears in town and says he thinks they will run a Liberal Coalitionist. I have delayed our people as much as possible; the Liberal Association met yesterday but I do not yet know result. The P.M. was good on Constantinople and the opposition funked a division.

I spoke on Friday on the Franchise Amendment Bill. It was a case of trying to talk the Bill out and I put in a 25-minute speech at very short notice. However there were sufficient supporters to pass the closure.[4]

Sunday 14 March   I have had to pay two visits to Stockport. When I first went down the Unionists were quite determined to run against Leigh who was nominated by the Liberals as a Coalition candidate. I returned to town and saw Bonar. He wired for the chairman to come and see him in town. He did not come but sent his Vice Chairman. Bonar heard through Fiddes the Liberal secretary that Salisbury wrote to encourage the Unionists in their defiant attitude. After a lot of to do the P.M. got Wardle the second M.P. for Stockport to resign. I then went down again and found things much easier. Now Unionists and Liberals run one candidate each and work happily together. Bonar told me ten days ago that he and L.G. were arranging fusion. L.G. is to address the Liberals in House of Commons next Thursday and something further may be heard.

Direct action for nationalisation has been signally defeated at the Trades Union Conference. The Labour leaders realise what a bad effect the threat of it has had on their election prospects.

Sunday 21 March   Last Tuesday the P.M. addressed the Liberal Ministers on the subject of fusion. All were bound to secrecy and Guest and Edge stood at the door to impress on each man as he went out that there must be no word to the press. Next morning *The Times* had a full account and the *Glasgow Herald* fuller still. L.G. addressed his Liberal supporters in the House on Thursday and Bonar spoke at Worthing on Friday, both on this subject, but no definite step has yet been taken towards coordinating our organisations.

Asquith made his first set speech on Monday last on question of prices. Instead of cursing the Government he blessed it. L.G. had come down to speak, but refrained. Thorpe, a new member, made a good maiden speech in this debate.

Chilcott was in Berlin during the *coup d'état* of last week. He says the French government has a much better staff there than we do. The whole country is very short of cereals, and farmers are exporting what they have on account of the high prices they can get abroad. The English are quite popular in Berlin, but the Germans simply hate the French and the French are making themselves as objectionable as they can.

Lloyd George to Sanders 27 March 1920

PRIVATE & CONFIDENTIAL

My dear Sanders,

In connection with the arrangements made for maintaining the essential services of the country in the event of serious industrial disturbances, it has been arranged to adopt the procedure of having Commissioners, which was instituted towards the end of the railway strike, but to more clearly lay down their functions and to get them into touch with their work and responsibilities before the industrial disturbances arise.

There will be thirteen altogether; eleven for England and two, on a slightly different basis for Scotland.

A good deal of the preparatory work has been laid down on paper and I shall be glad if you will be one of the Commissioners.

Hamar Greenwood will be Chief Commissioner in London. Your reports will be sent to him and he will act under the general control and direction of the Supply and Transport Committee of the Cabinet, of which Eric Geddes is Chairman.

As the matter is urgent, I shall be glad if you will communicate with Hamar Greenwood to-day.

Ever sincerely,
D. Lloyd George

Wednesday 31 March House just adjourned for Easter. There was some excitement at beginning of last week over a meeting of the Unionist Reconstruction Committee. They took up quite a hostile attitude about Home Rule. Bonar was in rather a stew about it. I never thought there would be much trouble. A Carlton Club meeting was suggested by the malcontents. All that came of it was a meeting between Bonar and Neville Chamberlain who was in the chair at the meeting. The Home Rule debate has been on the last two days. Carson made the speech of the debate. Austen and Bonar good. The P.M. not at his best. The majority was better than I expected. Some 20 Unionists voted against the Bill. The debate was favourable to it. But there is a feeling that nothing will come of it. On the other hand Scanlan, a former Nationalist M.P., said to George Younger: 'Be sure you get this Bill through.' James Craig says Southern Ireland will accept it because of the financial provisions.

Trouble with the miners seemed likely for a bit but has died down. In that connection the P.M. wrote me letter appended. I promised to act but the whole thing is now postponed.

No further step towards fusion has been taken on our side. But Asquith and L.G. have made speeches which will keep the two wings of the Liberals apart. That may clear the air and tell us what constituencies really are Coalitionist Liberal.[5]

Wednesday 15 April   House reassembled on Monday. There was some excitement during the recess over the Government note to France. People in the country were furious with L.G. The real facts are that Millerand definitely undertook not to move without consent of the Allies. He then did so thinking to confront the Allies with a *fait accompli*. His idea is to show that he is a bigger man than Clemenceau. Cambon is furious with him. Our Government were bound to make a protest, but cannot disclose the whole case without showing up Millerand.[6]

Sunday 2 May The chief business lately has been the budget. The business interests in the House were strong against the increase of Excess Profits Tax. Austen has been quite firm about it and the opposition on the resolution stage collapsed ridiculously. L.G. made his speech about San Remo on Thursday.[7] Not in such a fighting vim as usual except when he launched out at Northcliffe. I had a talk with him the same evening, and asked him why the French would not have Clemenceau as President. He told me the opposition came from the military party and the Catholics and was led by Briand and Foch. They thought he ought to have insisted on the Rhine provinces being given to France. L.G. said Clemenceau wanted Pétain not Foch in supreme command. Foch was pushed by L.G. himself.

I had a serious talk with Scovell the Co.Lib. chief agent the other day as to their organisation. He says they will try to form their own committees and then have joint committees with the Unionists. The split with Asquith gets wider every day.

Saturday 15 May   The Government had a strong time at the beginning of last week over the Indemnity Bill. At dinner time Edmund quite thought we might get beaten. Bonar then took matters in hand and very skilfully got us out of the difficulty at least for the time.

The Liberal split is now definite. Gordon Hewart told me that at the meeting at Leamington the distressing thing was that Runciman, Harcourt and Donald Maclean were on the platform and did nothing to get the

Coalition Liberals a hearing.[8] On the other hand men like MacCullum Scott seem to have asked for trouble. The result should be to force the Coalition Liberals to set up an organisation of their own which is all to the good. Holman Gregory told me that he had no doubt his own agent was Asquithian. He got Herbert Raphael his President to move at his annual meeting that notice be given to the agent. The result was that the Association kept the agent, but elected a new President. He also told me that Maclean told him that the reason Asquith is now so very flat in the House is that he has been so long accustomed to a cheering crowd behind him that he simply can't get on without it. He is good as ever on the platform.

All reports from Ireland are just as bad as can be. Wilson the Irish Solicitor General told me that if the Home Rule Bill is passed he thinks Southern Ireland will elect a Sinn Fein Parliament which will at once declare an independent republic.

Wednesday 23 June   The Conference of the National Union was held at Birmingham the second week in June. All went off very smooothly. J.C. Williams was in the chair and effectively but rather arbitrarily stopped awkward resolutions.[9] It seemed to me that about five-eighths of the audience were for the Coalition and the rest against. Bonar addressed a mass meeting. He spoke on excess profits, negotiation with Russia, and Ireland. His audience was really against him on all these questions and there was no enthusiasm. After the meeting he said to one of the local people that it was very unlike the last Conference in 1913 when he attacked L.G. for 45 minutes amid great applause. The local man replied: 'There would have been just as much enthusiasm if you had done the same tonight.' Bonar told me he narrated this to L.G.! We stayed with the Neville Chamberlains. Austen was there. He talked about Kitchener; said all who were in the Cabinet with him agreed that there never ought to be a soldier as War Secretary again. It meant that they never got expert advice on any military question as K. would have no appeal from himself.

Home Rule drags on slowly in the House. A little knot of Conservatives, W. Guinness, Hoare, Hills & Co. do most of the talking. The debates very dull.

The City is much annoyed at the E.P.D. [Excess Profits Duty]. Although things seem all right in the House, the Government is getting more and more unpopular among Conservatives. We lost the bye election at Louth, but this was largely due to the eccentricities of Turnor as a candidate.

Saturday 10 July   There was more excitement over the Dyer debate on Thursday than there has been since the War. A lot of Conservatives absolutely saw red about it.[10] Montagu's opening speech was as tactless as anything could be. Whitley gave a curious ruling that there could be one division on the Labour party's motion for reduction and another on that of the Conservatives. If both had gone together the Government might have been beaten. Rupert Gwynne made a very violent attack on Montagu. He had old scores to pay off dating back to the silum question long before the war. The Government really had a good case; a good many men voted against merely because Montagu had made them angry.

Still much talk about E.P.D. When Chamberlain first prepared his budget he put it at 40 per cent. The Finance Committee of the Cabinet raised it to 60 per cent. Now the Northcliffe press agitates to turn Chamberlain out in favour of Worthington-Evans who was a prominent member of that Committee. The debate comes on tomorrow – I expect some small concession will be made, but nothing very vital.

We have had trouble at the Central Office. Jenkins[11] who was appointed Chief Agent has broken down. His nerves have gone altogether. On Wednesday last he was so bad that I told Younger we must get him out at once. So he is sent off on a holiday and Malcolm Fraser put in his place. Work had not been heavy. Jenkins is simply unequal to the responsibility. I think Fraser will do well. He refuses to take a salary.

Sunday 18 July   Budget safely through Committee. Austen did very well. Strong opposition both to E.P.D. and the corporation tax. The Liberals insisted on a special day for discussing repeal of Land taxes. That was an excellent thing for us, as on that Conservatives voted for the Government with enthusiasm. Montagu was severely heckled one day at question time, but came out rather well and had the sympathy of the House.

Bonar Law to Sanders 27 July 1920

Private

My dear Sanders,

Sir Hamar Greenwood acted as Chief Civil Commissioner in the organisation set up to deal with the conditions which might arise in the event of a strike affecting the national life. He has had to give up the position which at the request of the Prime Minister has been assumed by his successor Mr Kellaway. For this purpose the country was divided into eleven areas each under a member of the Government and I should be greatly obliged by your agreeing to act as one of those in charge of an area. I understand that this would not mean any serious encroachment on your time except during a strike.

Yours sincerely,

A. Bonar Law

Sunday 1 August   L. spent a week in the constituency trying to get up the women's organisation. She found great apathy and a strong feeling against the Government among many of our good supporters. There is no doubt that Conservatives are getting very sore. E.P.D., Dyer, Home Rule and dealing with Bolshevism have annoyed them. There are letters from all over the county showing the same thing.

Worthington-Evans tells me that with regard to Poland we are gambling on the expectation that the Bolsheviks are so anxious to trade with us that they will give up military advantages to obtain our good will. If they take the opposite line we may be in a very tight place. If Germany likes to tear up the treaty and join hands with the Bolsheviks the situation will be very serious indeed. The French are most anxious to occupy the Ruhr district which would throttle Germany economically. Evans says he did a very good deal at Spa over money matters. The ten millions we have to pay towards German food over the coal deal is more than balanced by the ships we take being valued at present price, not at that of the time of the armistice. But we advertise any pecuniary advantages to France and Italy but say as little as possible about what we get ourselves.

Horne quite thinks there may be a coal strike. The miners were so very mild and conciliatory when they met him that he thinks they are likely to be dangerous. The Government hope to make 50 or 60 millions out of the coal export trade to make up for having never got E.P.D. out of coal. That is what the miners object to. Horne thinks if a strike is to come, next autumn would not be a bad time for it. The railways have good stocks in hand; manufacturers would not mind going slow for a bit just then as orders are not so plentiful as they were. The miners funds are about three millions which would last about three weeks.

Thursday 12 August   Ireland and Poland have been the recent excitements. Hamar did well on the Coercion Bill, but except for L.G.'s reply to Asquith the debate was dull. Dillon lunched with T.P. and Devlin to arrange details. They have got four or five fellows in prison on murder charges that this Bill may enable them to hang. E.T. told me that Hamar spoke to Carson one day about some criticism he had made. Carson replied: 'You must not mind what I say. I may say lots of things you don't like but I will back you up in any way I can.'

In Poland things are going much as I feared. The Labour party leaders are doing all they can to make things difficult in England. L.G.'s speech on Tuesday was not considered very wise.[12] If he means to deal with the Bolsheviks it is no good to abuse them publicly. There is a very strong feeling among Conservatives like Sir R. Hall, Gen. Davidson, Cockrill, Fortescue Flannery and J. Rees that Poland is not worth any expenditure of men or money by us. On the other hand the French are out for blood.

Their latest move has caused the adjournment of the House until Monday.

The South Norfolk and Woodbridge elections gave a striking contrast between the Coalition Liberals organisation and ours.[13]

Monday 18 October The coal trouble interfered a good deal with my holiday. I was summoned to London for committees several times, and was told off to go round the West Country and report on preparations to meet emergency. I found things pretty satisfactory. The feeling in the West is all against the miners. I held meetings the first week in October in the coast places in my division and found that so. The Labour party seem to have their tails down. Horne has won golden opinions by his handling of the matter. L.G. said he would not receive the Triple Alliance people if Horne did not wish it, and promised to back up Horne in every way. He has done so and is now very strong against the miners. I met W. Bridgeman at lunch at the Talbots yesterday. He is very anxious for a settlement; he says Brace and Hartshorn dined with L.G. after the strike was declared and are doing all they can to find a way out. The Government will move the adjournment tomorrow, and the debate is to be as conciliatory as possible. Bridgeman believes the miners would be only too glad to find some way out. The Government are still considering financial clauses of Home Rule Bill, and will be rather glad that it should not come on at once so that they may have time to put down amendments. I saw Charles Craig three weeks ago. He declared the 'Reprisals' in Ireland would settle the country in six months. On the other hand Fitzgerald, whom I met on Exmoor, told me that on more than one ocasion the premises of good Unionists had been burnt by mistake.[14]

We had a Women's Conference and meeting at Exeter on 30 September. It was a great success. Lucy in the chair at the meeting and did very well. There were over 1,000 there from all over the West Country.

Thursday 11 November Armistice Day. The Unknown Warrior idea has caught on with the public. At all counts it gives me a morning off.

Coal strike settled and really on better terms for the employers than those refused in the former ballot. The miners' leaders were desperately anxious to get out, and the confused settlement was really the datum line disguised. Labour stock is very low just now. Brace gets a permanent job for his services; the goal of the Labour leader. We finished report stage of Home Rule Bill last night. Its progress has been wonderfully quick. We got through the committee stage on Friday afternoon; Guinness and his friends had down about fifteen pages of amendments that they did not move and Hogge and Kenworthy coming in about 3 p.m. found the whole thing nearly finished. Hamar is convinced that they have broken the back of the murder conspiracy in Ireland. My namesake Robert Sanders tells me they have got the names of the gang now and are gradually hunting them down. There are few trials as the men usually resist arrest and get shot right away.

The Agriculture Bill will give trouble both with us and in the Lords.[15] Up to now Boscawen has been accepting amendments from the Labour benches, a mistake in tactics as the real opposition is from the old Tories. Guest and I had an amusing interview with Bottomley over the Wrekin election. Our object was to get Townsend to make such a declaration that we could with decency support him; as a matter of fact our supporters refused to do anything else.[16] Bottomley avowed that he wanted to become a Privy Councillor and tried to make a deal on that. When we had turned that down altogether we got a very good declaration of support for the Coalition, whereupon we magnanimously refrained from running another candidate.

Sunday 21 November   There has been trouble in the House over Addison's Ministry of Health Bill. It got a very bad reception on second reading. George Younger had a talk to Bonar about it and Bonar said that though the Home Affairs Committee had passed it, he and the P.M. had never looked into it. Result is that Bonar announced withdrawal of about half the Bill and modification of the remainder. On the top of that came the introduction of the new Licensing Bill. Shortt told Edmund Talbot that it was quite a harmless affair, but it has raised an awful outcry. At one of our whips' conferences I brought up the question of the Home Affairs Committee. Edmund took it to Bonar, who said that was all right. He and L.G. killed that committee a day or two ago. Younger has now got a small and sensible committee set up to go into the licensing question especially as regards hours and try to get an agreed bill. The real trouble is that Fisher and Addison who are strong Radicals produce these Bills without realising how much the Tory party is against them.

Sunday 5 December   I returned to work on Monday last. It has been a dull week. The only excitement in our House was on Friday afternoon when we were mortally afraid the Government would get beaten over the Ministry of Food's supplementary estimates. Our own people thought it a good opportunity to give us a nasty shake in the interests of economy. However, we eventually won by 88 to 60. The feeling for cutting down gets stronger and stronger.

At dinner the other night Bonar was talking of L.G. He said the only time he saw him really down during the war was for half an hour on 18 March 1918, when the news of Gough's defeat came in; but at the end of the half hour he was wiring to Wilson to suggest the brigading of one battalion of American with each of our brigades. Another story of him is that on one occasion someone said to him at a time of trouble 'Life is very worrying just now.' 'Yes,' he replied, 'but it's d---d interesting.'

Another story going about. Mrs Asquith asked Balfour: 'Well what do you think of the book?' 'What book?' asked Balfour.[17]

Saturday 18 December   As usual at the end of a session we have been having late nights. At one time it looked as if we should not get through before Xmas. The Wee Frees came out against the Dyes Bill and threatened obstruction but caved in at the last moment.[18] We sat up all one night on the Health Bill, and then the Lords threw it out on second reading. Salisbury and Selborne had no part in that. It was the work of the pure backwoodsmen. The campaign in the Harmsworth press against extravagance has had the effect of rallying members to the Government. Monsell and Sutherland consulted Pool of Lewis & Lewis as to bringing a libel action. He began by saying he has a retainer for the *Daily Mail*, but advised that action would be foolish. However Remer is going to try it on. My picture was among the gallery of 'wasters' in the *Daily Mirror*. Lambert's motion gave the Government a good opportunity. Austen made a very convincing speech and we had a huge majority. Bonar made a very good speech on the subject at Edinburgh. The papers hardly reported it, but we are publishing it as a leaflet. The Government meetings have gone very well, better than last year. But there is likely to be trouble in the country over unemployment which is getting worse and worse.

I went abroad on 19 December.[19] The House rose on the 23rd after a 22-hour sitting on the Lords' amendments to the Agriculture Bill. The Government certainly attempted to cram too much into the autumn session. The Home Rule Bill went through more quickly than was expected. Worthington-Evans who was in charge in the absence of Walter Long handled it very skilfully. He refrained from making unnecessary speeches himself, a temptation to which most Ministers give way. But in spite of the time saved on that Bill it was only possible to prorogue before Xmas by frequent late sittings. The introduction of Addison's Health Bill was a great mistake, and other small Bills were introduced and pushed through that were not really urgent.

The result of the Dover election was a surprise.[20] When the vacancy occurred the local chairman and agent came to see me with John Astor. They told me there was great indignation at the Harmsworths' pressuring to select a candidate and I went away thinking it was all safe. However, both the *Daily Mirror* and *John Bull* were used as election papers and Polson was undoubtedly a telling speaker. It was the Tory vote that carried him; and the extravagance cry is undoubtedly making many good Tories hostile to the Government. On my return from abroad I went with Fraser and Poole of Lewis & Lewis to consult Carson about proceedings against the newspapers involved under Clause 34 of the new Franchise Bill.[21] It was rather a curious interview. Carson gave us excellent political advice but knew nothing about the law on the subject at all. However, he urges that in the public interest we ought to take proceedings. We shall probably do so.

The Times has been publishing reports that there is to be an early dissolution as well as predicting a break up of the Government. It imputes some deep laid plot to George Younger. I hear from him that the whole thing is pure invention. He told me that Edmund Talbot is anxious to give up the position of Chief Whip and that I am likely to succeed him. The papers have got hold of the same story,[22] but I have heard nothing of it from Edmund himself, though I saw him in London. He has been laid up but has recovered and gone down to Cornwall. Walter Long is still very seedy and will have to resign. He told Younger that all the Admiralty Lords say we must build capital ships if other powers do so, but the matter is being held up for the present year. I cannot get any information as to how the Cabinet Committee on the Second Chamber is getting on. Curzon is chairman, but I don't know if it ever meets.

CHAPTER 9 NOTES

1   F.E. Smith had written a piece for Lord Northcliffe's *Sunday Dispatch* on 11 January, in which he had laid down the programme for a coalition to follow after fusion of the Unionist and Coalition Liberal parties. He had written again on 25 January to reply to criticisms. Lord Birkenhead, *F.E., the Life of F.E. Smith*, pp. 345–7.
2   Labour won the by election in the Wrekin Division with 38 per cent of the vote, the rest of the vote being divided between Bailey (Coalition Liberal) and an independent who was backed by Horatio Bottomley.
3   Asquith returned to the House of Commons by retaining the Liberal seat at Paisley on 12 February.
4   This was a private member's bill to equalise the franchise for men and women and to abolish plural voting. The bill was obstructed in committee by Sir Frederick Banbury, with the tacit approval of the government, and eventually dropped. David Butler, *The Electoral System in Britain since 1918*, p. 20.
5   That is what constituency *parties* were Coalitionist Liberal. Many parties had not had to make a final choice between Asquith and Lloyd George and were trying to avoid making such a choice.
6   The French intervention in Germany had been decided on unilaterally and the British note of protest to Millerand, the French Prime Minister, was couched in very sharp terms indeed. Public opinion in

Britain, however, assumed that Lloyd George was backing the defeated enemy against the recent ally – which in a sense he was. Paul Cambon was the French Ambassador in London.

7   There had been a conference of the Supreme Council at San Remo during April, a further unsuccessful attempt to settle the question of reparations.

8   This was the general meeting of the National Liberal Federation at Leamington, held the previous week, during which the Asquitheans demonstrated that they were in control of the party machine and declared all out war on the Coalition Liberals.

9   J.C. Williams had been a Conservative M.P. 1892–5, was Lord Lieutenant of Cornwall and a leading figure in the National Union, Chairman of the National Union 1919–20.

10   Brig.-Gen. Dyer was relieved of his command after the massacre of 379 Indians during riots at Amritsar. Many Conservatives, who were fundamentally opposed to a policy of conciliation anyway, believed that the Government should have stood by its local commander instead of disowning him.

11   William Jenkins had been Liberal Unionist Agent for the West Midlands before coming with Boraston to Unionist Central Office in 1912. Joint Principal Agent 1915 and Principal Agent from April 1920.

12   The Labour Council of Action to prevent Britain from aiding Polish forces against Russia was in full swing in early August. The Russo-Polish situation and the expected fall of Warsaw to the Russians had interrupted real negotiations between Britain and Russia and had probably ended Lloyd George's desire to make a trade deal anyway. E.H. Carr, *The Bolshevik Revolution*, vol.III, p. 278.

13   South Norfolk was lost to Labour by a Coalition Liberal and Woodbridge was held by a Conservative. However, the results were hardly comparable for an Asquithean Liberal intervened in South Norfolk but not in Woodbridge.

14   Charles Craig was Unionist M.P. for South Antrim. 'Fitzgerald' could be any one of a dozen officers of that name.

15   The Agriculture Bill of 1920 kept up the wartime agricultural wages boards for another year, this being unpopular with many Conserrvatives.

16   Townshend was the candidate of Horatio Bottomley, running on a platform of national economy. After defeat at the Wrekin by Bottomley's candidate in 1919, the Coalition parties were understandably unwilling to risk another defeat.

17   Mrs Asquith's book, in which Balfour figures prominently, was *The Autobiography of Margot Asquith*, which had been published in October and had been very widely reviewed.

18 The Dyestuffs Bill restored protection to the industry after wartime controls had expired in 1919 and was opposed by Asquitheans on grounds of free trade.

19 This section must have been written later, although there is no date heading, and covers the whole period from Sanders' departure to the new session.

20 Sir Thomas Polson had won Dover on the Rothermere campaign of Anti-Waste in what had always been a safe Conservative seat.

21 Under clause 34 of the 1918 Representation of the People Act, it 'became an offence for virtually any expense to be incurred in the promotion of a candidate without the agent's express permission.' D.E. Butler, *op.cit.*, p. 9.

22 Sanders' diary has a clipping from the *Sunday Times* of 6 February 1921 attached at this point from the political column:

> 'I shall be surprised if Sir Robert Sanders does not succeed Lord Edmund Talbot as chief party whip, for he is just as well versed as a whip in Parliament as he is as a whip in the field, which is saying a good deal. What Sir 'Peter' Sanders does not know about members and hounds is not worth bothering about. If I dared to paraphrase a maxim of Rochefoucauld, I should say that it is not until one has lived with dogs that one really understands the ways of men.'

Chapter 10 1921 'Bonar says he has done with politics for good'

Sunday 20 February Session opened last Tuesday. The King's speech is unsatisfactory in its reference to the House of Lords question. The fact is that Curzon's committee of the Cabinet has made no progress at all. F.E. told Younger he thought the report of the Bryce Committee rotten, but he has no plan of his own. There is sure to be a row with Selborne & Co. on the subject. Edmund Talbot has been offered the Air Ministry and declined it; he stays on till Easter as Chief Whip. Hewart has insisted on being L.C.J. as a right and the bar support his claim.[1] He will be a loss to the Government. The P.M. made a very powerful speech on the unemployment amendment. It was very noticeable how all our men howled at Bob Cecil when he interrupted. He was sitting on the front opposition bench for the first time.

Sunday 27 February The latest is that Hewart stays and is to take charge of the Licensing Bill. Finlay may be L.C.J. He is pretty old but quite hale and hearty. Younger, Fraser and Carson went to see the P.M. the other day as to proceedings re Dover election. The P.M. seems very anxious to avoid them, as he has ideas that he may be able to square Rothermere. It is agreed to wait till the pending elections are over. Meanwhile Beaverbrook and the *Express* are playing the same game againt Boscawen at Dudley on the Canadian cattle question.[2]

The Government nearly got beaten on Friday on Mond's estimates.[3] Things looked very bad and we only got 88 to 78. I urged on Edmund at the beginning of the session that Bonar or Austen ought to make an opportunity for a straight talk with the Conservatives on expenditure. Otherwise we shall have trouble on every vote. I am afraid Hamar has got into trouble over the Tudor and Crozier business.[4] It looks like a misunderstanding all round, but wants explanation. The feeling against the Black and Tans seems growing both here and in Ireland. Hamar's speech on Monday last did not go down so well as his previous efforts.

Sunday 13 March As a result of Friday division of 25 February Bonar agreed to the idea which I had pressed from the first day of the session that he should meet the party. After a lot of hesitation on his part it resulted in a lunch given nominally by Edmund Talbot at the Constitutional. Two private members were put up first to voice the causes of discontent in the party. Wilson Fox did it quite admirably; it was a most difficult job. He was clear and forcible without being in the least offensive. Bonar was not up to form in his reply. Still the function did good. Bonar is really tired out and wants a thorough rest. We have had a very strenuous time in the House lately. There are an awful lot of supplementary estimates, and a good deal of criticism of them; the result has been many latish sittings, and yesterday a sitting on Saturday. It is just possible now that we may get ten days at Easter, but that depends on the reception given to the German Reparation Bill. That is generally regarded as economically unsound, but it is possible the P.M. may induce the House to rush it. If not it might take a fortnight in committee.

Much discussion now about the Speakership. The present position is that the Government will propose Whitley unless very strong pressure is brought. There is a strong party for Ernest Pollock. Stanley Baldwin is also mentioned.

The party is furious with Beaverbrook over the defeat of Boscawen at Dudley. Coming just after our sensational victory at Woolwich it was particularly annoying.[5] About 20 seats have been offered to Boscawen. He has decided to go to Taunton. Our agents advised against anything in the London neighbourhood for fear of an Anti-Waste candidate.

I was sent down to speak at Birmingham last Thursday in place of Horne to an audience of 1,000 women. The whole thing was well worked and most successful. The women's organisation is coming on well.[6]

Sunday 20 March Bonar came into the Whips' room on Saturday 12 March after his return from Glasgow. I thought he looked better than before he went away. He talked about the Speakership, etc. and was in rather good form. Last Sunday he played four sets of tennis. That night he collapsed. On Wednesday night Edmund told us of his resignation and on Thursday the P.M. announced it to the House, breaking down as he did it. The secret was well kept and it came as a complete surprise to the House and to the press. The P.M. is very much upset. He says he would like to resign too. During the war there was the hope of victory to stimulate; now there is a succession of worries without compensation. Bonar says he has done with politics for good. The moment he was definitely out of it he got ever so much better. I expect he will be quite well by the end of the summer and the general idea is that he will come back. Personally, I don't think he will. Austen is the inevitable successor. There is to be a party meeting tomorrow with Edmund in the chair to elect a leader of the party in the House of Commons. A little intriguing is going on. F.E. came to the Lobby and informed his friends that he was drafting a Second Chamber Bill that would enable him to lead the party. A deputation consisting of G. Hamilton, Norton Griffiths and Grattan Doyle called on the P.M. to ask him if he would lead the party. Hamilton told me he was very nice to them, chaffed them and put them off in a kindly way. They threaten to move the adjournment of the meeting tomorrow.

The week has been strenuous; perpetual late sittings, but the Easter recess is now assured. Our men have stuck it very well. We have always had sufficient to closure.

Thursday 24 March   The party meeting was as successful as possible. A most thoroughly gentlemanly affair; not a word said that any one need regret. The features that stood out were Frank Mildmay's speech about Bonar – quite perfectly done – and the great ovation that Edmund Talbot got at the end.

The Government has offered to nominate Whitley for the Speakership, but he has not yet replied. Meanwhile Bull is going round getting a protest signed, and curiously enough is being assisted by the Attorney General and the Lord Advocate.[7] On the other hand Walter Guinness and his friends are keen for Whitley. The election is to take place on April 11.

Before departure for the Easter recess Edmund asked me if he might assume that I was ready to be his successor if he gave up the job. I said yes. He came up to town on Easter Tuesday. After seeing the P.M. he wrote to me to say I was either to be Under Secretary of State for War or Chancellor of the Duchy. He wanted me to be Chief Whip, but the P.M. insisted on Leslie Wilson. Leslie did not want the job at all, but was told to take it or leave it. He never saw the P.M. or Austen, only Edmund. Monsell and George Stanley are shifted too. I have not yet found out the reason of breaking us up. George Younger does not know and says Bonar would not have had it. It may be the P.M. thought we had a little too much influence. We were certainly a happy family. I never had or knew any row or ill feeing in the room during my time there. Edmund's taking his new position is heroic.[8] He had declined the War Office as well as the Air Ministry, and naturally was pressed a good deal before he consented to become Viceroy. He has been promised the full backing of Rome, and that may have a great influence.

Of the other new appointments that of McCurdy as Co.Lib. Whip is most curious. He is a particularly bad mannered fellow, just the reverse of Freddie Guest.

So ends my life as a whip.

Edmund Talbot to Sanders 30 March 1921

Dear Peter,

I have to write this in a great hurry and cannot go into all the details of the proposed changes. But so far as our room is concerned, the P.M. wants you to take either Under Secretary of War vice Peel, or Chancellor of the Duchy vice Bal who is to be Board of Works vice Mond, who is to be Health vice Addison who is to be 'without Portfolio'.

Peel is to be offered Chancellor of the Duchy and to answer for the War Office in the Lords. If he refuses this you are wanted for Duchy. Leslie Wilson is to come in my place, Bobby is to go as Civil Lord Admiralty and George Stanley as Financial Secretary War Office in place of Williamson who retires.

This all I can say at present. I shall be in London till Saturday evening perhaps go away then for week-end. I do not want to put on paper at present what is going to happen to me. I said I preferred you as my successor but P.M. wants to make rather sensational changes.

Yrs: E.T.

Edmund Talbot to Sanders 1 April 1921

My dear Peter,

Things have been so pushed all day I have not had time to write and now P.M. has arranged for the list to be out tomorrow so you will see before you get this that you are Under Secretary for War, Peel having decided on taking Duchy. You will also know my fate – it's an awful business and I tried to get out of it, but then felt I could not refuse. How the Whips' room is going to get on during the next fortnight I can't think, because you and Bobby and G. Stanley go, and Gibbs and Jack have to be re elected as well as Bobby. I think you and George Stanley will have to lend a hand.

I don't know if you have any ideas as to new whips. I told Leslie Wilson I thought Harry Barnston would do for one. Jack Gilmour suggests Buckley who is a Lancashire member which would fit in well. Leslie Wilson is very diffident about succeeding me, and would rather it had been you as indeed I should, but he finally agreed.

No need for you to return before Monday. I expect coal strike will upset parliamentary business next week.

Yours in haste,
Edmund Talbot

Younger to Sanders 4 April 1921
(from Hotel Lotti, 7 et 9 rue de Castiglione, Paris)

My dear Peter,

I don't quite know what to think about those new appointments. I had thought it was quite settled that you would take Edmund's place, certainly it was Bonar's intention that you should do it and I can't help feeling disappointed about that. Leslie Wilson is a cheery chap and quite a nice fellow but he knows nothing about the management of the business and I fear will find his job much more difficult than he probably imagines. Fancy him dealing amongst other things with Honours!! This must be a sealed book to him and he'll have a lot to learn.

This will I suppose mean your loss to the Central Office and that I naturally very deeply regret. It was good of you to take it on and no one appreciates more than I do how jolly well you have done it and what was the value of your work before and since the general election.

I must take counsel with you about the future when I return as I hope to do on Wednesday.

As to Edmund, I have known of this intention for some time and I earnestly hope that the patriotic sacrifice he is making will not be in vain. It is a fine thing to do, with all the grave risks accompanying it at the present moment, and both he and Lady Edmund, who seems now quite reconciled to it, deserve the greatest gratitude and admiration for their pluck. May they have every success and may they return in safety! I saw them on Friday night before coming over here. I was glad to see how cheerfully they looked on the venture, because it is a real venture. Some weeks ago when they first spoke of it to me he was quite convinced it was his duty to go if he got the promise of every help from Rome, but she was doubtful and rather turned against it. That is all changed now. Rome has spoken quite clearly and both are quite happy.

Good luck to you in your job! Keep Worthy in order. He needs it.

Yours ever,
George Younger

Sunday 10 April Started at the War Office last Monday. Worthy Evans called me in at once to see the C.I.G.S., A.G.[9] etc., as to the preparations for meeting disorder. A scheme was produced that was apparently prepared last autumn and which involved the embodiment of the Territorials. This seemed to be approved. Birch[10] the new boss of the T.F. told me afterwards that all sorts of pledges had been given to the T.F. that they should not be called up in aid of civil power. I told W.E. this and next day the Territorial Divisional Commanders were summoned to the War Office. They were unanimous that the T.F. could not be embodied. W.E. was called in; he got suggestions very quickly and in half an hour had got out the Defence Forces scheme that has now been adopted. I am struck by his capacity as an administrator; and his manners are better and less boisterous in the Office than in private life.

On Tuesday the P.M. sent for Jeffries, O.C. London District, commonly known as Ma Jeffries. He cross-examined as to what plan he had made for all sorts of possible and impossible emergencies and did not get much out of him. Before leaving Jeffries said he hoped that if he was put in a tight place the P.M. would not go back on him as he had on other people, Dyer for example. The P.M. wrote straight off to W.E. to say that Jeffries was not only insolent which he could tolerate, but incapable and that the safety of London must not be left in his hands. Would W.E. see to this at once? Result after some manoeuvring is that Cavan from Aldershot is placed in charge of the whole show.[11]

The work in the House has been full of coal discussion. The noticeable thing at first was the apparently genuine fury of the miners' members. That has been calming down during the week a little. Graham on Tuesday and Wednesday was the most truculent; on Thursday he was humorous and almost benevolent. Men like Clynes and Thomas are evidently very anxious to find a way out. After the announcement made by the P.M. on Friday the responsible Labour men see the red light, but I doubt if the miners' leaders could get the men back if they wanted. Stanley Baldwin, who has not previously come in contact with them, says they strike him as a particularly stupid lot and have no leader. I expect they miss Smillie who really was a clever man.

Sunday 17 April A week of melodrama. After much Government parleying had failed the mine owners asked M.P.s to meet them last Thursday and hear their case. One hundred and fifty to two hundred went including many of the most stalwart Tories in the House. Marriott in the chair. Evan Williams presented the owners' case and made such a hash of it that this Tory audience was disgusted. They decided to hear the other side and got Hodges to address them after dinner.[12] He made an excellent impression; but by dint of much heckling at the end they got him to say he was ready to discuss a temporary arrangement of the wages question leaving the National Pool over. On that Marriott, Leslie Scott, Hurd and Sam Hoare went to the P.M. at midnight. The result was the P.M.'s new offer, the miners' tardy refusal and the cancelling of the railway strike. The news of the last came up on the tape before either front bench knew anything about it. Thomas meant to come into the House and make an announcement, but took so long writing his notes that the House adjourned and he missed his bit of 'limelight'. The general impression is that a large proportion of the railwaymen would have refused to come out. Shackleton told me he thinks the Miners Federation will break up;[13] but I was surprised to find him strongly in favour of a National Pool.

At the start recruiting for the Defence Force was very slack. On Monday there were only about 5,000, but numbers increased as things got more acute, and we now have about 70,000. I went yesterday to see the canteens in Kensington Gardens run by the N.A.A.F.I. They seem admirable. Delighted at my going there. I thought they might rather resent it.

As to the Whips' room, Edmund told me the P.M. wanted to break it up because there were too many 'gentlemen' there. He said those were not the P.M.'s words but what it came to. I said: 'You have got gentlemen as your new lot.' Edmund said: 'Yes, we had to when we went into it.' The P.M. said he wanted me for an Under Secretary.

Saturday 23 April   The coal strike continues and there seems little sign of agreement. The P.M. got owners and men together yesterday but both sides were very stiff. However, he got them to promise to meet again on Monday. We have stopped recruiting for the Defence Force, but are not letting men go who have joined. Sir J. Beynon and a Mr Ward from S. Wales came to me on Thursday in rather a funk about the chance of trouble down there.[14] But next day J.C. Gould showed me a report from one of his men there that seemed much more peaceable.

At the beginning of the week I was put on a committee to consider the licensing question, Fisher in the chair. The proposals were fairly moderate, mainly about hours, no local option. But the Cabinet had now decided not to legislate this session. John Gretton's Bill yesterday afternoon was not pressed to a division; it was not very well received. He made the mistake of bringing in much too long and ambitious a Bill.[15]

Sunday 1 May   Dined with the Edmund Talbots last Sunday. She dislikes the prospects. He does not really. Henry Wilson wrote to him: 'How could you do it, how could you?' Edmund wrote back: 'Because I was brought up with cherry breeches not with a green coat.' He has the feeling that the honour of his regiment is involved.[16]

The strike situation is worse than ever. All quiet but no signs of the men going back. Willie Bridgeman says his last trouble is that Winston wants to interfere. Poor Willie has had a very hard time since he took on the job; most of the work falls on him but the limelight on other people.[17]

At the War Office we have had our little worries, the 5th Lancers and the Northumberland Yeomanry chief among them. I am beginning to take the measure of the various heads of departments. The way that most of the chiefs are down on the Territorials is quite remarkable. The Adjutant General and Quartermaster General most conspicuous in this way. The procedure of the Office strikes me as very cumbrous. A subject is raised; minutes are written from the various departments and the thing goes backwards and forwards for months without anything being settled. The establishment of the R.E. has now been tossed about for eighteen months in this way.

Neither Edmund nor Hamar nor George Stanley knew anything of Derby's visit to Ireland.[18]

The passing of Lowther was rather moving. He broke down when he had to read out the somewhat fulsome resolution about himself. He ought to have been allowed to say 'the motion on the paper'. Ronald McNiel's protest was well done and well received but the House would not stand Joynson Hicks on the same throne. As a matter of fact the Government took every care to ascertain the feeling of the House. I have no·doubt there was a majority for Whitley, but I don't think it was overwhelming.[19]

Sunday 8 May   Coal affairs still at a standstill. Baldwin tells me the Government think it wisest to stand aside altogether at present.

L.G.'s speech on reparations was very masterly, quiet and statesman-like. It killed what was expected to be rather a fierce debate. Worthington-Evans was really worked off his legs on the financial part of the question.

I went down on Friday and Saturday to the camps at Wimbledon and Wormwood Scrubs and had a talk with the C.O.s there. They report that the men thoroughly enjoy the outing and would like the strike to go on.

Allenby wired on 1 May that he wanted to detain troops in Egypt as he considered the situation 'dangerous'. Henry Wilson says when the Bull says 'dangerous' by Gad it means dangerous. But there is no further news from there.

Friday 13 May   We have been debating the Safeguarding of Industries Bill all this week. Quite amusing to hear the old tariff reform speeches on either side coming out again. Mond made about the best speech for the Bill; he has made great headway this session. The Wee Free whips played a very low down game. They bargained to get two days for the general discussion on the understanding that we got the resolutions by 8:15 on Wednesday, then went back on their promise and kept us up till five in the morning. The Speaker took a very firm line on Monday about an attempt to get the adjournment on the question of an Irish execution. I think Lowther would have granted it.

Two memoranda have been circulated to the Cabinet re Winston and the Sultan. Winston went to see him in Cairo and discussed politics with him; W.C. is strongly against the Milner policy.[20] He circulated an account of the interview to the Cabinet. His summary is: 'It is quite impossible to stay even a short time in Egypt without feeling how gravely our interests have been prejudiced by the Milner Report and by the lack of any policy in regard to it into which we have been forced by its premature disclosure.' Curzon has circulated in reply a most killing memo. A characteristic sentence is: 'I am clear as to this, namely that the Sultan displayed in this interview many of those characteristics which a closer familiarity with the regions which the Colonial Secretary has now taken under his wing will teach him are inseparable from the conversations of Oriental potentates, and indeed that His Highness consistently and successfully 'pulled the leg' of my colleague.'

Friday 27 May   Austen announced on Wednesday that miners and owners were asked to meet today. I have heard of no basis of agreement but the Cabinet seem very confident that something will be settled. In fact it is almost settled that the reserves will be dismissed on Monday next. The elections in Ulster are better than the Unionists expected, but the state of the rest of Ireland is worse than ever. McCurdy recommends intensive military measures in the summer and autumn.

Feeling against the exemption of M.P.s' salaries from income tax is increasing. The debate comes on next week.

The Government believe that the French were at the back of the Polish rising in Silesia but have no proof of it. There is however some proof that the Bolshevists are supplying Kemal with arms. Townshend is going out to Turkey and tells me that the P.M. has entrusted him with a mission to square Kemal. I am afraid it is not wholly to be relied on.

According to Scotland Yard the Sinn Feiners mean to have a shot at prominent men in England. It is rumoured that there were some in the neighbourhood of Chequers last weekend.

Sunday 5 June   On Wednesday the exemption from income tax for M.P.s' salaries was withdrawn, and free railway fares turned down by a small majority. Austen left the matter to the House, but Pollock told me he said he hoped Unionists would not vote against the motion. I did not vote at all. During Austen's speech which was quite able one felt the sympathy of the House was against him. The most noticeable thing in the debate was the anger of the Labour members at Donald Maclean's speech. They are very much annoyed at the whole thing.[21] The majority against railway fares was unexpected. If the Government had taken the whips' advice they would have left the whole question alone.

Lunched with Birch. Met Lord Home and Mr Justice Darling. Conversation all on fox hunting. Rather quaint.

Sunday 19 June   The miners have balloted and by a large majority decided to continue the strike. Bridgeman says the leaders wanted and expected them to vote for going back, but would not give any lead; just their attitude throughout. It is now thought that the men will dribble back by degrees. I have my doubts whether this will happen on any large scale.

Winston's speech on Mesopotamia and Palestine was a great success. It was pronounced the best thing done in the House for a long time and men on the Conservative side are talking of him as a leader.

The recent bye elections have been a blow to the Government.[22] At St George's a number of people would not vote for Jessel because he is a Jew. Even in the Carlton one heard this said. Neither there nor at Hertford is our organisation any good. At the latter place our people steadily refused to organise against Billing. I spoke at Ware and Hertford on the eve of the poll; meetings poorly attended and the whole thing with no life in it. The Bottomley and *Daily News* machine going strong in each case. The P.M. has now withdrawn his objection to legal proceedings and the Attorney General is keen for them, but Poole now thinks that it is too late to go on the Dover case. I am pressing to get something done and suggesting a petition at St George's as the best place. The Anti-Waste successes will make the position more difficult as to the debate on Addison's salary next Thursday. Horne spoke to me about that the other day and was very anxious to find a way out. He says Addison has done nothing at all since he has been without portfolio. Pike and Willie Bridgeman have told Leslie that they dislike voting for it. G. Younger has told the P.M. he will be beaten over it. But at present the P.M. means to treat it as a question of confidence.

At Oxford last weekend I met Princess Bluecher. She said her book originally filled two volumes but she was advised to suppress half of it, and is constantly pestered by American publishers to let them have the suppressed portion. She says that after the Marne, things were entirely out of the Kaiser's hands, and that the announcement of his abdication was actually made before his signature was obtained.[23]

The announcement that Part I of the Agriculture Act is to be repealed came as a surprise. The Farmers Union were consulted and while refusing to take any responsbility are rather pleased than otherwise, but they at present decline to advocate conciliation boards as suggested by Boscawen on the ground that they might lose members by doing so. It is probable that the wages board will lower wages to 40/- before it comes to an end. If they do that the labourers will not be able to make such a grievance of its abolition.

Friday 24 June The Addison debate yesterday fizzled. The P.M. promised that the Ministry without Portfolio should end with the session. That stopped the trouble, and there was no division on the main question. But the P.M. was not on form and his speech did him harm rather than good. The feeling in favour of a pure Conservative party is a little stronger now than it has been at any time since the armistice.

Monday 14 July Coal strike really over at last. I thought there would be trouble over giving the miners the ten millions, but it collapsed when it came to the point. The state of things in Asia Minor is better, Kemal has been making advances to Harington[24] and there are signs that he does not like the Bolshevists. On the other hand things in Ireland are very bad. One report that came to us at the War Office described our army as being besieged there and none of our information shows that we are in any way getting the better of the rebels. It is possible that the overtures to de Valera may lead to something,[25] but I am not very hopeful. In the House of Commons the chief difficulty at the moment is over the Railway Bill.[26] It gets on very slowly in the Standing Commmittee; as soon as one difficulty is squared another turns up. Banbury is dead against the Bill and is probably responsible for its slow progress.

Saturday 16 July Valera is over here. There is a cessation of bloodshed in Ireland bar Belfast. There is an expectation that something may come of it. Charles Craig really thinks it likely, and he is a fair judge. James Craig told me he had seen Asquith at the Court Ball and told him he ought to press de Valera to be reasonable. James declared Asquith would have more effect than anyone, a new light to me. Some Conservatives are a good deal perturbed at the idea of having any dealing with de V. They held a meeting at which Sprot proposed a resolution condemning such dealing altogether, but this was softened down to an expression of anxiety. Fraser spoke to me the other day about the state of our party in the country. At present he regards no seat as safe, anti-waste agitation being the trouble. He also told me that F.E. was quite avowedly intriguing against Austen and had some idea that L.G. might be given a rest for a bit while F.E. took command. Fraser was very anxious that L.G. should make another speech on the Maidstone lines to conciliate our party.[27] I spoke to Sutherland about this. I also told Lady Sykes who lunched with us the other day that her father ought to come back, as his return would do a lot to steady things.[28] It is true that the party is disgruntled; Imbert Terry predicts a repetition of 1906. I do not expect that, as Labour does not seem to gain much, so it is hard to see who is going to defeat us, but the feeling in favour of a pure Tory Government is certainly getting stronger. Addison has gone at last. He took advantage of his retiring explanation to make a bitter attack on the Government. Austen very dignified in his few words of reply. Bob Cecil said to me as we went out: 'They say a mad sheep is very dangerous.'

I have had some trouble at the War Office about reducing the number of Territorial battalions by 21, but I think all will go well as long as we are quite firm. Worthy is backing me well over it.

Thursday 28 July   Still trouble over the Territorial battalions and Worthy inclined to back down about a battalion in which Winston is interested. It is extraordinary how difficult the latter has made things with regard to the T.F. I have had charge of a little Bill to change the name of the T.F. to T.A., and Special Reserve to Militia. Have got it through Committee, the first time I have sat on one of the new Grand Committees.

The Government was beaten by two last night on an amendment to the budget. The Whips let people go for dinner and then Horne took a division while they were away. Austen said as the amount involved was small the Government would accept the decision of the House. Very little fuss or excitement over it. Last Thursday Addison and L.G. had it out. An undignified display on both sides. End of session to be between 19 and 26 August. This means the House of Lords will be much hustled. Doubtful how far they will stand it.

The Greeks seem to be upsetting all the predictions of our General Staff. If we can intervene and get a reasonable peace it ought to put things right in the Near East.

Sunday 21 August   We adjourned on Friday. The Lords kicked a bit, but no harm was done. At the War Office I have practically got my reduction of battalions as desired; even Winston has had to give in. The next difficulty has been the demand by the Treasury for further cuts. It is noticeable how the soldiers have been stonewalling on the subject. The only suggestion from the General Staff has been to abolish the T.F. However, Worthy has made out some considerable economies on the regulars and in the T.F. I have proposed cuts to the amount of one and a half millions without breaking into the 14th Division. There is an acute difference between Worthy and Winston over Mesopotamia, Worthy wishing to clear out, while Winston has a scheme of garrison by Air Force.

The most important thing in politics has been the attempt to deal with Sinn Fein. A few Conservatives in the House and many in the country are very angry at the Government having any intercourse with murderers, but on the whole the country approves. The terms offered certainly go to the very furthest limit consistent with safety. At the moment the question is whether they will be accepted. De Valera's speech reads as though there was no hope of agreement. But Fitzalan sends word that there will not be war again. T.P. and MacVeagh say the same. On the other hand Sinn Fein is recruiting and drilling in spite of the truce, and our press think there will be a split. Worthy tells me that if Sinn Fein keeps on procrastinating we shall put on a time limit. The Irish situation is the reason for adjournment instead of prorogation. I am off to Scotland today but may be wired for at any time. The position in our party is as bad as ever. It is significant that our candidate at Westminster calls himself anything and everything except Coalition.[29] George Younger told me that he had warned Austen that at an election our men must stand as Conservatives pure and simple, and that the P.M. must face that situation; that might mean the extinction of the Coalition Liberals. An election over Ireland is really being considered. I do not myself expect it. Fraser tells me that if a pure Conservative Government was formed F.E. would not serve under Austen, but would under Bonar. L.G. is trying to keep Bonar away in consequence.

George Younger to Sanders 23 September 1921
(from Central Office)

My dear Peter,

Many thanks for your letter of yesterday which I found here this morning. It is very good of you to ask me down to Bayford and I'd very gladly have gone and given you all my news if I hadn't been compelled to go home tomorrow. Two or three people have invited themselves to arrive on Monday at Leckie and as Jim and his wife are off to the North I must be there to receive them.

I am glad that you agree to give the *coup de grâce* to the *Popular View*.[30] McCurdy wrote me the other day asking whether I thought it was worth the money it cost as he certainly didn't. I let him know that if *he* didn't think it worth the cost I certainly couldn't be expected to hold a different view as it has throughout been run more as a Liberal than as a Tory organ. I said scrap it and I have instructed Fraser today accordingly, but we must issue something on our own as in certain cases *PV* is issued with a local cover (Worthy Evans does this) – so some substitute must be provided.

Louth has been thrown away by the d–d folly of Milton, the agent. *He* must be got rid of and it may prove an advantage to be beaten this time as a means of getting rid of him. By all means send letters to Hutchinson and Holt re. *PV*. If you will draft one Fraser, who has now returned to duty, will attend to it and send them for your signature.

Yours ever,
GY

Younger had recently been staying with Lord Fitzalan, the Viceroy of Ireland, and a man who as Lord Edmund Talbot had been a colleague in the Whips' room before the War. He reported to Sanders on what he had heard, in a postscript to the above letter.

. . . He is in great form, enjoys his work and if this d– Ireland is settled they'll all be tumbling over him. Everything is perfectly done, *with the minimum of ceremony* and all goes well. Her Grace is rather inclined to run out. She has so far succeeded in repressing herself. It was a relief to have me to loose off her feelings upon. She does not exactly love the Irish! GY.

George Younger to Sanders 1 October 1921
(from Leckie)

My dear Peter,

I have yours of the 29th. I am summoned to attend an important Railway meeting on Tuesday, so I am coming up to London for the day and return on Tuesday night. I expect to be at the Central Office from 1 o'clock or 1:30 onwards. I shall be very glad to see you any time. Let Mrs Tyndall know when you would like to be there.

This independent Conservative stunt[31] is going to add seriously to our difficulties and I should like to have some undertaking from L.G. at once. I am pressing Austen and think he is to attack the P.M. the moment he returns. My impression is that he will fail to get anything definite out of the little man, but it is right that he should have the first shot. If he fails and P.M. hangs on I fancy I shall find it equally difficult. We must then consider the propriety of forcing a decision one way or the other.

I am very glad you defeated the malcontents in Somerset. Why the devil can't they see that the thing will settle itself down if only they can exercise a little patience?

Yours ever,
G.Y.

Monday 3 October At the meeting of the Somerset Division of the National Union last week the Chairman of Bath and ex-chairman of Taunton moved that the Conservative party ought to throw over the Coalition. Their complaints were Ireland, opposition to France and giving in to Labour. I got the motion turned down, but it is significant. Saw Fraser today. He told me Tory revolt against L.G. was gaining head. Bonar has been urged by Younger to come back. L.G. wants to send him to America as our representative at the Conference. A curious item is that Derby has been urged by McKenna and Crewe to come out as Conservative leader.

The action against the *Daily Mirror* has begun at last. Hertford was chosen as the battleground and fines inflicted on some smaller counts against which Rothermere has appealed. The larger question of the clause in the last Franchise Act comes on this month. Our candidates won at Westminster and Lewisham, running as independent Conservatives.

Parliament is to meet on the 18th for a short time to deal with unemployment. After a lot of hedging the Irish conference is arranged for the 11th. Hannon who has been over in Dublin says that Sinn Fein will come to terms and then do all they can to get more.

Saturday 22 October I did a fortnight's campaign in my constituency at the beginning of the month. A 'Wee Free' Liberal has just come out against me. I was warned that the feeling against the Government is very strong, but had no trouble at my meetings and found in talking to farmers and others that though they grumbled they were quite good humoured. Altogether the tone was better than I expected.

At the meeting of the Nat.Union Executive on Thursday there was a good deal of hostility to the Coalition from Salisbury, Steel-Maitland and others. George Younger pointed out that if the Coalition broke up now we should not get Second Chamber reform. Duke of Northumberland has given notice of a motion adverse to the Coalition at the Liverpool Conference. That will probably be a somewhat lively affair.

Worthy Evans told me yesterday that our army is likely to have work soon both in Ireland and Egypt. In the latter place he says Raghoul is to be arrested; an outbreak will follow. Allenby says he can put it down with the troops he now has in Egypt. The Milner Report is to be discarded and the Egyptians told that we mean to remain in command. As to Ireland, Worthy expects an early break. After de Valera's wire to the Pope the Irish delegates have been told plainly that we shall stand no more nonsense. Michael Collins has gone to Dublin, and on Monday the conference meets again and may then break up. M. Collins and Duggan are apparently all for peace. Childers very hostile and bitter, Barton a nonentity, Gavin Duffy affable but does not commit himself. Collins seems to have attracted everybody. The secret intelligence says that there is division of opinion at Sinn Fein headquarters in Ireland.

Another trouble is that Ghandhi is probably to be arrested. I saw Lancelot Sanderson on Wednesday; he told me that the populace thought Ghandhi was divine, and his arrest must lead to trouble.[32]

Tuesday 1 November Saw Lady Fitzalan and Lady Midleton the other day. The latter told me that the Fitzalans had the curious story that Michael Collins was shot six months ago, and that the delegate over here is a substitute. A man generally abused just now is Cope, the Irish Under

Secretary.[33] He is said to have really gone over to Sinn Fein. The debate on Irish policy came off last night. L.G. did not seem to me very convincing, but the majority was enormous. The Government had a very strong case. No definite assurance was given in the debate that no tampering with Ulster would be allowed; but both Boscawen and Younger assure me the Government will be quite firm on the subject. L.G. threw out a faint hint that he might resign at any time. If he retired because he said he would not conduct a war with Ireland it would create a very awkward situation. The Duke of Northumberland's attempt to stampede the Northumberland Provincial Division fell flat. G. Younger went down to the meeting. The Duke made his speech which he had already sent to the Press, but moved no resolution.

Bonar is back and quite well again. He is restrained from coming to the House by his loyalty to Austen. The latter is rather losing ground. L.G. told Bonar he would be wanted very soon. He chaffed him on being the canny Scot who got out just when things were most difficult. Feeling against the Coalition seems as strong as ever in the country. Labour is in such a bad way that the fear of it is subsiding, and the chance of a pure Conservative Government is getting stronger.

Tuesday 8 November The *News of the World* on Sunday said that the Irish negotiations now turned on the question of Ulster and that the P.M. would resign if James Craig & Co. did not agree to terms. I pumped Worthy about this yesterday. He says Sinn Fein has agreed to all our conditions as to allegiance, etc., but want to have an All Ireland Parliament with subordinate Parliaments for North and South, the All Ireland Parliament to be elected in the ordinary way without any special advantages for the North. The Northern Parliament to keep all the powers it now has, but the All Ireland Parliament to take over finance, subject to safeguards. James Craig has been consulted and is ready to do what he can, but doubts whether his people will accept any such terms. If there is an absolute deadlock the Government will resign. Worthy suggested Clynes forming a Government and going to the country with a vote-catching programme. That is a real danger.

Sunday 27 November The Liverpool Conference on 17 November was a very great success. It was creditable to the Conservative party. The speeches were not bitter, and all were most anxious to avoid a split. The Die Hards had several motions on the paper but withdrew those that were combative in favour of a colourless one of Gretton's. F.E. had been down just before and put up Salvidge to move an amendment hoping for peace at the Irish Conference. This was carried by a very large majority after Worthington-Evans had given very clear pledges as to the limit of concession to Sinn Fein. These pledges were satisfactory and everyone went away in a good temper, even the South of Ireland deputation. Austen and Worthy both told me they expected peace within a month. George Younger also sanguine. But the Cabinet has changed their policy since Worthy spoke to me last about it. They do not mean to resign in the event of Ulster refusing terms. Ulster has now refused the All Ireland proposal absolutely. Worthy told me last Wednesday that there was a new proposal that Ulster would accept and that would work all right but the doubt was if Sinn Fein would agree to it. I urged on him how important it was that in the event of a break it should come from a refusal of terms by Sinn Fein not by Ulster. He told me he was doing all he could with that in view. He says that the Ulster men attach a lot of importance to keeping members in the English Parliament.

I had to go down at very short notice on Wednesday last to take a meeting at Hull that Worthy was to have addressed. A very good meeting. 3,000 there. Went off quite well. I was amused at the elaborate police preparations. Three detectives slept in the garage at the house where I stayed!

Sunday 4 December   I came up to town on Friday last after a day or two in the country. Went to see Worthy who is ill in bed and rather bad. He wants me to stay in town in case he should be totally unfit for duty. He gave me details of the last offer to Sinn Fein and asked me to look over the plans to be put in force in case of a rupture; the latter are strenuous and pretty complete. He told me Henry Wilson saw red over the whole business. I saw H.W. yesterday and there is certainly no doubt about that. He is very much down on the P.M., says he does whatever Michael Collins tells him and so on.

Thursday 8 December   Ireland squared and nearly everyone happy. The members of the Cabinet bubbling over with joy and excitement. Bar a certain amount of verbal eyewash such as 'Free State', the terms are practically the same as those offered in September. All the fuss about partition, and the oath of allegiance has been bluff on the part of Sinn Fein. T.P. was right when he said in August that having once come out of the trenches they would never go back again. I don't think there will be any serious opposition to the scheme; Ulster leaders were consulted privately and agreed to the boundary commission. Parliament is to meet on Wednesday next for a short session.

Sunday 18 December   Opposition to the agreement stronger than I expected. In the debate the two conspicuous features were Carson's speech in the Lords and Bonar Law's in House of Commons. Carson extraordinarily bitter but a great effort in oratory. Bonar got a tremendous reception on his reappearance. His speech was very helpful. I had a long talk with him on Friday. He is all for the settlement now; but he thought at one time the Government would let Ulster down badly and in that case was quite prepared to come out against them and thought that 90 per cent of the Unionist party would have backed him. He said he could not understand how L.G. could have imagined that the Ulster leaders would come in or that a press campaign would be likely to induce them to do so. He told me that it was not true that the Ulster leaders had been consulted privately about the boundary commission. This is absolutely contrary to what W. Evans told me. He said he himself had discussed the matter with James Craig and that he approved it. Lady Fitzalan says that James comes and talks to Edmund and says all is well and Ulster will probably join in a combined assembly before long and then next day all the Ulster people make these furious speeches. My own impression is that Ulster is exasperated by the foolish press campaign and is making the most of technical points in consequence. Dail Eireann has not yet ratified.

Goulding made me a small bet last Wednesday that there would be an election before Easter. His inspiration is from F.E. who apparently despairs of an acceptable scheme for Second Chamber reform. I spoke to George Younger about this. He is going to press Austen all he can to insist on a Second Chamber Bill.

A week ago Lord Bath came to see me at Bayford to tell me that there was great indignation in Bath at Foxcroft's Die Hard attitude, and that the resolution moved by Bagshawe at our County Executive meeting and supported by Foxcroft was quite against the views of the Bath Conservative Association. He warned me that Foxcroft might lose the seat in consequence of his attitude. The cross currents now are curious. My own impression is that the hostility to the Coalition is chiefly from the upper class, and that lower down Coalition is preferred to Toryism. But this varies in different parts of the country.

CHAPTER 10 NOTES

1   Hewart's 'right' to become Lord Chief Justice was the traditional right of succession of the Attorney General. It was not in fact exercised until 1922, Lord Trevethin occupying the position for just one year.

2   Sir Arthur Griffith-Boscawen was seeking re-election at Dudley after his appointment as Minister of Agriculture and the *Daily Express* was exploiting the situation in order to run a campaign on one of Beaverbrook's favourite themes, the 1917 embargo on the importa-

tion of Canadian cattle. A.J.P. Taylor, *Beaverbrook*, p. 181.

3   Sir Alfred Mond was First Commissioner for Works and, like many Ministers, the subject of demands for greater economies. In the Geddes economies of the following year, his Department's spending was hardly cut at all.

4   Major-General Henry Tudor was Police Adviser to the Royal Irish Constabulary and Brig.Gen.F.P. Crozier was commander of the Auxiliary Forces. Crozier resigned after press criticism of outrages by the Black and Tans.

5   Ramsay MacDonald had been defeated by a Conservative at Woolwich East on 2 March; Griffith-Boscawen was defeated at Dudley on the following day.

6   Although there had been a Women's Unionist and Tariff Reform Organisation before 1914, it was only when women got the vote in 1918 that they were introduced into the official Party Organisation. The women's side of the Organisation rapidly became the pacemaker in enthusiasm, finance and membership. By 1921 there were 1,340 branches. C.P. Cook, *The Age of Alignment*, p. 39.

7   These were Sir Gordon Hewart and T.B. Morison respectively, both Coalition Liberals.

8   Lord Edmund Talbot was created Viscount Fitzalan and appointed Viceroy of Ireland, neither the first nor the last time that a Chief Whip was appointed in a desperate attempt to solve the troubles in Ireland. As a Roman Catholic and a civilian, he could at least hope to start with a better chance of achieving something than had Lord French, his predecessor.

9   Chief of the Imperial General Staff and Adjutant-General.

10 Lt.Gen.Noel Birch was Director General of Territorial Forces, 1921–3. As the author of several books on riding and as a keen and experienced huntsman, Birch was a highly appropriate choice for the territorials. See diary entry for 5 June.

11 Gen.G.D. Jeffries, G.O.C London Area 1920–24, had been a Divisional Commander in the Army of the Rhine. Gen. the Earl of Cavan, C.in C. Aldershot 1920–22 and A.D.C. to the King was a more political soldier than Jeffries and a future C.I.G.S.

12 Evan Williams was a prominent coal-owner and President of the Mining Association. Frank Hodges was General Secretary of the M.F.G.B.

13 Sir David Shackleton had been a Labour M.P. but was then Permanent Secretary to the Ministry of Labour, subsequently Chief Labour Adviser to the Government. His prediction of the break-up of the M.F.G.B. was not borne out until the aftermath of the strike of 1926.

14 Sir John Beynon was a Deputy Lieutenant in Monmouthshire and a prominent local industrialist.

15 Colonel John Gretton was Conservative M.P. for Burton from 1918 and Chairman of Bass, Ratcliff and Gretton, brewers. A diehard Conservative and a regular spokesman for 'the trade'.

16 Fitzalan had served in the 11th Hussars, known for their cherry-coloured breeches, and Sir Henry Wilson's career began in the Rifle Brigade, noted for its green uniform.

17 Bridgeman was Parliamentary Secretary at the Mines Department under Horne, and later under Baldwin, as President of the Board of Trade.

18 'On 22 April, Lord Derby crossed to Ireland, incognito as a travelling salesman, and had a long but fruitless conversation with De Valera.' Tom Jones, *Whitehall Diary*, vol. III, p. 55.

19 J.W. Lowther, Speaker since 1905, had announced his retirement on 25 April. McNeill, Joynson-Hicks, Bull and Dennis Herbert objected to the way in which the Government took the views of the House for granted in nominating Whitley's successor as Chairman of Ways and Means before Whitley had been elected Speaker.

20 This involved the abandonment of the British Protectorate over Egypt, replacing it with 'free bilateral agreements'. A.M. Gollin, *Proconsul in Politics*, p. 592.

21 Maclean moved to reject the proposal to exempt M.P.s' salaries from income tax, a plan that was strongly supported by Labour M.P.s. His speech was continually interrupted with personal abuse and heckling (such as 'Dirty Dog, Dirty Humbug', 'Be truthful if you cannot be clean Donald.') *The Times*, 2 June 1921.

22 Westminster St. George's was won by the Anti-Waste League when Walter Long was elevated to the House of Lords and the traditionally-Conservative seat at Hertford was not regained when the wartime adventurer Pemberton Billing stood down.

23 Evelyn Mary, fourth Princess Bluecher von Wahlstadt had recently published her memoirs with the title *An English Wife in Berlin*.

24 General 'Tim' Harington was C.in C. Black Sea and Turkey area, 1919–1923.

25 On the King's initiative, the Cabinet had reopened negotiations with De Valera, using Smuts as an intermediary.

26 This was the Bill that rationalised the railways into five groups and tidied up their finances after seven years of government control. It had a rough passage into law, because Labour M.P.s wanted less decontrol and Conservatives wanted rather more.

27 Lloyd George had addressed a meeting of Kent Conservatives at Maidstone in May and urged the case for continued cooperation, with

sacrifices from both sides to make fusion possible. M. Kinnear, *The Fall of Lloyd George*, p. 95.

28   Isabel Sykes, wife of Sir Frederick Sykes M.P., was the daughter of Bonar Law.

29   The Westminster, Abbey by election was narrowly held by the Conservative candidate on 25 August.

30   *Popular View* was a party magazine jointly produced by Conservatives and Coalition Liberals since 1919 but never very effective. It was, however, the only organisational step taken towards fusion and so its abandonment at this stage was rather symbolic.

31   This was Lord Salisbury's decision to found a Conservative Party independent of the Coalition, far more significant in propaganda terms than in terms of its political power or influence. See M. Cowling, *The Impact of Labour*, p. 74.

32   Sir Lancelot Sanderson, Conservative M.P. 1910–15 and Chief Justice of Bengal 1915–1926.

33   Alfred Cope was actually Assistant Under-Secretary for Ireland. The confidence of Lloyd George in Cope was shown by his appointment as head of the National Liberal Organisation 1922–4.

Chapter 11   1922 'There may yet be time to avert the catastrophe'

Friday 6 January   I have had to spend a lot of time at the War Office over the Geddes Report, Worthington-Evans having gone to France for the conference. Geddes cuts are drastic, but the General Staff is more amenable than I expected.

A great fight is now going on as to an election. Austen wrote to me just before Xmas to ask me my opinion and what I thought as to effect in the West Country. I have replied that I am all against an early election though I don't think we should lose many West Country seats. Tory discontent with the Coalition is on the increase in the West. I dined with G. Younger on the 4th. He is all out to stop an election and has written the P.M. that if it takes place the Conservatives would run independently of the Coalition. Downing Street has been working the press as usual; now Malcolm Fraser is working it in the opposite direction. Conservatives that I meet are very strong against it. George Stanley thinks Labour would sweep Lancashire. Gould says it would upset S. Wales just as industry is improving. The Coalition Liberal whips are for it from some idea that they can capture the old Liberal organisation, quite a delusion. F.E., Winston and W. Evans are for it. I am inclined to think they will be beaten.

Austen Chamberlain to Sanders 22 December 1921
Strictly Confidential[1]

My dear Sanders,

I see some revised talk of a General Election early in the New Year. I have my own views as to the wisdom of this course, but I want to check them by those of one or two of my colleagues. I naturally turn first to Younger. I have asked my brother for an opinion on the Midlands, and I should be very glad if you would give me your views of how such a move would be taken in the West Country.

Would it be regarded as an unfair attempt to snatch a victory?

Would it be resented as an undue disturbance of the country in a moment of great trade depression?

How would it affect the Coalition, and, within the Coalition, our own Party?

Would the Party be better or worse if the election were deferred for another eighteen months or two years?

Would the Coalition be stronger or weaker by that time, (a) if it remains a Coalition, and, (b) if the interval has been used to make it into a national party?

Do not sacrifice your Christmas Day to answering these enquiries, but if you can find time to give me your views in the course of the next ten days I should be very grateful.

Yours sincerely,
Austen Chamberlain.

Sanders to Austen Chamberlain 2 January 1922

Strictly Confidential

Dear Chamberlain,

In answer to your letter of 22 December, my own view is against an early election. A great many Conservatives would consider it a breach of faith to have one before the Second Chamber question is tackled. I feel sure Labour would gain a good many seats on account of unemployment and I think a large proportion of the Coalition Liberals would lose their seats owing to the absence of local organisation.

I don't think it would be regarded as unfair, but there might be complaints as to disturbing trade.

So much for the country in general. As to the West Country, i.e. Bristol, Somerset, Dorset, Devon and Cornwall, the Coalition now hold 30 seats out of 32. Ainge, the district agent, would like an election in the spring and thinks we should lose two seats only. I consider he is too sanguine. Our danger is Tory abstention – the old Conservatives are more dissatisfied than ever and some may even support a moderate Liberal. Farmers are independent and difficult and publicans very dissatisfied with the Licensing Act. As to the future, I cannot prophesy. In most seats held by Conservatives we should get more votes as an Independent Conservative Party than as Coalitionists, the Liberal element that would vote for us not balancing Conservative defections. How far this defection can be checked depends on policy. If trade improves, taxation is lowered and the Irish policy is successful, or if Labour appears more formidable in these parts than it does at present, I think that many would come back to us. The Licensing Act will do less harm as people get accustomed to it.

As to a fused party, I think it might help in the Coalition Liberal seats. In Conservative seats I doubt its doing so, and it may lead to the running of more Independent Conservatives. In any case, the arrangements for it would take some time to work out. It would have helped us greatly if it had come two years ago.

To sum up – I do not like the idea of an election before Second Chamber reform. I think we should lose some seats in the West, but not very many. Our danger is Tory discontent with the Coalition. A fused party, though personally I should like to see it, will not gain us Tory votes.

Yours sincerely,
R.A. Sanders.

Circular letter from George Younger to Conservative Constituency Chairman[2] *9 January 1922*

UNIONIST CENTRAL OFFICE

PRIVATE

Dear Sir,

I think it very desirable to address you on the subject of the present rumours with regard to the possibility of an early General Election.

I have no information that the Prime Minister contemplates an early appeal to the country, but the decision on such a question constitutionally rests with him, and not with either his Ministers or his supporters. So far as this Office is concerned, we should most strongly deprecate any appeal to the country at the present moment. There is no crisis; the Government has up to now been most loyally supported by the Houses of Parliament; it received a vote of confidence at our Conference in Liverpool, and there seems to be no justification whatever for precipitating an Election at a time when industry is so depressed, unemployment is so serious, and the greatest need of the country is a restoration of industrial confidence. Any signs of improvement in the conditions of Trade would be seriously prejudiced by the dislocation which an Election inevitably occasions, and for that reason alone it ought to be discouraged.

So far as our party is concerned, forming, as it does, much the larger wing of the Coalition, there would be an emphatic protest against an appeal to the people before the electoral programme on which the Coalition was elected is completed. Every effort must first be made to cut down expenditure and to make every economy compatible with efficiency. Only by so doing shall we be able to lower taxation and free money for the expansion of trade which will in turn reduce the present grave state of unemployment.

One of the chief planks of the Government's policy was their promise to reconstitute the Second Chamber, and restore the balance of the constitution. Only a Coalition like the present could successfully deal with that vital question, and the Government has given the most specific pledges to deal with it in the coming session of Parliament. They command a majority which can secure a reasonable settlement of what is admittedly a difficult question, and there would be bitter resentment if they lay down office before a serious attempt had been made to fulfil those pledges. When returned they asked for the confidence of the electors in order to have a government in power which would steer a clear course through the difficult period after the war; which would consider, from an unprejudiced point of view, every question that arose for a settlement, in the national interests alone, and not in those of any Party. They have, I think, done excellent work in that respect, although doubtless many mistakes have been made, but the time has not yet come when it could be said that they have fulfilled their task. Much still remains to be done before the country can be said to have been steered into smooth water, and in our view that task ought to be completed before any further appeal for a fresh mandate is made.

Our supporters of the Coalition have honestly endeavoured to keep before them at all times the national interests, and the national interests alone. This is no time to consider either Party or personal interests, and it cannot, I think, be said that an electoral upheaval at the present moment could be otherwise than inimical to the most important interests of the country. Already Unionist Members of Parliament are declaring that, in the event of their being forced into an Election, they will stand, not as Coalitionists, but as Independent Unionists. That will, of course, mean the end of the Coalition, and the great opportunity of the combinatiion still doing real service to the country will have been lost, and will never be likely to recur.

I believe you will agree that the foregoing views correctly interpret the feelings of our friends as a whole.

I am,
Yours very truly,
George Younger.

Sunday 8 February Election off for the present at all events. House met yesterday. On Monday afternoon there was a meeting of Unionist Ministers called by Austen to discuss the situation. Austen, Horne, Curzon and F.E. spoke very strongly on the necessity for the Coalition on grounds of Imperial policy. G. Younger, Leslie Wilson, Bridgeman and Amery spoke strongly of the restiveness of the Conservative party both in the House and the country. Barlow, on the other hand, declared that in Lancashire the Coalition is a source of strength. I saw Derby yesterday and he confirms this. The fact seems to be that the unpopularity of the

Coalition is mainly with the middle class, but it is very great among that class. Our leaders do not realise and cannot apparently be made to realise how very fast the main body of the Tory party is slipping away from them.

Tuesday 14 February   Amery and Mitchell Thomson and I had a long talk on the Irish boundary question.[3] We agreed that all the junior Ministers ought to act together. Leslie Wilson impressed on Austen the very strong feeling existing on the subject. Austen's speeches have made things a little easier, but the language of the agreement is ambiguous. The Ulstermen say they would fight rather than allow large districts to be cut off. The only way out seems to be to appoint as Chairman someone who is sure to decide as we want; but that seems a poor game. Austen saw a deputation of Die Hards yesterday. He satisfied Joynson Hicks but not Gretton or Banbury. George Younger tells me that Bonar says he never knew L.G. so down. He looks regularly tired out. G.Y. expects him to resign before long and wants Austen to form a Government and carry on. At the election we are to stand as Conservatives pure and simple. F.E. is suffering badly from the old trouble – a surfeit of alcohol.

Saturday 18 February   Irish Bill passed second reading. Opposition mustered 60 only, a good deal less than expected. Gordon Hewart was to have made an announcement giving his interpretation of the boundary clause, but Churchill stopped him at the last moment because he thought it would add to the difficulties of Michael Collins. However, Austen in his speech at the end gave a pretty satisfactory assurance on the subject. Allenby has been over about Egypt. He wants to give the Egyptians a free government without guarantees and bargain with them afterwards. This apparently the Cabinet have accepted.

At the Speaker's dinner last night Freddie Guest got hold of me and we had a long talk on the Coalition position. What he put up to me was what did the Tories want to get as consideration for sticking to the Coalition. Would any legislation or assurances given by the Government rally them to L.G.? Or would it be better to part, if so let us part as friends. I would not commit myself, but promised to try and get Younger and him to meet. Saw Fraser this morning and discussed the whole matter with him. He quite thinks the Conservatives could get a majority on their own. I suggested that L.G. might stand down voluntarily after an election and give general support to a Conservative Government. Fraser thought it worth while to try and work this. He is to have confab with Younger and Austen tomorrow.

Friday 3 March   Guest and Younger lunched with me last Monday. F.E.'s 'Cabin Boy' speech had occurred the Thursday before.[4] F.G. put the point very clearly that if the P.M. was thrown over by the Tories he would certainly drift to the left and that we should find ourselves with all other parties united against us. G.Y. was undecided. He said that he did not now think the Tories could get a clear majority. The recent bye elections were not cheering.[5] I put in a plea for the plan of L.G. inviting us to form a Government if we got a majority after an election.

Tuesday was the royal wedding. L. and I were in the Abbey. All very well done. Next day news came out that L.G. had written to Austen on the subject of discontent etc., in the Conservative party. W. Evans spoke to me about our prospects if we formed a Government. Yesterday Guest came to me again and asked me to put up the conditions on which Conservatives would continue to support L.G. He confessed that L.G. would not have me as Chief Whip because he thought I was too Tory; but Guest now suggested I should be Chief Whip and take Younger's place as well. I told him any ousting of Younger would be resented intensely. Later in the day Leslie Wilson came to pump me as to whether it was constitutionally possible for the same man to be Chief whip and Chairman of the party. The press makes a great point of L.G.'s anger with Younger. The latter says it is very funny to see it suggested that he wants to stay on, when he has tried to clear out for at least two years.

Tuesday 7 March   Had another talk with Guest on Sunday evening. The gist of it was a proposal on his part that in return for certain concessions as to places in the Government, declarations of policy and so on, we should put our Central Office under the Chief Whip, and undertake to turn down candidates who would not stand as Coalitionists. I told him such a proposal was quite useless as the Conservative party would not have it. After a good deal of chat he said he should advise L.G. to resign as we wanted to get everything and give nothing. Yesterday I saw him again and he said L.G. had caved in and was much disgusted about it.

Friday 10 March   Edward Wood told me on Tuesday that Winston had asked him if he would take a peerage and become Under Secretary to the India Office, Winterton succeeding him at Colonial Office.[6] He was very loath to go to the Lords, and asked me what I should do. I told him I should certainly not advise him to go there before his time, and suggested that he should propose to Austen that there should be a Secretary of State for India in the Lords, vice Montagu. Yesterday came the announcement of Montagu's resignation. There was tremendous cheering in the House, very marked indeed. I have been trying to urge that Devonshire should succeed. I gather that the Coalition Liberals acknowledge that Conservatives are entitled to a larger representation in the Government. A Conservative at the India Office would do a lot to pacify our Die Hards.

After F.E.'s speech at the City Carlton,[7] Cuthbert James said to me: 'We Die Hards have had to put up with a good deal, but the hardest blow of all is to be patted on the back by F.E.' They were chaffing one another and in the best of form; rather quaint after their passage of arms in the House on Wednesday. Winston said to me that he thought F.E. had taken such a patriotic line during the Irish negotiations. If he had broken away while Austen was committed it would have been such a chance for him to become leader of the Tory party. I told him I did not think the Tory party would ever have F.E. for leader; they would want someone more stable if less brilliant.

Sunday 19 March   The Wolverhampton election was a great surprise to the Labour men. They made sure of winning and men who went down to speak for us were not happy about it. But our canvass figures were very good; it was curious that there should have been such a general impression that we should lose. Henry Wilson's speech on Army Estimates was a very artistic performance. His voice is impressive; he was slow and quiet and sat down just at the right moment.[8]

The meeting of Unionists called by Goulding and Hannon to pass a vote of confidence in L.G. was a fiasco. Goulding did not turn up and Sam Roberts[9] took the chair. A lot of Die Hards came in. Things looked ripe for a row. But Pretyman and George Lane Fox intervened and impressed on the meeting that the great thing was unity in our party. Eventually the meeting adjourned *sine die*. Leslie Wilson tried to issue an official account, but the papers had quite accurate information of what passed. It will make L.G.'s resignation more likely.

George Stanley says it would never have done for Derby to accept the India Office. India is bound to increase her import duties. Any such increase makes Lancashire furious, and if Derby were responsible it would injure his influence in Lancashire. Boscawen told me Ghandhi's arrest was sanctioned by the Cabinet in October. It was hung up by the Indian Government.

Thursday 30 March   Peel's appointment as Indian Secretary well received and Winterton as Under Secretary very popular. Peel told me Montagu has left him in a most difficult position as regards finance. L.G. has returned sooner than expected. He is very well and was getting bored in Wales. There is to be a motion next Monday approving the Genoa Conference. Leslie Wilson told me the motion was to be one of confidence in L.G. so framed as to make a dividing line. I told him I thought that a mistake. The terms now proposed seem harmless; and the proposals to the Bolsheviks are so stiff that I should not think that they would be accepted. L.G. seems quite ready to go on with present conditions for the present at least.

I had an interview with the Licensed Victuallers of my division last Friday. They are furious over the Licensing Bill. As they never had the wartime restrictions they look on the curtailment of hours as most unjust. I am afraid they will take of lot of smoothing down.[10]

Wednesday 12 April The Genoa motion quite successful. L.G. very dull, I think on purpose. Bonar and Austen both good. Just over thirty Tories against the Government. Austen in excellent form two nights later when Joynson Hicks moved a private member's motion against the Government.

W. Evans has gone to Genoa. He explained before leaving that it is expected that de Valera will declare a Republic at Easter. In that case we hold Dublin and Queenstown and blockade the rest of Southern Ireland. We keep a cordon on boundary of Ulster.

There is trouble over Canadian cattle. Winston has induced the Government to give a day to discuss it. They will not agree that if a motion is carried time is not to be given for a private member's bill. Boscawen threatens resignation in that case and many under secretaries would follow him. A small Cabinet has turned down the inclusion of fabric gloves under Part II of the Safeguarding of Industries Bill – Baldwin is to bring the matter up again when more are present.

Tuesday 16 May Genoa has not been much good to anyone, but in spite of much newspaper writing the country seems to care very little about it. With L.G. there and Winston laid up politics have been very quiet lately. Austen has been doing well in the House. The budget is well received. Boscawen got the concession to farmers after a struggle.

Saturday 27 May I was away at the Somerset County Show when the Government defeat occurred. The adjournment was moved just before the dinner hour. The whips put up Macquisten to keep the debate going, but he was not practised enough to keep in order and the division came when a lot of our men were absent. Last Monday when Austen moved a supplementary estimate there was a lot of ill feeling about it on the ground that it was moved merely to scare off men who had voted against the Government. That was true.[11] There was a lot of fuss also about the P.M.'s resolve not to speak first in the Genoa debate. Jack Gilmour told Austen he should resign if the whips' advice on a matter of tactics was so entirely ignored. L.G. gave in. But the Genoa debate was a poor affair, the only amusing part being L.G.'s second speech attacking R. Cecil. The luncheon yesterday went off well, but there was no crowd there. All Irish news is very bad. The only hopeful thing I hear is from Jerry MacVeagh who says that the agreement means that de Valera knows he is beaten and is making the best terms he can.

Sunday 25 June About 3 o'clock on Thursday last news reached the House of Henry Wilson's murder. I think young Sam Roberts was the first to bring it to the Treasury Bench. John Baird was told off at once to get particulars from the Home Office. I never knew the House so agitated.[12] Questions went on, but members kept making mistakes in asking and ministers in answering them. It was a relief to all when Austen moved the adjournment. There is a disposition to blame the Home Office and Shortt's unpopularity may make difficulties, but if the murderer is ready to lose his life no police protection can give absolute safety. Henry Wilson was a most attractive personality. He was not a success as a General in the field, but was a great military statesman. About Ireland he was a fanatic and very nearly had trouble at War Office in consequence. Locker of Punch said to me in the lobby 'Curious that the P.M.'s two ablest opponents should be gone in a week.' Northcliffe of course was the other. He is reported to have gone off his head altogether.

There was a great newspaper shout about the reprieve of Ronald Tree. He is said to be the son of Lady de Freyne. This got about only the name was changed to Lady de Frere (Vesta Tilley). De Frere wrote to the papers at last to deny all connection. Shortt's answer when tackled in the House was quite conclusive.[13]

Sunday 2 July Irish debate on Monday last after Henry Wilson's funeral. Bitter things were said by Ronald McNeil and others, but Winston really took the wind out of their sails to start with by saying that the Government would now insist on Collins & Co. standing no more nonsense. Bonar spoke forcibly on those lines. I had a talk with him afterwards; he said he had been very disturbed at the way things had been going, but agreed with me that it had been hard to point out the precise moment at which interference would have done good. On Wednesday we got the news of the attack on the Four Courts. The first intelligence at the War Office was that the Free Staters had commenced operations at an early hour and had now adjourned for breakfast. At the moment it looks as if Collins means to see it through; if that is so all may yet be well.[14]

We have had some very late nights over the Finance Bill. Beer duty now safely through Committee. Horne would make no concession about it, as the Treasury does not believe in the increase of consumption being sufficient to help out a drop in the rate of duty. I am afraid we shall lose voters in the country over this question.

There is trouble again over the Honours question. Robinson's peerage 'put the fat in the fire'. Crawford said that unless an inquiry took place Salisbury & Co. meant to refuse to let any legislation through. Now Robinson has declined and L.G. has promised a day for discussion in the House. I hear that Dudley Ward was responsible for Robinson. Vestey was George Younger's man. It is high time the whole business was stopped. I managed personally to keep clear of it at the Central Office.[15]

I travelled up from Leicester on Thursday with Blane a local M.P. who got in in 1918 and does little in the House.[16] I pumped him as to his views. He thinks L.G. the best leader; Austen not known enough among the rank and file; Worthington Evans popular among them. Says Lord Derby would be the best Conservative leader as the country looks on him as straight and honest. I asked him if Edmund Talbot was very popuar. He said not with the rank and file, as he took no notice of them. He considered George Gibbs the most popular whip.

Wednesday 5 July   Winston had a great success last night in the debate on Palestine. He kept the House in roars of laughter and withal made a very good case for the Rutenberg concession.[17] The fact is that it is a very risky speculation that the ordinary businessman would not touch. I am afraid the Government are doing all they can to shirk the House of Lords question; only the other day the National Unionist Council passed another unanimous resolution on the subject, so the friction with that body is likely to be greater than ever.[18]

I sat next the P.M. at dinner at the House on Monday. He was very interesting. Said he looked on Joe Chamberlain as the greatest parliamentary speaker of recent times. Remarked what a pity it was that such a great mind as Dizzy's was wasted for constructive purposes for 40 years while he was in opposition. Said Harcourt was absolutely hated by his colleagues but popular with the rank and file of his party to whom he was very forthcoming; he was the best of company.

Saturday 15 July   The resolutions on the Second Chamber question that are to be submitted to the House of Lords have been published, and are ridiculously inadequate. I have seen the Cabinet papers on the subject. Curzon submitted a well thought out scheme by which the ultimate solution in cases of deadlock was to be a joint sitting. This was attacked by Winston, Fisher and Mond who want really to leave the Parliament Act alone; their views have prevailed. Ancaster tells me the Lords will never swallow the present proposals, which would greatly diminish the hereditary element and give little increased power in return.

There was a debate last Wednesday in the Lords on the Canadian cattle question. Walter Long spoke strongly in favour of removing the embargo on the ground that an absolute pledge was given, but advocated a month's quarantine. Feeling was all against the embargo and the debate was adjourned on the motion of Lord Harris. Next day George Lane Fox, Fitzroy and I had a talk with Boscawen. He was all for a compromise, and said if he fought the thing out and was beaten he must resign. I was all for fighting the main question before trying to deal. On Friday letters appeared in *The Times* in one of which Lord Lincolnshire said:

'Boscawen must go.' Result that night Boscawen said he was all for fighting it out.

The honours debate comes off on Monday. The Government are going to agree to an inquiry. Probably that will stave off the trouble for the time; but the inquiry may be pretty awkward.

Wednesday 19 July The honours debate was rather futile. The P.M.'s speech very dull. Ronald McNiell livened things up by making charges against Waring and Williamson that have since been indignantly denied.[19] At the end Linky Cecil talked it out on purpose. He told me it would have been the sort of rotten division that would have been no good to anyone.

We had a meeting at Ministry of Agriculture yesterday about Canadian cattle. Decided to fight in the Commons and possibly compromise in the Lords. The more I see of it the more impracticable it seems to me to find a satisfactory compromise proposal. Had a talk with Leslie Wilson this morning. He and Younger are going to tackle Austen this afternoon on the question of Coalition. The point to be pressed is that if after the next election the Conservatives come back a strong party they should have the leader in case there is a Coalition government. Derby has written opportunely on the subject, and the question must be settled very soon.

Friday 21 July As a result of the interview between Austen, Leslie and Younger, Austen summoned a meeting yesterday of Conservative Ministers outside the Cabinet. I was called to speak first and pointed out that if we let things drift we should lose many seats, that the Coalition Liberals would lose still more and that many of the Conservatives who returned would not support a Liberal P.M. I said that we wanted a Conservative Prime Minister and Conservative preponderance in the Cabinet. I was surprised to find how generally my views were supported not only by my immediate friends but by Pollock and Leslie Scott and by Scotch members. I was also surprised and pleased at the way Austen received my suggestions. I had of course assumed that he was to be leader. He said he would lay the matter before his colleagues in the Cabinet and seemed to think it quite likely that the P.M. would step aside quietly, and advise his colleagues to go on. Altogether it was a satisfactory pow-wow. The men who were there seemed pleased with the way I had put the case.

In the House today Ronald McNiell apologised for what he had said about Williamson, but refused to withdraw anything as to Waring. Stanley Baldwin told me that Balfour produced a lot of Foreign Office papers that were not at all favourable to Williamson and the City had a very bad opinion of both Waring and Vestey.

Saturday 29 July   Austen has spoken to the P.M. who has no objection to retiring. He wants to write a book for which he has been promised fabulous sums. But the Conservative members of the Cabinet, especially Balfour, do not look kindly on the idea at all. They have resolved to hang the matter up till the autumn. Leslie now proposes a meeting of all the Conservative Ministers, but has not yet broached the subject with Austen who evidently regards the matter as settled for the present.

Last Tuesday Sir A. Hunter gave a dinner at the House of Commons to General Higginson who is 96 years of age. There was a 'most distinguished gathering' from Duke of Connaught downwards. The old man spoke for 20 minutes without a note, without hesitation and in beautiful English. A most impressive speech.[20]

Friday 4 August   We had an Under Secretaries meeting on Wednesday at which I was put forward to be first spokesman at a meeting of all the Unionist members of the Government held yesterday at the House of Lords in the Moses Room.[21] At the latter meeting after we had stated our case we were treated to a violent harangue from F.E., followed by shorter and more moderate speeches from Balfour and Austen, the gist of which was that things were to go on just as now. Everyone was very annoyed at F.E.'s speech and the comic thing is that Austen has abused him for it and let us know through Leslie Wilson that he has done so. We have talked it over and agreed rather against my advice to sit tight until the autumn though many of us, including Leslie Wilson, are to tell our constituents that we shall not feel bound to support a Liberal P.M. after another election. F.E. told George Younger that the P.M. had no intention of clearing out, but you don't know what to believe.

I saw Fitzalan on Wednesday. He told me he was not going back to Ireland till October as no one consulted him there at present and he was better out of the way. He takes a more hopeful view of the position there; thinks well of Griffith and hopes for the best from Collins.

Sir Malcolm Fraser to Sanders 7 August 1922

Private

Dear Sanders,
    Many thanks for your note and for the important information it contains. Younger sent me full details of the meeting and I gather you made a very admirable opening statement which had the support of the Junior Ministers. I really believe Austen fully realises the gravity of the position and is desperately afraid of the party falling to pieces under his

leadership. But equally I think he does not quite feel capable of himself handling the future – particularly if *all* his colleagues do not stand by him. Were he assured of their solid support, he would I should say, come out like a flash. F.E. wants frightening and if the Junior Ministers can do this the rest of the sheep will follow through the gap made by F.E. in his stampede for the nearest horizon. Perhaps on the whole it is better to wait awhile – and then all move together. But from the party point of view it would have been better for the whole to have moved *con amore* rather than to wait until circumstances force them to do so with indecent haaste!

My compliments to your Lady,

Yours

Malcolm Fraser

Sunday 1 October   Since writing above Griffith and Collins both gone; but Cosgrave who is now at the head of the Free State Government seems inclined to run straight.

I came up yesterday on account of the Turkish business. Late on Friday night 29 September, orders were sent to Harington to give the Turks a short time limit to clear out of the neutral zone and in default of compromise to bombard them from land, sea and air. The Cabinet are anxiously awaiting the reply. But up to a late hour last night no reply of any sort had come. Meanwhile plans are all going on for mobilisattion of two divisions; and the question of calling out the Territorials is already under discussion. W. Evans told me it was ten to one on war. He said he did not see how we could have avoided the present position. It is the fact that we have been trying to deal with Kemal for over a year, but could get no reply from him. Yet the French have dealt with him all right. I think feeling in the country in spite of the *Daily Mail* and the Labour party is with the Government; but of course war will not be popular.

Malcolm Fraser lunched with me on Tuesday 19 September. He told me that the previous Sunday at Chequers the party of Ministers there assembled had decided to go to the country as a Coalition exactly on present lines. L.G. had seen Bonar and asked him whether he ought to resign. Bonar said he thought he ought. Fraser much perturbed at Government decision. He does not think the Coalition will get a majority at all. He had had an hour's discussion with Chamberlain. C. had said that the difficulty was that if L.G. went it was doubtful if any Coalition Liberals would remain. He also said that the members of the Cabinet supporting L.G. had some flair for electioneering and he thought an election would turn out much better than our agents supposed. Since then appended letters have passed.

Sir Malcolm Fraser to Sanders 22 September 1922
(Central Office)

My dear Sanders,

On hearing result of the Chequers meeting Bonar had thought a split in the party inevitable. If Turkish crisis blows over he thinks P.M. will have a General Election right away. If it does not and if Turks attack our troops he thinks P.M may equally try a Khaki Election; he regards last Saturday's Turkish manifesto as written with an eye to such an end. I ventured to suggest that if Turks attack our troops it might have quite an opposite effect on the public psychology. They might equally turn and rend the Coalition for mishandling the situation. He thought if an election were rushed the Die Hards would try and call a Conference of the Nat.Union. Austen was in most difficult position. If he went to P.M. now and said he was sorry but he could not carry his party farther into the Coalition, the P.M. might quite rightly say: 'What is your proof – get a conference of your people throughout the country and defend the Coalition to them. Until you have done this and failed how can you possibly say your party won't follow you?'

B.L. recognizes that the one chance of reuniting the party is to go to the country separately and on the understanding that if we came back with a sufficient majority the P.M. would be a Conservative. But he hardly sees how Austen can break with the P.M. Speaking quite academically he thought only A.J.B. or he himself could reunite the party. A.J.B. certainly would not and he could not as things were at present. I am not quite so sure what his attitude would be if a conference of the party asked him to come forward. In any case I doubt his health enabling him to stand the strain.

Have today received letters from Leslie Wilson and G.Y. in reply to my memo giving details of Chequers meeting. Both are aghast and G.Y. is coming back specially tonight instead of next Sunday.

Forgive this note counched in telegraphic terms but am snowed under and am just writing a long letter to Leslie.

Yours,
M.F.

Sanders to George Younger 23 September 1922

Dear George,

Fraser has told me of the latest developments. It looks as if we may be rushed into a Coalition election before the party has a chance of expressing any opinion on the subject. I think that procedure would lead to great resentment among many members of our party besides the Die Hards. Would it be possible to have a meeting of the N.U. Council before any definite announcement is made and have the straight issue put whether the party is ready to support a Liberal P.M. in another Parliament? I don't see that Austen could object to that, and it would clear the air one way or the other.

I expect you will see Leslie Wilson. I should like to know what his position is. I am inclined to think it would be better for those who consider the course proposed to be absolute folly to resign as soon as it is announced, but I should like to know what others think. We ought to act together if possible.

I am afraid you are put in a pretty awkward position too. It is all rather damnable.

R A S

Leslie Wilson to Sanders 24 September 1922
Hunthill, Brechin

My dear Peter,

Malcolm Fraser tells me you know all that has been happening so I won't repeat it – but only say that I am appalled at the decision arrived at by Austen at Chequers.

I have written very strong letters to him and G.Y. is seeing him and the P.M.

I've given him a pretty broad hint that I shan't be able to accept the decision but I am just sending you this line to suggest that we none of us, unless forced to do so, take any action independently but let us all act together if action is necessary. I shall be back at the end of the week but don't want to come before and George agrees with me entirely and will, as Chairman of the Party, put the case to Austen and the P.M.

It's very difficult being here and it's my only real holiday this recess! So I do want to stay the full week!

Yours,
Leslie

Younger to Sanders 25 September 1922
UNIONIST CENTRAL OFFICE

Confidential

My dear Peter,

Very many thanks for yours of the 23rd inst. The fat is properly in the fire if our mandarins persist in the policy they appear to have adopted at Chequers. I am to see Austen to-morrow afternoon, and shall let him distinctly understand that such a policy amounts to an inevitable split in the party; that he is not justified in making any public declaration on the subject until he has consulted the whole of his Ministers, senior and junior; and that also the party ought to be given an opportunity of expressing its view before anything is finally settled. He may not like this but I shall insist upon it.

After all he is only Leader in the House of Commons, but even if he were Leader of the party, it is his first duty to try to preserve party unity, and to adopt a policy which he knows perfectly well will rend us in twain, without at all events taking steps to ascertain that the great majority of the party is behind him, would be, in my opinion, an outrage. I certainly could not be the instrument for carrying out any such policy, and I am very glad to see that your view clearly coincides with my own.

I hope there may be yet time to avert the catastrophe which threatens us. I am writing quite shortly, and I am glad to tell you that Leslie Wilson is completely in accord with me, and has written Austen in no uncertain terms as to his own position. It is, as you say, a damnable mess, and I have lost all confidence both in the Government and in the lot who represent us in the Cabinet.

Yours ever,
George Younger

Younger to Sanders 27 September 1922
UNIONIST CENTRAL OFFICE

My dear Peter,

I enclose a rough Memorandum of what passed between me and Chamberlain last night. I send it to you very confidentially, as you are all to be called together next week. I am glad that, in the meantime at all events, I have put a stopper upon any premature declaration, either by Austen or anyone else.

I go home to-night, but shall be here again on Sunday morning.

Yours ever,
George Younger

Confidential Memorandum of an interview with Mr Chamberlain on Tuesday, 26 September 1922

We discussed very frankly the position created by the decision of himself and one or two other Ministers at Chequers a week ago on the subject of the future election policy of the party. He maintained that it was practically in accord with his Oxford speech, in which he had stated that the Government would appeal to the country as a Government. I pointed out that while he had no doubt said so, most people held on to the terms of his previous announcement to the N.U. Council, and that they had not read into the statement anything which amounted to a continuance of the Coalition on its existing basis, with the present Prime Minister as leader.

I pointed out that in the view of the Central Office the Chequers arrangement was a disastrous one; that it was obvious it meant a serious split in our party, and that it was impossible to forecast the extent of such a split; that it would be fatal to the electoral results, and probably fatal to the party for many a day to come seemed certain, and that I hoped this decision would be regarded as provisional until:

(1) He had consulted the whole of the Unionist Ministers, both senior and junior, and ascertained their views about it, and

(2) Even if after an interview with these Ministers it was decided to adopt the Chequers policy, it would be impossible, without tricking the party, to promulgate it publicly without ascertaining the party view of the proposal.

As the National Unionist Conference was called for 15 November, any election before that date, without having consulted the party, would be regarded as a piece of sharp practice, and even of political trickery; and that I must beg him to consider most carefully the propriety, in the event of a sudden election, of adopting the course of announcing this policy to a special Conference of the party.

In the circumstances, at the present time, frankness and pluck were necessary, and a straightforward statement of the position by Ministers themselves with their reasons for proposing a continuance of the existing arrangements might have considerable effect on the minds of those to whom it was addressed.

It should be a different kind of Conference from that of the National Union itself, and it probably should be called together in a different way, but it ought to include all delegates appointed to attend the N.U. Conference in November, together with all Members of Parliament, and such others as might be thought to add to its representative character. The programme would be arranged beforehand, there would be no complications arising out of the rules which guide the procedure at our ordinary conferences, and it would enable Ministers to attend in force, and to take the most prominent part in the proceedings. We should be trammelled by no resolutions, except those submitted by Ministers themselves, and upon those a direct vote could be taken.

He seemed to regard the proposal as worthy of consideration, and I left him with the promise that he would, in the meantime, arrange to make no public declarations of any kind, that he would see all the Ministers as early as possible next week, and that he would think over my suggestion of avoiding, by means of a special conference, any kind of appearance of dodging the party.

I might add as a postscript that I was fortunate enough to meet Sir Robert Horne late in the evening. I put my proposal about a conference to him, in the event of the necessity for an election arising before 15 November, and was very pleased to find that he thought the suggestion an excellent one, that it would get them out of many of the difficulties which had actually presented themselves to him, and that he would whole-heartedly support the suggestion I have made.

G.Y.

27 September 1922

Monday 2 October Harington's reply came yesterday; things are much easier at Chanak. H's former report had fairly frightened our General Staff, and it was on their advice that Friday's message was sent. Now Harington says the situation there is not dangerous and asks to be left to deal with it. He is to meet Kemal tomorrow. W. Evans still thinks there will be war. The Government have information that Kemal is feinting at Chanak and massing his troops at Ismid for an attack on Constantinople. We have already said he was to get that by conference, but now F.E. and Winston want to go back on that and keep the Turk out of Europe altogether. How they propose to do it goodness knows. The Government have got hold of a dispatch from General Lyautey[22] who is in command in Morocco, saying the Germans cultivated the Turk in order to hit England, that England is now 'the enemy' and that France ought to follow the German example. This is supposed to be Poincaré's policy.

Tuesday 3 October Kemal is not meeting Harington, but is sending Ismet to do so. There looks to be no reason why things should not settle down, but the Government is very jumpy. Philip Chetwode says Curzon has saved the British Empire when some of his colleagues were doing their best to ruin it.[23] The *Daily News* prints a letter from F. Maurice who is its correspondent at Constantinople, saying that the Government has been saved by Harington from rushing into war. Maurice is staying in Harington's house. As a matter of fact the orders to Harington were caused by his alarmist message and were sent on advice of General Staff.

I saw Leslie Wilson yesterday. He hopes to get the conferences proposed by Younger. He says he cannot stand on the terms settled at Chequers. Saw Fraser later and suggested that Younger should sound Derby as to his attitude. He might be the man to pull us through this. Leslie told me that very bad things might come out as to L.G.'s people trading in honours.

Called on Aubrey Herbert who has lost his sight altogether; he is in bed and under treatment. He told me that a year ago he had in his pocket a draft treaty with Kemal giving him less than we are now offering him. L.G. would not look at it.

Thursday 5 October   Crisis seems to have subsided. I leave town today. George Stanley tells me Derby has definitely left the Coalition. He wrote to Austen to say so, and Austen has asked him to say nothing at present.[24] He speaks in Lancashire on 21st. I put it to George what a good thing it would be if Derby came out and gave the party a lead, and George said he would write to him last night.

Leslie Wilson to Sanders 5 October 1922

My dear Peter,
    I send you herewith a copy of a letter I have just sent to G.Y. I don't think I can add to it but the position is most unsatisfactory and I hope by Monday to get something more definite from Austen, Yours,
                                    Leslie Wilson

My dear George,
    After waiting two days, I saw Austen yesterday. He did not come to London on Monday or Tuesday as there was no Cabinet.
    We had two hours together but I fear with little result except that he has promised to see Derby and Walter Long and that he will, at an early date, call together his Conservative Cabinet colleagues and then probably the junior ministers. He is backing down on the special conference and says he does not see the difference between a special conference and the Nat.Union meeting in November when he would be able to go and put his case in answer to some one of the resolutions.
    Altogether he is very disturbed – says he is between the devil and the deep sea and after what I had told him said apparently he would have very few friends if he pursued the Chequers policy! Which is true! His argument is that if the P.M. is asked to go, he will, but that the National Liberals will also go and join the Wee Frees, getting rid of Asquith and putting Winston at their head. The result then of a general election would be that we might have a majority over either the Wee Frees or Labour but certainly not over both, whereas if we went as a Coalition, whatever individual candidates might stand as, there would have to be a Coalition against Labour after the election and all would join this rather than have a Labour Government. I pointed out that many of ours would stand pledged definitely not to serve under Lloyd George, but he said they

would have to forget that in face of the greater national danger of a Labour Government.

I also pointed out that to pursue this course would make administration from the Central Office quite impossible and must inevitably lead to such a split in our party as would take years to heal, if it ever were healed.

Apart, however, from this, there was the immediate question to be settled (which could not be delayed) as to how he was going to deal with the N.U. meeting. Undoubtedly a resolution would be passed there, if nothing was settled before, and he would find himself in an impossible position at the Albert Hall meeting, advocating a policy which had been rejected by the N.U.

He ended by remarking that it would seem best that he should retire to cultivate his garden and that it did not seem advisable for him to lay down any old port at No.11!

I have met many during the last few days at the Carlton and elsewhere, but not one who is not most anxious for some agreed line of policy to be come to before the N.U. meeting. There is a movement going on, headed by Walter Long, William Bull and about 20 others who are meeting to try and bring some definite proposals to Austen. That is the reason why I suggested Austen seeing Walter Long.

At any rate the idea which he has and which was undoubtedly agreed to at Chequers, namely, that there should be a very early election and no time given to anyone to argue against the decision, is definitely abandoned – and a good thing too! I told him if that had been carried out, he would have been accused of trying to trick the party and the only thing to do was to take the party into his fullest confidence in the best possible way; but he must first consult his colleagues and afterwards the party representatives in the constituencies.

Austen was cheerful but he has fully realized the gravity of the situation. I was able to bring many concrete cases to show how the P.M.'s stock has gone down to nearly zero. He does not believe this is the case – but I am sure of it.

J.T. Davies told me that he did not see how L.G. could be P.M. after the next election and foresaw himself that there would be such rival claims for Austen and Bonar that we should ask A.J.B. to take the lead for a year until our differences were settled. It may be that we *shall* have to look for a *tertium quid* – as a solution to the difficulty.

I am off to Exeter to speak there tomorrow. Shall be up next week on and off. Anyhow up all Monday when I will see whether he has made up his mind at all and hear the result of conversations with Derby and Long.

I believe that there is a great chance of uniting our party if he will take it. I'm not afraid of the secession of the National Liberals. They really have nowhere to go and I don't see how they can go to the Wee Frees or that the

W.F.s will take them. Of course, it suits them to go as the Coalition is at present moment formed. They have everything to gain by doing so and nothing to lose. Our case is the exact opposite!

Yours ever,

L.W.

Sir Malcolm Fraser to Sanders 7 October 1922
UNIONIST CENTRAL OFFICE

Confidential

My dear Sanders,

I saw Lord Derby last night. He said that he was strongly against the Government's foreign policy, particularly in relation to France, and that he could no longer support the Coalition. He had to-day seen Austen Chamberlain.

He did not wish to embarrass the Government while the Turkish crisis lasted, nor did he wish to do anything which would split the party, but he felt that unless the party broke away from a Coalition under Lloyd George, it must be split, with no hope of its being reunited in the near future.

He fully realised the danger of letting the Labour party in. He did not think the Conservatives could return with a majority on their own. He was all in favour of working with those Liberals who would work with a Conservative majority, on the same lines as did the Liberal Unionists in the old days. He thought that Die Hardism *per se* was a negligible quantity and was on the decline. On the other hand, there was a growing distrust of Lloyd George, and a growing danger of internecine warfare within the party from a great mass of moderate Conservative opinion which was arising against the present Government.

He felt that he could no longer hold Lancashire for the present Coalition. He was cordially received at the various meetings which he attended, and they did what he asked them, largely because of the influence he happened to have in Lancashire, but he felt the whole time that the real feelings and the better judgement of the meetings were against the lines which he had advised. He was emphatic that Sir Archibald Salvidge had no influence in Lancashire outside Liverpool, and said that it was generally recognised that Salvidge was only the mouthpiece of Birkenhead.

In view of his unwillingness to embarrass the Government in any way at the moment, he was in a quandary as to what to say in a speech which he had to make to the local Labour committee on the 21st, and particularly in a speech which he had to make in the near future at the St Stephens' Club on foreign policy.

He felt that he would soon have to resign his position as Chairman of the Lancashire Provincial Division. This would bring matters to a head, as he would have to outline his reasons for resigning, and if after his resignation and having given this explanation they re-elected him, it would bring matters to a very definite head. It would also leave his hands free to act as he thought fit in the future.

He had recently seen Bonar Law, whose position and feelings appeared to be similar to his own, though Bonar Law hesitated to take any definite action at the moment.

Yours
M.F.

Sanders to Leslie Wilson 8 October 1922
(War Office)

Dear Leslie,
Many thanks for yours. It comes to this; that according to Austen a friendly arrangement is rejected, and the Coalition Liberals say if you won't have L.G. we take the field against you. I should not be frightened by that. In the first place I think it is bluff; the Wee Frees would not have them; they are actually supporting Die Hards against Coalition Liberals as I know for a fact. In the second place Maclachlan reckons that if the Conservatives stood against all comers they would get a clear majority.[25] I think his opinion is on the whole the best you can get. If we went to the country under Derby or Bonar, I quite think it would be so. I don't know what Walter Long's attitude may be.

I think the important thing for the moment is that we should not drift into the N.U. conference without a clear understanding as to the issue to be put to it, and the decision we want to get from it.

I shall be at the War Office on Wednesday next.

Yours,
R.A. Sanders

Leslie Wilson to Sanders 12 October 1922

My dear Peter,
I rang up this morning but found you had gone out of London. I hope I've got your right address!

This is just a line to say that after very carefully thinking over the matter, consulting G.Y., Malcolm Fraser and Bonar, I wrote last night to Austen to say that if the Government announces a dissolution and goes to the general election as a Government and our party is asked to support the Coalition as it exists today, without any opportunity being given by its leaders of expressing its opinion, I must publicly dissociate myself from such action.

I am very nervous from all I hear of what the P.M. may say on Saturday. He may say we will accept the challenge and take the verdict of our countrymen!!!

G. Younger is at the moment with Austen. I thought I'd keep away today having done my bit!!!

Yours,
Leslie

Thursday 19 October   This has been an awful week. Last Sunday L.G., F.E. and Worthy Evans dined with Winston. Fitzalan and Leslie Wilson there too. It was decided by the Cabinet Ministers in spite of protests of Edmund and Leslie to dissolve on Saturday next (21st). A meeting of all Unionist Ministers called for Monday afternoon and one of Unionist M.P.s for today. Junior Ministers lunched with Amery before the meeting. We decided that we should insist on a Unionist Prime Minister, or resign. Went on to the meeting where Austen announced that the composition of the Government next Parliament must be left an open question. Amery stated our views, not very well. Then Pollock went back on us and backed Austen. I insisted that we must have a Unionist P.M. and asked for a free hand at the Carlton meeting, which was granted. I also asked Austen when he would like to receive resignations and was told by F.E. to wait till after the Carlton meeting. Had another meeting next morning which Stanley Baldwin and Boscawen attended. They said they and Curzon were coming out. That evening I had a meeting at Bridgwater and said I wanted a Conservative premier and that I was going to resign on Thursday, an announcement that was received with total apathy, much to the amusement of Peel who had spoken for me. Meanwhile Younger was at work in London to get Bonar to come out as leader. Meetings of Under Secretaries went on. On Wednesday night Sam Hoare came in and told us that a meeting of 35 M.P.s at his house that morning had decided to support a resolution moved by Pretyman in favour of the party breaking away from the Coalition altogether. It was said that the Government quite expected to win at the Carlton meeting. This morning the Newport election result came as a cheering surprise. I am told the liquor question had a good deal to do with it.[26] The Carlton meeting was at 11. Bonar's speech turned the whole thing. Balfour failed quite pathetically to grip the meeting. There was no ill feeling, all most gentlemanly. I think the result staggered Austen and F.E. The Government has now resigned and Bonar goes to the King tomorrow. The feature of the Carlton meeting was its extraordinarily restrained and kindly atmosphere. No harsh or excited words.

Lloyd George to Sanders 19 October 1922

My dear Under Secretary,
I write to inform you that I have tendered my resignation and that of the Government to the King this afternoon. I understand that His Majesty will be graciously pleased to accept these resignations as soon as he is assured that an alternative Government can be formed.
    I should like to take this opportunity of thanking you for your valuable services during your tenure of office under my premiership.
Ever sincerely,
D. Lloyd George

Monday 23 October   Meeting at Hotel Cecil today to elect Bonar leader of the party. All unanimous, but the supporters of Coalition did not attend. Fraser asked me if I would see Freddy Guest and try to do a deal as to seats in the country. He came to see me in Eaton Square this evening. He thinks this can be arranged, says L.G. is genuinely afraid of the Labour party, that he is going into the election on the lines of the Leeds speech and that he expects relations to be quite amicable after the election.[27]

Wednesday 25 October Yesterday I was offered and accepted Ministry of Agriculture. The manner of it was quaint. Stanley Baldwin dashed in about 7 p.m. 'Peter will you take Agriculture?' 'Yes love to,' I said. 'All right that's settled,' and off he went. Went to the Palace this morning and kissed hands as P.C. and then took oath as Minister. Stamfordham[28] told me the King said what a good thing to appoint a Master of Hounds. So far it is a real old Tory Cabinet. Of the House of Commons members, most of us are intimate friends. It is curious that Peel, Baldwin and I were all in the Upper Sixth at Harrow together.
    I saw Freddy Guest and McCurdy yesterday and think I have fixed up an arrangement by which we discourage opposition in their seats and they advise their followers to support us against the Wee Frees. Rothermere is trying to get a step in the peerage as the price of his support.

Saturday 25 November I had a strenuous election and was returned by a majority of 119 only the figures being:

Sanders	11,240
Morse (Lib)	11,121
Williams (Lab)	1,598

The small majority was a surprise. There was a curious wave of Liberalism in parts of the South West. We lost Taunton and N. Dorset and two
seats in Wilts and only just kept Tiverton. Being a Cabinet Minister is a
handicap rather than otherwise; you have to be so careful about promises. The chief things worked against me were low wages and Field
Punishment No.1[29] which I had to defend as Under Secretary for War. I
had to go to town on the day of the count and left Lucy to go in. She
had an awful time. Taking the country all through the result was very
satisfactory. During the election I prophesied in public that we should
get a clear majority and added that I expected 335 seats and hoped for
350. We got 344 so I was not far out. The deal with the Coalition
Liberals did not come off and we took several of their seats including
Guest's.[30]

Cabinet has been mainly occupied with the Turkish trouble. The
Government is very anxious to get out in peace, but has left the
negotiations to Curzon who really has a free hand. Bonar announced
during the election that he did not mean to interfere in the work of the
departments as L.G. had done. Following out that policy he has refused
to see a deputation of unemployed who have marched to London.
Great trouble was threatened in consequence but up to now all has
been quiet.

Parliament opened last Thursday and for two days past we have been
treated to wild speeches by the wild men returned from Scotland.[31] The
Canadians are pressing us to go ahead at once with the Canadian Cattle
Bill. Both Bonar and Devonshire want to do so. I have represented that
the Bill is contentious, that it is not yet ready and that farmers would
resent its being rushed. But it is quite possible they may insist on taking
it.

Sunday 17 December Parliament was prorogued on Friday after a very
strenuous three weeks. We took the Canadian Cattle Bill and got it
through, but I had to drop the clauses relating to the other colonies, and at
one point in committee I was in difficulty, simply through insufficient
knowledge of the Bill. We had trouble with the Ulstermen about the
provisions for detention of all imported cattle, but after making their
protest and getting well beaten they did not obstruct. There was an
agricultural amendment to the address and L.G. took part in the debate on
it. He was very moderate but was treated rudely by the Labour men. He
asked for an inquiry as to how agricultural development had been

promoted in foreign countries and Bonar agreed. I have settled with L.G.
that the inquiry should be conducted by three professors in spite of some
protests from Labour men and others.

There has been a certain amount of Labour rowdiness but it has been
not so pronounced as the papers make out; and there have been several
late night sittings, but we have been asking the House to do too much in
the time; there has been little real obstruction. Bonar has got hold of the
House already; the Labour men are never offensive to him as they were to
L.G. His refusal to see the unemployed deputation has turned out all
right.[32] The ill feeling between Liberals and Labour is very apparent. It
culminated in an attack on Asquith by a man called Johnstone, the editor
of *Forward* who accused him of corruption over the Soudan loan and
refused to withdraw.[33] Ramsay Macdonald is in a very difficult position as
leader and has done very well. Curzon seems likely to bring Lausanne to a
successful conclusion. It will be a great triumph if he does. The Turks were
ready to agree to everything else if he would give up Mosul, but he has
refused even to discuss that and the Turks are gradually coming into line all
the same.

Bonar has had a conference with the Allied Premiers. He found
Poincaré perfectly friendly and polite, but very intransigent on the
reparation questions. There was very nearly a rupture but Bonar got
Poincaré to come in last Monday morning and said how sorry he should be
to start with trouble with France and eventually Poincaré agreed to put the
whole thing off till January.

George Younger to Sanders 28 December 1922

My dear Peter,
Many thanks for yours of the 23rd which I find on arriving from home
this morning.

I must heartily reciprocate your good wishes both to Lady Sanders and
yourself, and hope you'll have a Happy New Year and a successful one in
your new job. It won't be easy to meet your difficulties, but I hope you
manage all right.

I knew about Townley and Gretton told me himself that he had offered
his services to Bonar.[34] You may be amused to hear that Bonar has never
even mentioned it to me. I don't know whether that may be regarded as a
clear indication of the value he placed upon the offer.

I told John that it was a whole time job and that unless he gave up other
things and devoted himself to the office *he could not match the work.* I
think it rather surprised him and it seemed to cool his ardour.

I'm most anxious to be relieved and have urged Bonar to apply his mind to the position. The strain is too much for me now and I must have some rest or I'll crack up: I think my sacrifices for the party must come to an end. These, however, have been well repaid by the result of the election with our party more solid than ever.

Yours ever,
G.Y.

CHAPTER 11 NOTES

1 This is the letter from Austen Chamberlain referred to by Sanders in the diary entry of 6 January, together with Sanders' reply (AC 32/2/6 and AC 32/2/16 in the Austen Chamberlain Papers at Birmingham University). Austen Chamberlain wrote to Sanders, Neville Chamberlain and J.C. Williams to ask each of them about feeling in their area on the question of a Coalition election, presumably because he no longer trusted the information about local feeling that was reaching him through Younger and Central Office. The information from all three, however, coincided with Younger's advice.

2 This was a circular sent to all local party chairmen from the Chairman of the Party Organisation. Although it seems to argue the case in favour of the continuation of the Coalition, it formed an important part of Younger's press and publicity campaign against an early coalition election by informing the local parties that one was in the air.

3 The decision to revise the Irish Boundary through an independent commission was bitterly resented in Ulster and among Unionist M.P.s. When it finally met, the commission made virtually no changes at all. See Tom Jones, *op.cit.*, III, p. 189.

4 On 23 February at the Constitutional Club, Birkenhead had described Younger as the cabin boy who was usurping the authority of the ship's captain, a sally that provoked an instant response from Younger's supporters and a sharp rebuke for Birkenhead from the National Union. The National Union Executive was only prevented from passing and publishing a denunciation of the Lord Chancellor by the promise of Worthington-Evans to see Birkenhead and persuade him to moderate his language.

5 The government had lost all three of the seats that it had defended in by-elections in late February, at Manchester Clayton, Camberwell North West and Bodmin. All had been narrow defeats but all had been suffered by Conservatives and so the alibi of poor Coalition Liberal organisation could not be used to explain them away. Youn-

ger was no doubt expecting to lose Wolverhampton West on 7 March, a seat that was in fact comfortably held.

6   6th Earl Winterton (in the Irish Peerage) had been a Conservative M.P. since 1904. He became Under Secretary at the India Office with Viscount Peel as Secretary of State in the Lords.

7   This was all part of the government's attempt to heal the breaches in the party, which had been caused in part by Birkenhead's previous speeches. As the Diehards correctly recognised, it did not reflect any real changes of attitude. Maurice Cowling, *The Impact of Labour*, p. 142.

8   Field Marshal Sir Henry Wilson had recently been elected a Conservative M.P. after retiring from the army. His maiden speech of 20 minutes was a strong attack on the Government's domestic record and received an ovation from Unionist M.P.s. Bernard Ash, *The Lost Dictator*, p. 275.

9   This was Sir Samuel Roberts Bt, M.P. for Sheffield Ecclesall since 1902 and a keen supporter of coalition; his son, also Samuel Roberts, was M.P. for Hereford (although he subsequently moved to the family seat at Ecclesall) and a strong believer in the independence of the Conservative party. It was not unknown for them to be paired on sensitive votes, so as to avoid a family split in public.

10   The 1922 Licensing Act was an attempt to tidy things up from the patchwork of controls that still remained since the war. The 1921–2 agitation showed that this was one of the issues for which the Lloyd George government was most strongly resented. A number of Conservatives believed that the Coalition Liberals had taken advantage of the war to introduce restrictions that they had always wanted and which might some day lead on to prohibition. See C.P. Cook & John Ramsden, *By-Elections in British Politics*, p. 35.

11   F.A. Macquisten had been an advocate but was a relatively new M.P. and one who had not served through the procedural battles of 1911–14. The government was defeated over the question of teachers' pensions, a subject where increasing expenditure seemed to demonstrate a lack of faith in public economy. The supplementary estimate of 26 May made a much larger increase in educational expenditure a matter of confidence.

12   Sir Henry Wilson was assassinated off Eaton Square by I.R.A. gunmen at about 2.30 p.m. on 22 June, the last assassination of a British politician in London until 1979. The murderers were arrested only after a hectic chase through the West End in which a policeman was slightly wounded. The House of Commons was adjourned at a time when no accurate information was available, for Austen Chamberlain announced that three policemen had also been killed. M.P.s can rarely have felt so unsafe as they went about their business.

13 Ronald Tree had been reprieved by the Home Secretary on the ground of insanity, after a particularly atrocious murder. The reaction of the popular press was predictable but extremely violent.

14 The Four Courts had been seized by rebels against the Free State government on 17 April and had become their Dublin headquarters until the Government moved in with large forces, including artillery, on the morning of 28 June. A pitched battle was still being fought in the streets of Dublin.

15 The peerages for Robinson and Vestey finally brought the honours scandal to a head. Dudley Ward was a Coalition Liberal Chief Whip. Robinson eventually solved the government's problem by refusing the offer after the public outcry. The final comment of Sanders casts an interesting light on Younger's subsequent claim that he had never had anything to do with selling honours (Younger to Baldwin, 27 August 1927, in the J.C.C. Davidson Papers.) For all of this see Tom Cullen, *Maundy Gregory*, p.110.

18 On 9 May, the National Union Executive had passed a belligerent resolution describing continued failure to reform the House of Lords as 'a breach of the understanding upon which the continued allegiance of the Unionist Party to its leaders depends.' When Salvidge moved to delete this phrase, so obviously offensive to Austen Chamberlain, he could find no member of the Executive to second his motion, although it was a packed meeting that included nine M.P.s and seven Conservative peers. Presumably the silence of Neville Chamberlain, Younger and Sanders betokened their agreement with the resolution as passed. On 27 June, the National Union Central Council reiterated these views with two unanimous motions passed by an attendance of 270. The warnings to Austen Chamberlain could hardly have been clearer.

19 Waring and Williamson had both received peerages recently; Waring was accused by McNeill of having traded with the enemy and caused a sensation when Waring himself replied from the Distinguished Strangers' Gallery: 'It is a lie.' Tom Cullen, *op.cit.* p. 115.

20 General Sir Archibald Hunter had been a Conservative M.P. since 1918; General Sir George Higginson had commanded the Brigade of Guards in the Crimea.

21 The Moses Room was the largest of the Committee Rooms of the House of Lords, so called because of a tapestry hanging there.

22 Marechal Lyautey, a reactionary and highly political soldier, was French Resident-General in Morocco.

23 Lt. Gen. Sir Philip Chetwode had spent most of his army career in India and the Middle East and was Deputy C.I.G.S. in 1922.

24 This anecdote is an interesting commentary on the independent

influence of the Stanleys; Lord Derby had not been a Minister since 1918 and had had no direct connection with the government since returning from Paris in 1920, but the news that he was seceding from the coalition was thought to be an important step.

25 Leigh Maclachlan, Chief Organiser at Conservative Central Office and a long-serving professional agent.

26 Victory by Reginald Clarry, Conservative, over Liberal and Labour candidates in a rough contest which featured the drink issue prominently. See Cook and Ramsden, *op.cit.* pp. 14–43.

27 On 21 October, Lloyd George spoke at Leeds and tried to keep open his options for a future alliance with the Conservatives and so destroyed the chance of Liberal reunion. Trevor Wilson believed that this speech 'finished him as a force in the election.' Trevor Wilson, *The Downfall of the Liberal Party*, p. 245.

28 1st Lord Stamfordham, Private Secretary to the King.

29 There had been Liberal and Labour demands for the abolition of Field Punishment No.1, which could include tying to the wheel of a field gun but was more often merely hard labour. The Army Council insisted on retaining these powers and, as Under Secretary, Sanders had to defend them in the House of Commons. (*Hansard*, House of Commons, 5 April 1922.)

30 There was in fact a continuation of the Conservative-Liberal pacts in many areas, especially in Scotland and some Northern towns, but there was no national deal. M. Kinnear, *op.cit.* p. 144.

31 These were the Clydeside M.P.s who had made such a breakthrough for the Labour left in the Glasgow area. See K. Middlemas, *The Clydesiders*.

32 Law refused to see a deputation of unemployed himself and this did in fact turn out to be a shrewd move; the delegation was sent for political purposes but he neatly turned the tables on them by using it as an occasion to show that his Ministers, unlike Lloyd George's, would be truly independent. Robert Blake, *The Unknown Prime Minister*, p. 476.

33 Tom Johnstone was one of the most vociferous of the Clydesiders.

34 Colonel Gretton had offered himself to Law for Younger's post as Chairman of the Party, but the choice of such an intransigent Diehard would have been needlessly provocative.

Chapter 12   1923 'A real old Tory Cabinet'

Sunday 28 January   The conference with the French at the beginning of the month broke down very quickly. Philip Lloyd Graeme who was there said Bonar managed things extraordinarily well. Certainly after breaking with the French the feeling left behind was much more friendly than after one of L.G.'s patched up agreements. The Rothermere press is now urging that we ought to support the French, but the country seems indifferent on the subject. After professing to back us at Lausanne the French are now inclined to let us down and Curzon is losing his patience. In the U.S. Baldwin and A. Geddes strongly recommended acceptance of U.S. terms, but Bonar would not have them at any price and told Baldwin to come home.

At home nothing exciting has happened. None of the defeated Ministers has yet got a seat. George Younger told me seventeen had refused to have Boscawen, but Fraser told me a week ago that he was to have Doyle's seat at Newcastle. Fraser also told me that it was owing to him that so many National Liberal seats were contested by Conservatives. The L.G. people tried to bluff him out of it, but he considered it the best chance of getting his majority and stuck to it. He did what he could to prevent opposition to ex-Ministers but without much success. Farquhar stopped our drawing on the party fund during the election, being one of the Trustees of the party Fund.[1] Luckily Fraser had collected and banked a considerable sum in his own name, Younger's being afterwards added, and that saw us through. It is not yet decided who is to succeed Younger. The papers mentioned Gretton. I asked him about it and he said he had not been approached but would like the job. Fraser thinks he would never do. Pike Pease who is to have a peerage is being considered.

Bonar wants to have as few Bills as possible in the coming session. I am struggling to get a Rating Bill with the agricultural assessment reduced to 25 per cent, but that is still in suspense.

Sunday 4 February   There was a Cabinet on Tuesday on the U.S. debt question. After Baldwin had stated his case for acceptance of terms offered, Bonar said he was so strongly against acceptance that he would not personally consent to it. He stated that he did not regard the debt as an ordinary one and hinted at repudiation. The feeling was very strong the other way, and a decision was postponed till next day. On Wednesday we held a meeting without Bonar in Cave's room in the morning. Cave and Baldwin, while dissenting from Bonar, advised giving in to him in the last resort. Both had been pressing him without avail to modify his attitude. Derby said he looked on Bonar's attitude as inconsistent with honest dealing and thought he would have to resign. It was arranged that Cave, Baldwin and Devonshire should see him again before the Cabinet and we dispersed very much perturbed. On getting to the Cabinet Bonar said at once that he had not realised how fatal his resignation would be in the party and gave way. So all is well.

Viscount Younger to Sanders – 18 February 1923

My dear Peter,

Very many thanks for your kind congratulations.[2] I've been quite snowed under and have been reduced to quite a formal reply, but I must send you a few words of very cordial thanks for all you kindly say in your letter.

You know that the row last year wasn't an easy one to have, and you can appreciate what I always tell Bonar, that my successor will find it an easy job to serve him as both his chief and P. M., compared with mine, when a constant eye had to be kept on L.G. and his supporters, with unpleasant rows at intervals.

I hope he'll make up his mind soon, as the office work now is pure drudgery, with a greater volume of work than ever, and there is no interest in it now.

I doubt the success of 'the wreckage' in some of the present contests, but we were told we must make every effort to secure seats and it has been a thankless and difficult task. I take no kind of responsibility for the result. We tried at first to pick and choose, but latterly had to take what we could get and just run the risk.

I think this decision to deal equally with all protected houses – the only possible and fair course – may just help Bosky to get back. Without it he would possibly have had little chance. I hope he is not going to prove the Masterman of our party.[3]

Again many thanks not only for your congratulations now, but for the pleasant and successful time we had together at the Central Office.
Yours ever,
G.Y.

Saturday 24 February   The latest trouble is over the Rent Restriction Acts. Onslow's committee recommended that rents should be decontrolled as to the highest rented houses this year, the next in 1924, and all in 1925. Boscawen and Stanley are now fighting suburban seats and this was at once seized on, and they were attacked by middle class householders. Boscawen got the Cabinet to agree that decontrol of the two highest classes should take place in 1924. Then he told the electors he would not agree to its taking place then if there were not plenty of houses built by that date. Today there was a Cabinet at which he fought for general decontrol in 1925, but failed to get that and the latest proposal is decontrol of the two highest classes in 1924 unless Parliament passes a resolution to the contrary. It is a bad business, from which there is no really satisfactory way out. The Government majority sank to 22 on a private member's motion to give universal old age pensions, a subject on which many had pledged themselves during the election. On the amendments to the Address as to the Ruhr and Mesopotamia we did well. George Tryon made a first class speech on pensions last Tuesday.[4] There is a very strong feeling about Winston's use of official information in his articles. L.G. and F.E. are said to be going to follow his example. Bonar stated explicitly the other day he considered Winston's revelations inconsistent with the Privy Councillor's oath.[5]

Friday 2 March Leslie Wilson and Malcolm Fraser both tell me that Catterell, who is standing against Boscawen, is financed by Oliver Locker-Lampson.[6] Harrison who is one of Rothermere's men assures me Rothermere knows nothing of it. Godfrey Locker Lampson impressed on L. that Bob Cecil is very anxious to join the Government. I had to receive the King at the Islington Horse Show on Wednesday. Queen Alexandra was there wonderfully alert and interested in the jumping. The King absolutely radiant because a horse of his took a premium.

There was a little discussion in the Cabinet on Wednesday morning about applying the Safeguarding of Industries Act to France and Belgium, Lloyd Graeme anxious not to, Amery the other way. Derby told me that if Amery had his way he and Devonshire must resign.

Sunday 11 March The result of the bye-election is a great blow.[7] The Labour people never thought of winning Liverpool. I think the chief cause was resentment at being made a convenience for defeated Ministers. But no doubt the suburban middle class man is afraid of the abolition of rent restrictions. Greaves-Lord; M.P. for Norwood, tells me the feeling in his very Tory division is intense.

The N.F.U. have been attacking me for saying the Government will not go for subsidies or protection of food stuffs and has been publishing letters on the subject.

Sunday 18 March   Stanley Jackson has been appointed to succeed George Younger and Reggie Hall Malcolm Fraser. The first came as a surprise. I did not think Jackson would take it. They should both do well.[8]

There is trouble over agricultural wages in Norfolk. On Friday delegates from the N.F.U. and the Labourers' Union came to see Bonar. He wanted to avoid them, but I got him to do it. He was very uncompromising telling them that he had no remedy for their ills. I think the interview may do good as showing that the Government does not mean to be squeezed. I have been putting up proposals for a tax on imported malting barley and I think that may be adopted. If so it will do a lot to pacify the eastern counties farmers. On Friday afternoon we got a Merchandise Marks Bill through second reading. I had to speak on behalf of the Government and pleased our own side I think.[9]

The event of the week has been the arrest of the Irish conspirators. Willie Bridgeman has been most naive in his speeches in defence, but the party is all with him. Pat Hastings made an awful failure last Monday in the debate on the subject.

Thursday 29 March   House adjourns today. Bonar has been troubled with a relaxed throat and has not been able to speak in the House. He took the chair at the Cabinet on Wednesday last and had an acute difference of opinion with Curzon on the subject of the report of the Cabinet Sub-Committee on Iraq. Bonar wanted to postpone the peace with Turkey, Curzon to get a decision at once. Eventually it was decided to postpone till after Easter.

There is an agricultural strike in Norfolk which is causing further trouble for my department. There is to be an agricultural debate as soon as the House reassembles. Bonar and Baldwin are now considering the idea of reducing farmers' assessment. I think it will be done.

Sunday 15 April   During the Easter recess the agricultural economists issued their interim report. They say very little as to what may be learnt from foreign countries, but have taken up very crude ideas suggested by English pundits. I saw Bonar about it last Monday, having circulated recommendations during the recess. Bonar wanted to adopt nearly all the proposals including wages boards. I told him I thought farmers would be all against that. I then got Robbins of N.F.U. to lunch with me that day and sounded the agricultural M.P.s in the afternoon. Next day got Pretyman, German, chairman of N.F.U. and Robbins to see the P.M. They said they were all against wages boards unless accompanied by subsidies or general agricultural protection. Cabinet Tuesday evening adopted proposal to reduce assessment of agricultural land for rating to a quarter and referred question of barley duty, wages boards and other smaller matters to a Committee. I then went off to Surveyors Institution dinner where I was principal guest. As I was leaving the hall some time after 10 p.m. a reporter told me the Government had been beaten. George Lane Fox went down and found this was true, then went to the Carlton and heard the details. The whips had told members to be back at 9:30. In the course of the debate Boyd Carpenter made a statement about the Lytton report that was not considered satisfactory, but the whole thing seemed fizzling out. Clifton Brown, P.P.S. to Baldwin, went to see him at Boyd Carpenter's request and advised him that things were all right. The whips did not put up anyone to keep the debate going and a division was called at 9:10. It looked as if the question would not be challenged but Wedgwood did so and Hope called a division. Herbert Nield got a few of our men to vote against the Government on account of the Lytton affair and the Government was beaten by five. N.Chamberlain moved the adjournment.[10]

Wednesday was the day fixed for the agriculture debate. Having got the rating concession I was quite happy about it. However, the motion as to supply next day came first and closuring that brought on the row. Lloyd George said to me in the lobby that the great mistake was closuring; in another half hour the debate would have fizzled. I doubt it. Anyhow the Speaker adjourned the House on account of the row and my announcement as to rating had to be made to the press. German had promised the P.M. and myself that he could undertake to stop the Norfolk strike. The Labour party could claim that in stopping business they were following a precedent set by us.

Thursday I had to start at 9 a.m. from Paddington to go down to Cirencester where the King was inspecting the Agricultural College. It rained all the time but everyone seemed quite happy. Lunched at Bathurst's. The King got me to sit next him after lunch; talked a lot about agriculture in a most Tory vein; all against a wages board. I told him German had promised the strike would be squared. In this the latter has played me false; it is still going on. Both H.M. and the Queen were perturbed at the Labour men having sung the 'Red Flag' in the House. I got back to the House soon after 6 p.m. and took part in the all night sitting on the Army Annual, a most futile affair. It merely killed a useful Private Member's Bill that was down for Friday.

Sunday 22 April Budget introduced on Monday. Reception favourable. Baldwin's speech sound without being impressive. I tried to get him to put agricultural proposals in, but the whole thing was arranged before they came on the *tapis* and he would not alter his arranged programme. In his reply on Wednesday he announced the arrangements as to agricultural rates. The Cabinet on Wednesday decided that the reduction should apply from 1 April and approved the proposal for a tax on malting barley. The Ministry of Agriculture vote was put down for Thursday last, and it was intended to have a general discussion during which I could announce the proposals of the Government. However, Wedgwood Benn supported eventually by his party, objected and Hope ruled out all proposals involving legislation.[11] Consequently the discussion was a mere supply affair of the tamest and most amicable kind. I got a private notice question addressed to me on Friday to enable me to announce the tax on barley and refusal to set up wage boards. I was able to announce on Thursday that the Norfolk strike was practically settled. Ramsay Macdonald cleverly stepped in at the right moment and got credit for a result with which he had little to do.

Last Sunday's papers declared Bonar was about to resign and heralded the return of Austen and F.E. This was worked by the latter. The report was denied at once, and the effect has been rather to pull the party together. For some reason I have not yet fathomed Rothermere has come round to us. I made a speech at the Constitutional on Tuesday on Agriculture, booming the Government policy all I could and the *Mail* and the *Mirror* gave it the biggest headlines.

Sunday 29 April   The reason for Rothermere's change is said to be that he has quarrelled with F.E. The latter is getting more and more disliked. Government stock seems rising. Neville Chamberlain did very well in introducing the Housing Bill. Bonar is off for a sea voyage. His doctor says that will restore his voice. He is quite sound otherwise.

I got my Salmon Bill through Grand Committee in two hours; rather a good performance as it has 93 clauses and there were four pages of amendments. On the other hand the Merchandise Marks Bill is not getting on at all owing to the obstruction of Royds, Hogge and Kenworthy. During the week I have had many dealings over the Canadian cattle breeding order. I think it is now just possible that it may be squared; but the breed societies all feel that Boscawen let them down badly. There was really some misunderstanding between him and their representatives.

Saturday 5 May   At the Cabinet on Wednesday Curzon produced his letter to the Soviet Government. It is very forcible. Cabinet approved. The terms will be published at end of next week. Nothing has yet leaked out. I think it will please Conservatives immensely and make the Labour people furious.

The case of Art O'Brien has been before the Court of Appeal.[12] They have not yet delivered judgement, but it is generally expected that they will go against the Crown. Willie B. says if they put him in prison he will grant himself a free pardon.

Friday 18 May I have got my Salmon Bill through all stages with general benediction. And I have got the Canadian breeding cattle business postponed till the Imperial Conference. It seems clear that the agricultural representatives when they told Boscawen to make the best deal he could did not understand the position, probably through their own stupidity. Boscawen always put things clearly enough.

The Court of Appeal has turned Willie down and the House of Lords ruled it has no jurisdiction. At a Cabinet on Monday it was decided to bring in a Bill not only granting indemnity but giving powers to lock the deportees up again if the Home Secretary thought desirable. That was altered on Wednesday owing to pressure from our own people. Inskip, Walter Guinness and Stanley Jackson were very strong against it. There was a row in the House on Wednesday night. Newbolt called Fitzroy a 'bourgeois'. Fitzroy told him to leave the House without giving him a chance to withdraw. Newbolt refused. Fitzroy sent for the Speaker. The latter was very weak but did name Newbolt, who eventually left quietly.[13]

Confabs with Krassin are still going on. The Russians are evidently anxious not to break with us, but I doubt their caving in altogether. Ronald McNiel spoke well on Wednesday and Thursday.

Friday 1 June Bonar's collapse occurred just after we had gone away for Whitsuntide. I did not come up to London. Baldwin wrote me: 'Dear Peter, I hope you will carry on. Let me have a line by Friday morning.' Bonar is believed to have cancer but he does not know it. Curiously enough the new Government is generally acclaimed and its position is strong at present. Curzon behaved very well. He got a great ovation at the party meeting last Monday. I think it was Salisbury who promoted an offer being made to Austen. When the latter went down to Chequers Baldwin told him he had offered the Post Office to Wothington-Evans. Austen said: 'He will be a hound if he takes it.' He has done so though.

The proceedings over the Indemnity Bill were rather a muddle and led to an all-night sitting on Tuesday. I got second reading of my Credits Bill on Wednesday without much trouble and managed to get Committee stage of the Financial resolution and my Consolidation Bill during the dinner hour without discussion.

Saturday 9 June On Monday the Agricultural Rates Bill came on for second reading. Neville Chamberlain introduced it and I wound up. The Labour Party opposed. Liberals were utterly divided. Mond spoke against it and Lambert for it. L.G. came in, heard that Mond had opposed the Bill and went out again. According to Winfrey he had said they could not oppose it as a party.[14] We got a very good majority on second reading. On the committee and report of the financial resolution there was a good deal of Liberal opposition, especially to the Scotch provisions which avowedly give relief to landlords. Thomson the Scotch Solicitor General was very weak in defence.

Chamberlain's new Rent Restriction Bill went through with a large majority after two days dull debate.

Thursday 21 June   I got my Credits Bill through committee last Monday in a single sitting. There is serious trouble over the proposed tax on malting barley which runs up against various foreign treaties. The departments discovered this accidentally long after the announcement had been made. I am not clear how we can get round it. On Tuesday night over budget the Radicals made a stupid blunder in refusing to allow Bull to withdraw an amendment as to valuation forms. The Government then allowed a division without whips and Bull's amendment was carried. Pringle & Co. furious.[15] The amendment marks the destruction of the last vestige of the Lloyd George land tax machinery. I hope we stick to it, but Joynson Hicks tells me the P.M. may give way on report. J. Hicks has done very well in the budget debate.

Wednesday 4 July   Budget just through. We stuck to the valuation clause in spite of a protest from L.G. and curiously enough from Austen. I got the Credits Bill through on Friday. Leslie Scott made a protest at the last moment against the rate of interest to credit societies which looked like giving trouble but fizzled out. The English part of the Rates Bill is through committee without much trouble. They had one day on the Scotch part on Monday and broke the back of the opposition; we take it again tomorrow.

I met Herbert Samuel at the Balliol Gaudy on Friday last and had a talk with him about Palestine. He thinks it is going well. The Jewish immigrants come from Poland, Ukraine and Roumania and are young fellows of the middle class full of zeal who settle to agriculture willingly. Bolsheviks they clear out quietly. He expects to continue a benevolent despotism as democratic institutions have been turned down. Men of all creeds work quite happily together in the local police. Asquith spoke at Balliol. I expected a treat but he was very feeble.

Went up on Monday to Alnwick for the Royal at Newcastle. A house party of big guns. Northumberland very hospitable. It was worth the journey to see such a wonderful old feudal castle. Saw the show in great comfort and came back yesterday night. Cabinet this morning. Curzon reported that the French are more difficult than ever over the Ruhr. Lloyd Graeme says all the trade reports are as gloomy as can be and that some European settlement is vital to us. We shall have to take a line that the French will resent.

Sunday 15 July Rates Bill got third reading on Wednesday last. It has passed very easily considering that the Scotch clauses give relief direct to the landlord.

The event of the past week has been the announcement as to policy with regard to the Ruhr. The trouble there is generally admitted to be doing immense harm to our trade just as it was showing some signs of recovery. There has been a good deal of discussion of the subject in the Cabinet. Curzon produced a draft that struck us all as not sufficiently friendly to France. The P.M. produced an alternative and eventually it was left to the two to concoct the exact form between them. It is contemplated that in default of agreement we should send a separate note to Germany. I asked Lloyd Graeme what the result is likely to be if we do so while France remains in the Ruhr. He expects a revulsion in France against Poincaré when the French find European opinion against them. I rather fear the result might be the exact opposite. The announcement was well received in the House. There may be ten or twenty of the Gretton type out against it.

Sunday 22 July Much time has been spent on Cabinet consideration of the notes to Germany and the Allies. The result on the whole has been to make them very civil to France. Curzon seems to think the French will be delighted with them, but doubts German acquiescence.

I had a talk the other day with Ramsay Macdonald on agricultural wages. He rather surprised me by telling me he was all against wages boards.

Sunday 29 July No reply yet from France or Belgium. The principal excitement of the week has been the 'Worthy' puff.[16] I don't know the inner history of it. I asked Neville Chamberlain if he knew the man who did it. He said: 'Yes of course, but I can't imagine his doing it while I was there.' On Wednesday Mitchell Banks made a slashing sort of platform speech on the Kenya question which so irritated Wedgwood that he came across to the front bench below the gangway and kicked Banks on the shins and called him a 'dirty swine.'[17]

I am having a lot of trouble over the question of a tax on malting barley. I shall probably appoint a committee to try to find a way out.

Friday 3 August House adjourned yesterday. There was a long discussion in the Cabinet about the Navy's Air Force on Tuesday. The decision was in favour of the Air Force contention by a fair majority.[18] The Admiralty worked the press over it for all they were worth. Bridgeman was called on with the Attorney and R. Cecil to inquire into the disclosure of documents from the Admiralty. There is to be a debate on the main subject in the autumn. As to the Ruhr the French and Belgian replies are as unsatisfactory as can be. Our policy at present is confined to publishing the despatches. Curzon to my surprise wants the matter discussed by the League of Nations.

More trouble over breeding cattle. Bledisloe is writing to *The Times* protesting, and the Royal has passed a resolution on the subject objecting to all imports of breeding cattle.

Lloyd Graeme at the last Cabinet produced a scheme for a duty on silk and other articles, but the matter was deferred.

Friday 10 August A Cabinet yesterday to consider the reply to the French. The P.M. and Curzon had prepared a draft that everyone else considered too combative towards the French. They agreed to modify it. Curzon is going away for a three week cure and is going to see Poincaré on his way back. Meanwhile it looks as if Germany may collapse. I see no hope of getting France to change her attitude in the least. We are making it clear that we are not prepared to renounce all claims either on Germany or the Allies.

Sunday 16 September Everyone has been and still is holidaymaking. I have had more newspaper correspondence over Canadian cattle. Pretyman made a useful contribution to the discussion. Strachie seized the chance of having a political dig at me.

Italy and Greece have provided the sensation of the summer. I think the factor that has brought the trouble to what seems a satisfactory conclusion is that France is much impressed by the anxiety of the smaller nations that the League of Nations should not be flouted. That made Poincaré press Mussolini to name a date for evacuation of Corfu.[19]

Lucy and I have just spent a couple of days at Boulogne where I attended the 'Grande Semaine du Poisson' as Minister of Fisheries. French hospitality was immense and almost embarrassing. I was received with a band playing the National Anthem and a guard of honour of sailors. Déjeuners and diners of course. Poincaré came down on Thursday. There is no doubt as to his popularity. His reception was most enthusiastic. His programme was well arranged, but the minor staff work was badly done. The progress round the exhibition for instance was a regular hustle. I sat next Poincaré at the dinner. I congratulated him on his reception. He said he knew he was very popular now, but the French were very fickle. He envied English Ministers their holiday; he said a French premier never got a holiday, but then he did not go on so long as a rule. He was not talkative on the whole. He has an escort of mounted gendarmes, the ships were dressed and altogether the arrangements were such as we make for royalty but not for Prime Ministers. I had to make a speech in French at the dinner. I had it carefully prepared and read it out. It really went down very well. Maurice the head of the Fishery Department was a first rate G(eneral) S(taff) O(fficer).[20]

Thursday 11 October Have been kept busy at the economic conference. Bruce, the Australian P.M., made rather a notable speech on Tuesday strongly for tariff and preference. Stanley Jackson lunched with me that day. He says Lloyd George and F.E., with the Rothermere press will go strongly for protection. He thinks we must go for it first even if it involves an immediate election. I said tariff for manufacturers, subsidy for wheat. I have had talks with Strutt and Pretyman who both advocate subsidy. I had previously proposed it in a memorandum to the P.M. for his interview with the Farmers Union. That came off this afternoon. After a long paper from the N.F.U. had been read the P.M. asked them what they suggested, and eventually they agreed to put up a scheme. Earlier in the day we had a meeting at the Colonial Office on the cattle question. The Canadians Grisdale and Marshall were most fierce and we did not get much forrader.

Tuesday 23 October Cabinet today. The P.M. stated that he meant to announce at Plymouth that he was going for a tariff. He considered an election within six months would be necessary. The chief objection came from Bob Cecil. Derby took it much more happily than I expected. Curzon did not at all like the idea of an early election, and was doubtful how the country would take the new policy. The P.M. said he would subsidise food, not protect it.

Sunday 11 November Ten days ago Bonar died. Very generally mourned. The crowd on the day of his funeral was remarkable when one remembers how little he advertised himself or was advertised in his lifetime. Cancer which had been in his throat went down and poisoned his lungs. He had a great influence for good during the Coalition. He used to get his way with L.G. without a fuss. It was after his departure that the Coalition got into trouble. He certainly did a big thing for the party a year ago.

I had a talk with Maclachlan the other day about election chances on the tariff programme. He said he had not evidence enough to make a prediction. The farmers have put a programme of £1 an acre subsidy on arable land with a 30/- minimum wage. Maclachlan thought that would go down like anything. The scheme has been referred to a Cabinet committee. I have just had a talk to Salisbury who is in favour of a subsidy to all agricultural land arable or not. There was a Cabinet on Friday when question of an election was discussed. Most of the House of Commons men were for one at once. Amery wanted to wait till the budget had been brought in. Curzon, R.Cecil and Salisbury want to defer as long as possible. On that day Ludendorf had just seized power in Bavaria. Since then he has collapsed, so that the foreign situation is not so critical.[21] Jackson and Hall are for an election at once. I impressed on the P.M. the necessity for a very early statement on agriculture, and that in case of an early election our candidates must be warned not to pledge themselves to exempt particular articles from a general tariff.

Friday 16 November   Parliament dissolved today. The P.M. announced on Tuesday. After a lot of talk I have got the agricultural programme practically on N.F.U. lines. I announced it at Cirencester on Wednesday night. I had a very good meeting. Went to Isle of Wight yesterday and had good meetings at Ryde and Newport. The feeling in the House on Tuesday was very curious. At lunch time our people were very angry at the idea of an election. As the afternoon went on they got better and by dinner time were quite keen. There has been a good deal of newspaper excitement about the approaches to Austen and F.E. The P.M. asked me on Tuesday morning what I thought. I told him the party would certainly resent the return of F.E. He said the latter was ambitious to leave a name as a great Lord Chancellor. I saw Derby just afterwards. He said it was decided that F.E. should come back and did not like it at all. I told him I thought it had not been decided yet. In the House that afternoon the party soon let it be known how much they objected. The Ulstermen said they would not take the whip if he was in the Government. Austen said he and F.E. stood together; a great pity. Everyone would be glad to have Austen back. There is a good deal of resentment in the party at not having been consulted about the protection policy and the dissolution. But there have been no resignations from the Government. Even Bob Cecil has come into line more or less. Clarke the Liberal member for the Isle of Wight crossed with me in the boat. He said a very curious situation was likely to arise among the reunited Liberals. Asquith is likely to lose his seat at Paisley and his followers would not have L.G. for leader.

Wednesday 12 December   I lost my seat at Bridgwater the figures being:

Morse	13,778
Sanders	12,347

I never held better meetings and was never better backed by my supporters. Outwardly all seemed very rosy, but the canvass told another tale and I was not much surprised at my defeat. A Labour candidate withdrew on the nomination day and the Labour party voted solidly Liberal. The new division is worse than the old Bridgwater Division, the western portion being Radical.

The general result came as a surprise to me. I thought we'd keep our majority. Liberals certainly managed to frighten the women with the idea of 'dear everything'. The P.M. at first meant to resign at once. Worthy, Joynson Hicks and Lloyd Graeme wanted him to do so, and hoped to get some combination under Balfour or Austen to keep Labour out. Willie Bridgeman went down to Chequers on Sunday and strongly urged him to meet Parliament. On Monday the P.M. saw the King, and the latter told him he ought to go on. At a Cabinet yesterday everyone approved. There was no sort of ill feeling shown by anyone. In the evening the P.M. told us he had seen Asquith who said it was the right course to take. Joynson Hicks said he had good information that Asquith dreaded the Labour party just as much as he did. There will no doubt be much intrigue before Parliament meets, but my own impression is that Liberals will support Labour. I am asked to carry on, as we shall probably be out by 18 January.

CHAPTER 12 NOTES

1   Lord Farquhar's mental illness caused the party great difficulties for a time, since party funds were lodged in accounts at his personal disposal. The problem was solved only by his death but, henceforth, all party funds were held in trust by at least three trustees, with provision in each trust for majority voting.

2   Younger had become a Viscount, a signal reward from Bonar Law for services rendered to the party over the past few years and a reply to those like Birkenhead who regarded Younger as one of the chief sources of trouble.

3   Griffith-Boscawen, standing at Mitcham, was defeated on the issue of the decontrol of housing. Charles Masterman had been a prominent Liberal whose career, like Griffiths-Boscawen's, was wrecked by successive election defeats.

4   George Tryon was a lifelong expert on pensions: he was Parliamentary Secretary for Pensions 1920–22, Minister of Pensions 1922–3, 1924–9 and 1931–5, and after a brief foray into other fields, his last post was Under Secretary for Pensions in 1940.

5   During February, *The Times* serialised Volume One of *The World Crisis*, the first of a long series of political memoirs of World War I drawing on government material.

6   Oliver Locker-Lampson had been P.P.S. to Austen Chamberlain and a close friend of Birkenhead; widely regarded as an intriguer and one of the most intransigent of the coalitionist Conservatives.

7   Labour had gained Liverpool Edge Hill on 6 March, without even having contested it the previous year, and the government had also lost Mitcham and Willesden East on 3 March.

8   Hon. F.S. Jackson, cricketer and soldier, had been a Conservative M.P. since 1915, known as 'Jacker'; Admiral Sir Reginald 'Blinker' Hall had been Director of Naval Intelligence during the war and a Conservative M.P. since 1918. Both were M.P.s and so neither could regard the job as full-time; in retrospect, neither appointment was particularly successful.

9   K. Middlemas and J. Barnes, *Baldwin*, p. 86.

10 Boyd-Carpenter had only just become Financial Secretary to the Treasury; the dispute was over the recommendations of the Lytton committee as to the employment of ex-servicemen in government departments. The government was thought to be delaying the implementation of their report by setting up another enquiry with impossibly wide terms of reference.

11 J.F. Hope was Deputy Speaker and Chairman of Ways and Means.

12 Art O'Brien, previously de Valera's London agent, had been arrested on the orders of W.C. Bridgeman, the Home Secretary, but the High Court had ordered his release in view of the complicated tangle of nationality laws in relation to a citizen of the Irish Free State in 1923. Bridgeman persisted in his campaign against Irishmen as undesirable aliens, and O'Brien was duly re-arrested a fortnight later. Tom Jones greeted this news warmly on May 22: 'Ran into Bridgeman, full of worries about the Irish deportees and the Indemnity Bill. I said I was glad Art O'Brien had been re-arrested as he was a treacherous villain.' (Thomas Jones, *Whitehall Diary*, vol.1, 237, London 1969)

13 J.T.W. Newbolt was a prominent left-winger, Communist M.P. for Motherwell, 1922–3. Edward Fitzroy was Deputy Chairman of Ways and Means.

14 Mond was a leader of the Liberal moderates and Lambert a prominent radical and had been chairman of the Asquitheans.

15 W.M.R. Pringle was a leader of the radical wing of Liberalism.

16 A paper on the political career and achievements of Sir Laming Worthington-Evans, the Postmaster General, had been circulated by the Post Office, raising the whole question of government public relations machinery.

17 Mitchell Banks had made an outspokenly imperialist speech in which he attacked Wedgwood's 'friends' as being unpatriotic. *The Times*, 26 July 1923.

18 These debates were about the control of the air forces to be used for coastal flying and in cooperation with the Navy, sparked off by the interim report of the Salisbury Committee on Defence which had

decided in favour of an integrated and unified air force – in face of the bitter opposition of the Admiralty. K. Middlemas and J. Barnes, *Baldwin*, p. 320.

19 This was also the view of Amery, cited by Maurice Cowling, *op.cit.*, p. 301.
20 H.G. Maurice had been in charge of Fisheries at the Ministry of Agriculture since 1912 and was a civil service protegé of Sir Robert Morant.
21 This was the abortive Munich *putsch*, now more often linked with Hitler than with Ludendorff.

Chapter 13   1924 'The feeling is all against socialism'

Monday 14 January   I have had much trouble over foot and mouth disease which has been very bad in Cheshire. However, I have succeeded in carrying on the slaughter policy and the Treasury has been liberal as to taking over the cost. It is rather hard under the circumstances that it should fall to me to have to stop hunting over most of the country. The N.F.U. were very strong that it must be done.

There is no doubt that the Government is to be turned out. Asquith's speech at the National Liberal Club has made it clear that he is not open to a deal and he told the P.M. so privately. That has put a stop to any overtures. Worthy, J.Hicks and Lloyd Graeme in the Cabinet favoured some such attempt, but were sat on. There has been much discussion over the King's speech. On the whole it is a conciliatory document. The question of whether protection remains the policy of the party is still open. The City is very frightened at the idea of a Labour Government and shares have fallen a lot. It is said that a good many Liberals don't like it, but I expect few will refrain from voting. Curzon has been rather unnecessarily provocative to France about the separatist Government in the Palatinate. It has not come before the Cabinet, but I doubt if his action is approved by most Ministers.

I have definitely given up Bridgwater.

Wednesday 23 January   Cabinet yesterday morning after the decision of the night before.[1] The P.M. went straight to the Palace to resign. New Cabinet announced last night. We all said farewell to the King this morning. I wrote last night to Noel Buxton my successor, who was at Harrow with me, to ask him if he would like to come down and be introduced by me. He came and was most grateful saying he was the most fortunate of his colleagues, no one else having been treated in the same way. He says Macdonald's idea is to show how respectable they are. The King seems to have been favourably impressed with Macdonald. Chelmsford's coming in has surprised everyone and no one more than myself. I knew him well at Oxford and read in the Chambers with him more than 30 years ago. I never expected him to do such a thing.[2]

The Liberals are said to be far from happy!

214

Sunday 13 April I have been getting a good bit of hunting since leaving office. The Labour Government's line has been great moderation. Many of our people are not anxious to get them out too soon. The Liberals are splitting up. I have been surprised to find how many of our people were backing Winston at Westminster. Jackson tells me Freddy Guest has already mapped out a little plan of seats where Conservatives and his friends can combine. As usual the giving is mostly to be from us. It seems unlikely that any Liberals who come over can carry their associations with them. I had a long talk with Hastings the Attorney General on Friday. Personally he is having a dog's life. He thinks our people can turn the Government out whenever they wish, but expects to hold on till November.[3]

In our party there is complaint that things are run too much by a little clique; Amery, Lloyd Graeme, Davidson, and rank and file never consulted.

Tuesday 24 June I have now been adopted as candidate for the Wells Division. The Conservatives there are playing up very well. Burford, the former Conservative member, got beaten at the last election. He is a Taunton farmer and representative of the N.F.U. It was not until it was absolutely clear that the association would not have him again that I agreed to come forward. Some of the farmers are rather sore. I have been trying to stir our people up about the Bill to put women on the register on same terms as men.[4] It will do us a lot of harm. I wrote Baldwin and Monsell and have talked to W.Evans, Neville Chamberlain and several of the whips. I am now assured that even if it passes the Commons the Lords will not let it go through; but the matter is difficult because so many of our people have pledged themselves to the principle. I gather that Baldwin is rather fading out. He hardly expresses an opinion at the Shadow Cabinet. I asked W.Evans who really pulls the strings. He says J. Hicks has more influence than anyone else.

The death is just announced of Royce, Labour M.P. for Spalding.[5] He had been Conservative candidate and was Conservative Chairman before 1918. Shortly before that election he came to me at the Central Office wanting a candidate. From my list he picked 'Paddy' Hannon, but when he took him down the Association rejected him and adopted another man. Royce himself then stood as Labour, got in and has been in ever since.

I had a talk with Neville Chamberlain last night. He thinks the West Country is the only place where the party is gaining ground. Douglas Hogg[6] says we shall lose seats in London. My own belief is that they are unduly pessimistic.

Tuesday 29 July   I lunched yesterday with Stanley Jackson to meet party representatives from various centres and discuss question of cooperation with Liberals. With the exception of Salvidge they were all very shy about it. Jackson says he has been trying for a long time to find Winston a safe Conservative seat, but they won't have him anywhere. He expects to make an arrangement just before the election with the Asquith headquarters by which both sides quietly agree to support the other in certain selected seats against Labour.

Sunday 10 August   The Irish Boundary trouble is not at all welcome to our party. Dixon, one of the Ulster Unionists, tells me that Michael Collins actually said to him that Lloyd George took him by the arm and said: 'If you sign this treaty you'll get Fermanagh and Tyrone and the city of Derry.' On the other hand at the time the treaty was before the House of Commons Winston showed me a written opinion by F.E. that the words could only mean a rectification of the boundary not an allotment of territory.[7] I believe F.E. to be perfectly right, but the Ulstermen don't want to risk anything. Londonderry says they will do all they can to ease the position, but the leaders cannot control the wild men. Clinton tells me he does not think the Lords would throw out a Bill adopting a Commissioner. Pat Hastings tells me he expects an October election. Both the Labour party and L.G. would probably welcome the chance of fighting on that cry.

Thursday 11 December   I won my contest in the Wells Division comfortably the figures being:

Sanders	12,642
Hobhouse	8,668
Young	2,726

I had expected a good Conservative majority in the country but was surprised at its being so overwhelming. The feeling against the Russian loan business was very strong, and in the West Country the feeling is all against Socialism.

   When Baldwin formed his Government he wrote to express his regret he had not been able to give me a place. Having missed the last Parliament spoilt my prospects. The Government is generally approved, the appointment most criticised being that of Steel-Maitland.[8]

   The House opened last Tuesday. There has been no excitement. The Labour men seem much tamer than I expected. Ramsay very ineffective in his first speech. No strong note of opposition has been heard so far, L.G. as mild as milk.

Friday 19 December   House adjourned today. Week has been spent on amendments to the Address. I spoke on Egypt last Monday. The attack was so mild that little reply was wanted. Duff Cooper, 'Lady Diana's husband', made a very good maiden speech. The Liberals tried to get up some fireworks on Wednesday on the subject of Baldwin's statement as to Safeguarding of Industries Bill. They exaggerated of course, but there is sure to be trouble both over that and over the committee that is to spend a million on colonial marketing.

CHAPTER 13 NOTES

1   On 21 January, the Baldwin Government was formally defeated in the House of Commons on an amendment to the Address.
2   1st Viscount Chelmsford, a Conservative, had accepted the post of First Lord of the Admiralty in the Labour Government.
3   Churchill only narrowly failed to win the by election at Westminster, Abbey backed by some Conservatives and by moderate Liberals. 'Guest's friends' on the right of the Liberal Party were men like Colonel England, J.S. Rankin, and Austen Hopkinson. Many Conservatives felt that they were giving the Labour Government too easy a ride and Eyres-Monsell, the Chief Whip, had to deny that they were deliberately arranging for Conservative M.P.s to be absent in order to prevent the government from being defeated. (*Conservative Agents' Journal*, July 1924.) In fact, the number of Conservative absentees unpaired only exceeded the Government majority on one important vote: C.P. Cook, *The Age of Alignment*, p. 246.
4   These same private pledges, especially that given by Joynson-Hicks, were the influence that finally committed the party to equalising the franchise in 1928.
5   W.S. Royce was M.P. for Holland-with-Boston, the constituency that included Spalding; the Conservatives gained the seat after his death in a rather unusual situation.
6   Douglas Hogg, M.P. for St Marylebone and a leading London Conservative; in the event, the Conservatives gained ten seats in London in the autumn, but his gloom was widely shared in the spring.
7   There is no real doubt that the idea of a Boundary Commission was the device that enabled Lloyd George to get some form of agreement for the 1921 Treaty and it would be surprising if he had not described its implications differently to each side. Tom Jones,*Whitehall Diary*, III, p. 155.
8   Steel-Maitland's general unpopularity remained with him throughout

his career, perhaps due to his obvious ambition. Baldwin himself subsequently believed that he should have put him at the Board of Trade rather than the Ministry of Labour, to deal with the causes of unemployment rather than its consequences. K. Middlemas and J. Barnes, *Baldwin*, p. 283.

Chapter 14   1925 'The Government might stay in for 20 years'

Tuesday 16 February   House met a week ago. I saw Chelmsford one day during the recess. He told me that at a Cabinet meeting one day, the Cabinet was definitely informed that the Russian treaty negotiations were broken off. Next day the press announced that Macdonald had signed it; that was the only intimation they got.

Parliament has been quiet. Willie Bridgeman tells me he very nearly resigned over the Navy estimates; but in the end the Cabinet met him halfway. There is trouble over the proposed agricultural conference. The labourers' unions have refused to join. E. Wood wants to drop it. The prevailing feeling among agricultural M.P.s is to go on. The unions represent barely one-tenth of the labourers. Another trouble is the Trades Union levy. The party wants it, but the Government is shy. Steel-Maitland thinks it will re-unite the Labour men who are now quarrelling among themselves.[1] I saw Hewart Lord Chief Justice last night. He said the Government might stay in for 20 years if it avoided two question, viz. protection, and the House of Lords.

Wednesday 18 March   Politics have been pretty dull during this session. But business has been going on pretty rapidly. The Labour party are not clever in opposition. I have taken the chairmanship of a standing committee, and so far have found Bills sent there go through very easily. I was not in the House when Kirkwood was suspended. Ronald McNiel who was there told me Hope was unnecessarily sharp with him, and that seems the general opinion.[2] Baldwin's speech on the Political Levy Bill was very remarkable. It was not in the least oratorical but intensely human and it carried the party when most of them disagreed with him.

I made short speeches on summer time and the army estimates.

Monday 18 May   At the time of the Easter adjournment the general complaint was beginning to be heard that the Government was doing nothing. Then came the budget and now the question is how it will be possible to get the work through. Winston's budget speech was a successful effort. He kept the House interested and sometimes amused for over two hours. His long explanation of insurance proposals was unncessary and not at all lucid. But the budget is popular among Conservatives. I never thought any Chancellor would have the courage to reduce the super tax. Beaverbrook has started a press campaign against the silk duties and the insurance proposals. They say the latter are to be taken on the floor of the House. Chamberlain introduced his Rating and Valuation Bill last week. I spoke on the second reading, urging that steps be taken to deal with distrust in rural districts. It will not be easy to get it through committee in a reasonable time.

We had a meeting at House of Commons the other day at which Selborne spoke on subject of Second Chamber. I took the chair. The meeting showed the hopeless divergence of views on the subject within our own party. Selborne urges rightly that we ought to concentrate on powers, while allowing that in a Government measure reform of composition must come in.

My own impression is that the Labour position is less strained. The P.M.'s appeals for peace have had an influence on the moderates. There seems less likelihood than I thought a few months ago of a big row this summer.

Last week Bobby Monsell sounded men as to whether I would be ready to go for the Speakership when Whitley clears out. Edmund Fitzalan made the same suggestion to me six months ago. The idea is that James Hope should be moved from the Chair of Ways and Means and I should take his place. I said I would be ready to fall in with the new proposal, though I would rather have a political job.

Saturday 20 June   The Budget has gone through committee after some very late sittings. The declaration of a large section of the Labour party in favour of Imperial Preference was a pleasing feature. Winston accepted in principle an amendment that I moved exempting agricultural land from the increase in estate duty. He had promised me and Courthorpe[3] that he would do so, and I got the *Morning Post* to write a special article that morning advocating the change. But it came as complete surprise to the Opposition, and both Liberals and Labour were furious. Wedgwood Benn has put in an immense amount of work in opposition to the tariff clauses. The whole job has really fallen on his shoulders as the Liberal leaders have attended very badly.

We have held two sittings of a special committee on Second Chamber question, and it now seems evident that the general opinion is that it is impossible to defend restoration of powers without radical reconstruction.

Monday 13 July   There is a general impression that the Government is losing popularity. The campaign in the Harmsworth press is certainly having some effect. The Farmers' Union is on the warpath. I had a talk the other day with Robbins their chairman. He declared that the feeling among farmers was that the Ggovernment was going out of its way to make things worse for agriculture. They hate the Rates Bill, Tithe Bill, and Government proposal to grant a million to help Dominion imports. With another section of the party Austen is looked on as hopeless at the F.O. I went down to the P.M.'s meeting at Bradfield in Devon. He spoke about agriculture very feebly. The effect in the country has been bad but on the whole I gather that the Devon people were pleased. We seem to be heading for a row over coal. That would have the effect of pulling our party together.

Went down yesterday to the Fitzalans. The King has made over Cumberland Lodge to them. Edmund's idea was that things were going badly for the Government.

Monday 20 July   Neville Chamberlain has made concessions on the Rates Bill which have squared most of the opposition on the standing committee. I doubt their disarming hostility in the country. The Summer Time Bill was squared last Friday. The promoters of the Bill accepted an amendment of mine which satisfied everyone but the Scotch and one or two English agriculturalists. The chairman of the Farmers' Union approved.

Bridgeman told me he thought he would have to resign over the cruiser question. He thinks the old Coalition lot in the Cabinet is rather anxious to force him out. I find the feeling among the younger members of the party by no means in favour of high naval expenditure.[4]

Sunday 26 July   Bridgeman has got his way. Amery and Balfour were on his side; all the rest apparently against him. But he was determined to resign and they were not. I gather that feeling ran pretty high. It is a setback for Churchill. But the Admiralty will have to cut down elsewhere. They have not played the game in that respect up to now. I was surprised at 'Blinker' Hall saying so rather strongly.

Coal question very threatening still. George Lane Fox says there will be a strike; Betterton, Under Secretary to Labour Ministry, that there will not.

I have been in the chair in standing committee on the new Unemployment Insurance Bill. The Labour people have been on the rampage and I have had stormy times. Buchanan[5] was reported to the House for insubordination. The Speaker said it was not his job, but he delivered a homily on the subject which had a good effect. Monsell promised to give a day if necessary for a motion to suspend. We got the Bill through all right on Thursday.

J.H. Whitley to Sanders 20 July 1925

Dear Sir Robert,

I have consulted Webster, and it is clear to me that I have no power to take any action with regard to disorder in a standing committee. On your Report only the Government could move any motion and it would be debatable (probably very undesirable at this period of the session!).

I think it is best to see if the action of yourself and your committee has the desired effect. If not, it may become essential for the Government to move – even at the loss of a Parliamentary day. I cannot even reprimand a member (for something not done in the House) except if I am ordered by the House.

I am inclined to think and hope that your action will not need more than the Report lying on the Table.

It may be that we shall have to give more power to Chairmen upstairs – but the proposal would be hotly contested.

Yours truly,

J.H. Whitley

Thursday 6 August   The party is thoroughly disgusted with the coal subsidy business.[6] Bridgeman, J.Hicks and W.Evans opposed it in the Cabinet. The only support seems to come from the young Scotch Conservatives. The vote will go through all right, but the prestige of the Government has had a very great blow.

We succeeded last night in getting a promise of a grant from the Road Fund to rural district roads, by opposing the Mersey Tunnel Bill, a palpable piece of Parliamentary blackmail.

Thursday 17 November   House reassembled yesterday. During the recess there has been a series of very bitter attacks on the Government and on Baldwin primarily in the *Mail* and the *Express*. I went to the N.U. conference at Brighton thinking there might be some stormy scenes. It was just the other way. The papers had gone too far and had the effect of rallying even the discontented. Baldwin got a tremendous reception though his speech was very dull.

Just before the adjournment Ashley asked me if I would try to tackle Winston on the subject of the road fund. Winston means to lay hands on it if he can, and has as usual established a funk. I wrote to Winston early in September and got a very civil but non-committal reply. I proposed a resolution at Brighton against any raid on the road fund and it was carried unanimously.[7]

Had a talk with Bridgeman and Lane Fox last night as to the coal business. They told me that on the very day of the surrender the P.M. said to the miners: 'There can be no question of a subsidy.' W.B. put down the sudden change to influence from Buckingham Palace. Lane Fox thinks there will be a strike in May. Bridgeman inclined to think not.

Monsell told me Austen wanted to have Oliver Locker Lampson as Under Secretary and that he had stopped it.

Friday 18 December Everyone agrees that the autumn session has been particularly dull. But Government stock has certainly gone up. The election results have been remarkable and have shown how little effect the press campaign has had.[8] The Liberal party seems in a greater hash than ever. L.G.'s absence during the Safeguarding debates was noticeable and gave Ronald McNiel an opportunity for a good hit, about the best speech of the session. Philip C.-L. was not a success in conducting the Safeguarding Bill, he is too provocative; Burton Chadwick the Under Secretary was really pitiable when anything was left to him.[9]

Bull, Campbell and I went to the Cabinet Committee on House of Lords. It consisted of Cave, Winston, Peel, Birkenhead, Salisbury, J. Hicks and Hoare. Winston and F.E. want to raise difficulties; Salisbury, Cave and J. Hicks seem to mean business. The discussion was quite friendly and Cave asked us to keep in touch with them. I told them there was no chance of getting any sort of agreement among our party on subject of composition.

CHAPTER 14 NOTES

1 This was the penultimate attempt of the Conservative backbenchers to reverse the Trades Union Act of 1913 so as to end the system of contracting out. The issue was brought to a head by F.A. Macquisten's private member's bill; Baldwin dealt with it, as Sanders relates, in his famous 'Give Peace in our Time' speech. Middlemas and Branes, *Baldwin*, p. 292.

2 David Kirkwood, a leading firebrand of the left was suspended from the House of Commons for defying the authority of the chair on 5 March. There is considerable evidence that, having allowed unusual latitude to Conservative opponents of the Labour Government of 1924, the Speaker and his deputies had to be unusually tough in 1925 and 1926 in order to re-establish the authority of the chair.

3 George Courthorpe was Chairman of the Parliamentary agricutural committee, 1925–8.

4 For this see R. Rhodes James (ed.) *Memoirs of a Conservative*, pp. 211–220.

5 George Buchanan, I.L.P. activist and Labour M.P. since 1922.

6 The coal subsidy had been extended for a further nine months on 30 July 1925, 'Red Friday'. Conservatives were as disappointed as Labour

was jubilant and Lord Salisbury sternly told Baldwin that the government had lost its 'moral authority'. H. Montgomery Hyde, *Baldwin*, p. 255

7   Wilfrid Ashley, Conservative M.P. since 1906 and a contemporary of Sanders at Harrow and in the Whips' room was Minister of Transport 1924–9. This is thus a rare case of a Minister organising support from the back-benches against his own senior colleague. Sanders seems to have emerged, as over the House of Lords in 1926–7, into the same sort of independent party position that he had played in 1917–18, organising beckbenchers against their own government.

8   The government had held all three seats that it had defended in autumn by elections and, in the only one with a contest comparable to 1924, their candidate had actually increased his share of the vote.

9   Philip Lloyd-Graeme had changed his name to Philip Cunliffe-Lister in 1924 and was President of the Board of Trade in 1925; Sir Burton Chadwick was a leading shipowner and Conservative M.P.; he remained at the Board of Trade only until January 1928 and then left the Government altogether.

Chapter 15   1926 'Everyone sitting tight about coal'

Friday 19 February   Proceedings in the House have been very dull so far this session. The Labour party has been obstructing supplementary estimates, not very cleverly. We failed to get any sort of agreement in our agricultural committee on the subject of the road fund. Consequently our own motion on the subject last Wednesday was not very effective. The feeling on the subject is strong, but Ashley tells me that Winston is not going to steal so much as he first intended. He is going to put on extra taxation for cars. The feeling about coal is much happier. Bridgeman says there will be no strike. George Lane Fox thinks there will be, but that other trades will not come in. Pat Hastings says it can be avoided if great tact is used and no one is irritated unnecessarily.

Wednesday 24 March   Dullness continues. There was a good debate on the Economy Bill. Neville C.'s answer to L.G. was the best thing he has done yet. He is being spoken of as the future leader of the party. I dined with Winston that night. He said he should never again try substituting one tax for another as in case of death duties for super tax last year. You get cursed for the death duties while getting no gratitude from the super tax payers.

We had a curious episode in connection with our House of Lords business. At a meeting of our big House of Commons committee a motion against any retention of the hereditary principle in a reformed House was carried. However, we decided to go on a deputation to the P.M. to urge him to deal with the matter next session. Some of us met a little committee of interested peers the other day; Sumner, Midleton, Northumberland and Fitzalan. I was struck by Northumberland agreeing that the Lords would be content with 100 in a new chamber.

Everyone is sitting tight about coal at present. I had a talk with Tom Shaw and was surprised how anxious he was that the matter should be squared. The general feeling in House of Commons is certainly that it will be. Personally I expect a strike.

There has been quite a lot of excitement over the League of Nations fiasco.[1] Austen addressed a big meeting in a committee room before the first debate in the House. He made it quite clear that he wanted to increase the membership of the Council. In that the feeling of all parties was against. And at Geneva he had to go against any increase. I can find no evidence that Brazil did not act on her own. The importance of the whole thing seems to me exaggerated. There is no sign that the peace of Europe is in any way endangered.

Thursday 22 April   There has been a great outcry on the Labour benches against the Economy Bill. I think it will probably gain them votes in the country, though my agent tells me it will have very little effect. With regard to coal, George Lane Fox expects a strike. He told me Baldwin had told Thomas that if there was anything in the nature of a general strike the Government might have an immediate general election on the question of clipping the wings of the trades unions. That frightened Thomas a good deal.

Thursday 6 May   We are now in the midst of a General Strike. In the House of Commons things have been very calm. Speeches moderate on all sides. I think the debates have made it clear that the Trade Union committee that proposed to negotiate had no authority whatever. The front bench Labour men are evidently in a blue funk. They would love to be out of it. I am told the real authority is in the hands of Purcell.[2] Thomas has been talking very big. He cut a really miserable figure yesterday. He made public use of a confidential document and made statements about his interviews with the P.M. that were absolutely untrue. I hear the P.M. will be prepared to repeal the Trades Disputes Act when this is over.

Sunday 16 May   The most notable thing of the debates on the strike has been Simon's speeches on the illegality of the general strike. Following on them came a decision last Tuesday by Astbury[3] in a Chancery court that the Trades Disputes Act did not apply to such cases. Next day the General Strike was called off. After a little friction the railways are now going again, Thomas & Co. having signed the most humiliating document admitting that they had committed a wrongful act. Lloyd George provoked an outburst from our side one day when he tried to make trouble about the *British Gazette* not having printed a pronouncement by the Archbishop of Canterbury and other ministers of religion. Horne and I made representations to the whips that it would be much better if our fellows would keep quiet and Stanley made an appeal to that effect at the meeting of the 1922 Committee. It had a very good effect. On Thursday Macdonald was listened to in most chilling silence. Their own side are too much down to cheer.

Meanwhile Government business has gone on rather quickly. The Merchandise Marks Bill came on for second reading on Wednesday.

Sidney Webb was moving the rejection, but all the Labour party cleared off leaving absolutely empty benches behind him. I was called on next and said there had been nothing like it since 'the boy stood on the burning deck'.

Wednesday 9 June   The coal strike goes quietly on. Except that there is a bad train service it is not making much difference to life in the West End. But of course many industries are hit. It is now more than ever clear that all the talk of a possible settlement before the strike was absolute eyewash. At present there seems to be an absolute deadlock. and the miners are getting considerable support from outside. Their propaganda has been worked cleverly enough to make many people think they are being badly treated. The Hammersmith by election was regrettable. But the result was largely due to the adoption of Gluckstein as the Conservative candidate. The choice was that of the local people, against the wishes of the Central Office.

There has been some discussion in the papers about Blain leaving the Central Office. He confided to me that he was doing so because Jackson would not support him in financing the organisation of derelict districts, in Wales for example. He said Linlithgow left for the same reason. Also that George Younger supported him in his proposals for expenditure. I saw Younger a day or two later. He did not confirm what Blain said and expressed the opinion that the latter was not worth the £5,000 a year given him by the party.[4]

The ructions in the Liberal party have caused a good deal of amusement. Asquith certainly has the support of the vast majority of Liberals in the country, but L.G. has that of the majority of the party in the House. It is comic that his majority depends on the adherence of Freddy Guest and his friends. F.G. told me he meant to support L.G. if he got certain assurances. He said: 'I would sooner trust him than Simon, wouldn't you?' I refrained from committing myself.

Saturday 3 July   The coal strike still goes on and causes comparatively little inconvenience. In the debates in the House there has been carefully engineered disorder. After the debate last Tuesday when the P.M., Bridgeman and Lane Fox were accused of voting for their own personal interest, Jos Wedgwood wrote to Lane Fox expressing his indignation at his party's attitude, and saying he regarded those three as the most honourable men in the House. There has been a good deal of comment on the Speaker's leniency. James Hope tells me it is carefully considered. He said to J.H.: 'These fellows want to pose as martyrs, and I don't want to give them the chance.'

Wednesday 14 July   Rowdyism was very bad last week. The climax was the scene in the House of Lords. Feeling against the Speaker is increasing. On Monday he read out in answer to a question a strong expression of regret about the House of Lords affair. The debate on Monday was very subdued. Both in that and the subsequent discussion on the coal estimate the Labour people seemed to have their tails down. But there is no sign yet of an end to the strike.

We are to go on a deputation to the P.M. on the 20th on the subject of the House of Lords. It falls on me to introduce. I am to speak and so is Lord Midleton. Our young Conservatives are as troublesome as ever. Skelton, who is on our committee, has now come to the conclusion that nothing ought to be done at all for fear of the Government being thought reactionary.[6]

Bobby Monsell went to the Speaker after the House of Lords affair and seems to have told him pretty plainly what he thought. When Bobby is annoyed his speech is very plain. Instead of telling him to mind his own business the Speaker took it quite calmly and afterwards wrote a letter of regret to him.[7]

Wednesday 21 July   Yesterday we had our deputation to the P.M. on the House of Lords question, about 100 M.P.s and 50 peers. All went well. I was rather afraid there might be general discussion and trouble. But after Midleton and I had spoken, the P.M. replied promising that the matter should be dealt with during the present Parliament. I thanked him and the whole thing was over in twenty minutes.

The electricity committee will probably finish tomorrow. It has been a long affair. The obstruction has been very cleverly worked by George Balfour and Nall. They have talked a lot themselves and have been very successful in drawing the Labour members. The latter support the Bill, but will not keep quiet.[5]

Wednesday 10 November   House met again yesterday. Coal strike still going on. That has been the sole political topic of the recess. It has struck me that the miners have lost the amount of public sympathy that was with them in the summer. On the other hand there is a lot of feeling that the Government ought to have stopped the strike somehow. In Somerset one result has been a heavy fall in the price of cheese. The farmers really are hit hard by it.

At Scarborough where the N.U. conference was held the cry was all for legislation to curb the trades unions. The Government will have to do something about it, and will probably get into trouble over it. I moved the House of Lords resolution, which went through without the least enthusiasm. The week after Cave, who was Chairman of the Cabinet committee on the subject, saw a little joint committee of the two houses that we had formed in response to a suggestion of the P.M. He told us the Cabinet committee's plan. It was very nearly the same as our own. We pressed on him the importance of getting on with it at once.

CHAPTER 15 NOTES

1 A French condition to the admission of Germany to the League of Nations in the aftermath of Locarno was the admission of Spain, Poland and Brazil to the League's Council as counterweights. Austen Chamberlain supported France but there was great opposition in Parliament, in the League and from the League of Nations Union. A compromise was finally agreed, but Brazil left the League rather than accept it.

2 A.A. Purcell, Labour M.P. from 1923 and President of the International Federation of Trades Unions, was a favourite bogeyman for Conservatives. Although a fellow-traveller and a stalwart of the Minority Movement, he was also under attack from the leaders of the Communist Party for his moderation. Roderick Martin, *Communism and the British Trades Unions 1924–33*, p. 80.

3 Sir John Astbury was a Judge in Chancery and had been a Liberal M.P. 1906–10. It is curious how many of the important legal pronouncements on the General Strike were delivered by Liberals – Asquith, Simon and Samuel as well as Astbury.

4 Sir Herbert Blain, Principal Agent at Central Office 1924–1926, had a stormy time there. He was an almost non-political efficiency expert who had done much to tighten up the organisation of Central Office and the party agents. He withdrew his resignation on this occasion, after receiving an assurance of support from Baldwin, finally leaving at the end of the year, after being 'sacked' by Davidson in a curious episode (R. Blake, *The Conservative Party from Peel to Churchill*, p. 231.) In the end, Davidson pursued Blain's policy so far that only 25 constituencies did not run Conservative candidates in 1919. Second Marquess of Linlithgow was Deputy Chairman of the Conservative party, 1924–6, Sanders' successor in the post.

5 George Balfour and Sir Joseph Nall were both industrialist M.P.s critical of the government's intervention in industry. The tactic of provoking inexperienced Labour M.P.s to speak by making wild statements, enabled opponents of a Bill to prolong its committee stage by allowing each of them to speak against the Bill each time somebody on the other side could be provoked into speaking in favour of it.

6   Noel Skelton, Conservative M.P. from 1922 and acknowledged leader
    of the Y.M.C.A. group of M.P.s. The author of *Constructive Conser-*
    vatism.
7   There were disorderly scenes in both Houses of Parliament on 8 July,
    begun in the Commons after an unexpected closure motion was put by
    the government and continuing in the Lords Chamber after M.P.s were
    summoned to the ceremony for Royal Assent. The Speaker had
    refused to take action against M.P.s for their conduct in the House of
    Lords. *The Times*, 9 July 1926.

Chapter 16   1927 'The Trades Union Bill absorbs attention'

Sunday 20 February   Since the end of the coal strike things have been pretty quiet in politics. It is curious that though the strike was the most disastrous blunder the trades unions ever made it has temporarily at least strengthened the Labour party in the country. Before Xmas both Park Goff and Cuthbert Headlam told me that in the event of an immediate election we should hardly hold a seat in the North. I had a talk in January to Maclachlan who had just become Chief Agent. He said he thought we had lost ground, but he thought is was only a temporary phase.[1]

The House met on 10 February. So far things are quiet even to dullness. The Labour people insisted on dividing on the China question against the wish of their leaders. Thomas spoke in favour of the Government and then paired against it. I spoke on the Liberal amendment to the Address about rating, and on a Tuesday evening motion on the Lords question. We did not carry the latter to a division as we had not whipped for it and the Labour people were there in force. We had a meeting the other day in Sumner's room and decided that resolutions on the subject should be introduced in the Lords if the Government did not object.

I was nominated by the Executive Committee last Tuesday for the Chairmanship of the National Union. Davidson said that Gretton the senior Vice Chairman wished to retire – Gretton told me afterwards that he did not wish to retire at all but that they were kicking him out.[2] The P.M. told me before the meeting that he wanted me to take it on. George Younger tells me that the party fund is now less than a million and lower than L.G.'s.

Sunday 13 March   I was duly elected Chairman of the N.U. Gretton continued as a Vice Chairman after a ballot. The meeting was quiet enough. It turned down the extension of women's franchise, and a motion in favour of the Factory Bill.

Wargrave told me the other day that he had been talking to Margesson, one of the whips, and asked him who would succeed if anything happened to the P.M. Margesson said: 'No doubt about it. Willie Bridgeman.'

Last Wednesday Neville Chamberlain addressed the Unionist agricultural committee on his Poor Law proposal. There must have been more than

100 there. They were all quite civil and friendly. But with the exception of Jack Hills and one London member who had got in there the whole committee was dead against the Minister. I had a talk afterwards with Bobby Monsell. He wants resolutions passed against upsetting the rural guardians and suggests that I should see the P.M. on the subject.

I saw the P.M. a few days later. He said: 'Get your committee to say what they honestly think. I have told Neville we cannot upset the party to pass his Bill.'

Monday 25 April   The budget has been a success. I should think that economically it is quite neutral, but it has very cleverly got us through present troubles without imposing fresh taxation. It has been a great disappointment to the Labour party. On the whole their stock seems rather low at the present moment. Their attitude to China has certainly done them harm.[3] The Trades Union Bill has certainly done a lot to please the malcontents in our own party. How far it will hurt us in the industrial districts is hard too say. Clem Edwards[4] who was one of our own tame Labour people tells me it will absolutely ruin our party. On the other hand the Labour men in the N.U. are enthusiasts over it.

There was a great struggle in the Cabinet over the vote for flappers business. Philip Cunliffe Lister told me that at the last moment he hoped to get the 25-year limit. Our own Central Office people are all against that. But they expect the extension as proposed to do us harm in the industrial districts. The fact is that hasty election promises have got us into a mess and we must just make the best of it.

I won the Heavyweight Point to Point for Lords and Commons at Leighton Buzzard on 9 April riding my own horse Black Button. There was only one other heavyweight starting and I had an easy ride, but in my sixtieth year it was a pleasing experience.

Wednesday 27 April   I saw F.E. last night. He was in a great state of mind about the flapper vote. He put the trouble down to Jix's answer in the House two years ago.[5] He thinks it means ruin to the party, and wants me to take steps against it. I told him the only way of escape was for the House of Lords to upset the Bill. That he did not cotton to at all. Said the Commons had made the mess and must get out of it. He says both F.E. and Winston were very much opposed to the idea. It was the P.M. who carried it in the Cabinet. He said the difference between the vote at 21 and 25 meant only 800,000 women.

Saturday 21 May   The Trades Union Bill absorbs attention now. It is very remarkable how the temperature has fallen as the debates have gone on. At first Ministers could hardly get a hearing. Now the proceedings are almost dull. Our reports from the country are that the Labour campaign against the Bill is falling very flat. The raid on Arcos is the other main topic. I have not been able to discover what has been found there.[6] The Labour people seem to be a good deal frightened about it.

I met Sir Francis Aglen, the deposed chief of Chinese customs, the other night. He takes a gloomy view. Says we ought never to have gone out of Hankow. It has damaged our prestige enormously. Headlam tells me the decision was made by the naval officer on the spot. Sir F.A. thinks there is little to choose between the various leaders. They are all ruffians. Unless a big man emerges civil war may go on for 20 years.

George Courthorpe who is Chairman of the Unionist agricultural committee has caused a bit of a flutter by putting down a protectionist motion at the Council of Agriculture. The Unionist committee are protesting, and it is remarkable how very strong they are against it. G.C. has now made it plain he speaks for himself only.

Saturday 2 July The House of Lords question is very much to the fore now. I approached the P.M. some time ago as to a resolution in the House of Lords. He said the difficulty was that whoever spoke for the Government would have to make some pronouncement and we wanted to avoid that at present. He said he looked on the question as the most difficult one in politics and evidently wanted to avoid it altogether. I reminded him of his promise to the deputation last year that he would deal with it in the present Parliament and asked him what I should tell my friends in the Lords who were submitting the motion. He said tell them to consult Salisbury. The debate came on on 20 June. Fitzalan moved. Early in the debate Cave announced the Government policy and F.E. next day said they meant to proceed with it next session. Some papers suggested that it was a put up job. As a matter of fact Fitzalan knew nothing about it. More than that neither the Chief Whip, nor the Chairman of the Party nor the King had been informed. The plan is quite different from and much inferior to that which Cave showed us last autumn. But it has sufficed to cause a lot of excitement. Monsell is furious. A lot of Conservatives, mostly youthful, are on the warpath about it. There was a motion on the subject at the Council of the National Union on Tuesday. There Shirley Benn and Spender Clay came out against the Government proposals.[7] The motion in support of the Government was carried by a large majority, but the opposition was sufficiently strong to make a good deal of impression. The Labour party are moving a vote of censure next Wednesday. I am afraid the Government is sure to run away more or less.

Monday 11 July On Tuesday last I moved the amendment to the Finance Bill on the subject of the Road Fund. We had put a lot of pressure on

Winston beforehand, and got a little more out of him than I expected. The agricultural committee had been very much on the warpath, but were quite pleased with the result. The debate on the Lords left the matter in a very unsatisfactory state. The malcontents were clever in putting up John Buchan.[8] He got in early with a maiden speech. He took the old fashioned Tory line that the House of Lords was the best assembly we could have and ought not to be interfered with. The Government was climbing down all through. I spoke under rather unfavourable circumstances. L.G. had just made a long and impassioned oration and people cleared out after it. Philip Cunliffe-Lister says they will go on with proposals about the Speaker and money bills. I am more inclined to think they will run away altogether.

Thursday 10 November   My chief political experience during the recess was taking the chair at the N.U. conference at Cardiff. It went off very well. The delegates were unusually anxious to support the Government even when it was obvious that they did not agree with it! This happened with regard to agriculture and education. In both cases the Minister in question was quite out of sympathy with the audience, but they voted for him. On the House of Lords question Londonderry was enlisted in the cause of the Y.M.C.A.[9] but the audience was all against him. In fact they would hardly listen to his supporters. He was very annoyed as about 40 M.P.s had asked him to take it on, but very few turned up to support him. We were staying at Tredegar where we were most kindly treated. I was provided with a mount for cubbing one morning! The Baldwins there. He was in great form. Very pleased at his Canada trip. She told me she thought the Government had much better leave the Lords question to be dealt with by the Labour party.

The *Daily Mail* has been running a great agricutural stunt all the summer. Marlowe[10] told me it was being done in the interest of L.G. It has certainly done our party harm. I was approached by the *Mail* on the subject of a tax on foreign malting barley and gave them a statement in favour of the proposal. It has attracted some attention and has made the *Mail* back a policy which L.G. is bound to oppose. From all I hear the agricultural position is very serious indeed.

Friday 9 December   We got Guinness to attend the Unionist agricultural committee a fortnight ago. He foreshadowed a further grant in relief of rates. That would be a good move. The arable sub-committee have brought up a very hot report on the subject of Bledisloe's speech which we have deferred.[11] Guinness is asked to come and explain the speech. Maclachlan the Chief Agent told me he thought things were going badly in the country and was anxious I should do what I could to impress it on

Ministers. The other night at a dinner to the Central Office staff Baldwin made a speech about the L.G. and Rothermere alliance and impressed on us that we ought to do everything possible to see that the League of Nations Union did not get too much into Radical hands.

The House has been very dull. The Labour party has now learnt the art of obstruction and has been practising on the Insurance Bill. They forced a timetable and the third reading is today.

I have been engaged in trying to get some agreement on the Lords question on which the Government may act. In conjunction with Kindersley and Bourne I have been meeting Spender Clay, Apsley and Macmillan as representing the Y.M.C.A., and have probably managed a deal.

Friday 23 December House rose yesterday. The event of the last few weeks has been the Prayer Book debate. It was of course clear away from party lines, and was run by amateur whips. Wolmer was more or less in charge among our people and Slesser in the Labour party.[12] On the Monday before the debate Wolmer and I were dining together. He told me he expected a majority of over 100 in the Commons but was not sure what might happen in the Lords. I heard a good deal of the debate in the latter place. The weight of oratory was certainly for the Bill. Bishop of Durham and Archbishop of York both good. Carson not really up to form against it. In the Commons it was just the other way. W.Bridgeman very poor to start off with. Hugh Cecil also poor. He did not expect to have to argue details and failed in doing so. On the other hand Jix and Mitchell a Labour man were both really eloquent in beating the Protestant drum. About the best defence of the Bill came from Dunnico, a Nonconformist minister on the Labour benches. By dinner time I thought the Bill would be lost. A good many men on our side had not made up their minds till the last moment and were turned by the speeches. W.Nicholson and Apsley were instances.

Bledisloe came before the Unionist agricultural committee to talk about his speech. He said his ideas were his own not the Government's. He was kindly received but not impressive. The barley duty is definitely turned down. I took the opportunity of a Liberal vote of censure on the agricultural question to make a speech on what my local Farmers' Union people say they want. If the Government will relieve rates that will go a long way. I talked to Monsell on Maclachlan's view of party prospects. He told me the Factory Bill and Neville's board of guardian proposals were to be dropped. I also took an opportunity to try to impress on Winston the unpopularity of the Government. He did not much like it!

The changes in the Standing Orders as to Private Members time proposed by a committee of which I was a member have been adopted.

They were largely my proposals and were not quite in accordance with the ideas of Hugh Cecil who was Chairman of the committee.

CHAPTER 16 NOTES

1   Sir Park Goff was M.P. for Cleveland and Sir Cuthbert Headlam M.P. for Barnard Castle and a Durham County Councillor. In 1929, the Conservatives lost half of their seats in the North.

2   Gretton had been a thorn in the flesh of successive Party Chairmen, so it is not at all surprising that Davidson should have wanted to be rid of him. In the event, Sanders was elected, and Davidson explained to the Central Council that by an oversight the Executive had nominated four men for the three Vice-Chairmanships; Gretton was one of the three elected after a ballot and he went on to be Chairman in 1928 (National Union Central Council Minutes, 1 March 1927). He celebrated his triumph with some trenchant criticisms of Davidson and the party leaders (National Union Executive Committee Minutes, 15 March 1927).

3   The Government's strong action in defence of British interests in China had been attacked as imperialist by Labour spokesmen but the popular mood had still not changed so as to make such attacks effective.

4   Allen Clement Edwards, barrister and author, Liberal M.P. 1906–10 and Chairman of the National Democratic Party, 1918–20. See Roy Douglas, The B.W.L. and the N.D.P. in the *Historical Journal*, 1972. It is interesting that Sanders should refer to an N.D.P. leader as 'one of our own tame Labour people'.

5   The Government announced its intention to equalise the franchise on 13 April after several months of Cabinet dicussions. Although Joynson-Hicks had promised a Bill in the House of Commons in January 1925, Baldwin and others had given similar pledges in 1924. H.A. Taylor, *Jix, Viscount Brentford*, p. 280.

6   This was a police raid, on the Home Secretary's orders, on premises shared by Arcos Ltd and the Soviet Trade Mission. The police did not find what was expected, but they found enough to prove that the Trade Mission was being used for espionage. Montgomery Hyde, *op.cit.*, p. 282.

7   Sir Arthur Shirley Benn and H.H. Spender-Clay had been M.P.s since 1910 and were both leading figures in the National Union, Benn being a past Chairman.

8   John Buchan, the novelist, had been elected as a Conservative M.P. on 26 April. It was uncharacteristic of him to take 'the old-fashioned Tory

2   A.M. Samuel had been F.S.T. only since December 1927; Herbert Williams was even newer as Parliamentary Secretary to the Board of Trade. Churchill had balanced the budget by imposing a tax on oil, intended to cash in on the increasing popularity of motoring. His climb-down was made by distinguishing transport oil from oil used mainly for heating and lighting. Harold Macmillan, *Winds of Change*, p. 241.

3   E.A. Fitzroy, the new Speaker, had been a regular soldier in the Life Guards and had been wounded at Ypres. Sanders made only the slightest reference to this, and in a situation where it is customary to cite all of the subject's achievements. The Labour reaction says much about their attitude to soldiers by 1928.

4   The Racecourse Betting Bill of 1928 set up the Totalisator system of betting under the Racecourse Betting Board. It met stiff opposition from Opposition M.P.s who objected to any state involvement in gambling.

Chapter 18 1929 'The defeat did not come as a great surprise.

Monday 11 February Since the House resumed on 22 January we have been devoting the whole time to the committee stage of the English and Scotch Rating Bills. Neville made a very good speech to start with and has been very masterly all through. But the guillotine has reduced the debate to a farce. Any number of important clauses have gone through without discussion. On the other hand Neville has met the representatives of the local authorities and has squared things with them, putting down in his own name amendments to meet their views. On the whole substantial justice has been done, but it is not by debate in the House that it has been obtained. The precedent is a bad one and will be used against us if the Labour party come in. The debates on the whole have been very dull. Criticism has been mainly captious and there has been no sort of case made against the main features of the Bill. The leading men of both the Liberal and Labour parties have kept away and the opposition has been led by Ernest Brown for the Liberals and Greenwood for Labour.[1]

There was a row at question time last Tuesday. Howard Bury asked a question about miners refusing work, and the Labour party were furious. They shouted 'Liar' and various other opprobrious epithets. For some time the House was quite out of hand. Our people thought the Speaker was too lenient. Eventually Churchill who was in command suggested that a question should be put down for next day and peace was restored. Next day there was a wrangle for three-quarters of an hour at the end of questions, but nothing much came of it.

I announced my resignation of my seat at Xmas time. We have not yet got a candidate and no local man is available. We hope to adopt a good outsider this week.

Monday 29 April We have adopted Major A.J. Muirhead as candidate for Wells. He was recommended to me by Lord Stanley and John Buchan[2] and seems to go down very well.

Things in the House are very dull. Latterly even divisions have come to an end. Everyone's thoughts are on the election. Our Central Office is very sanguine as to the result. They adhere to the idea that we shall get a majority of 50 or 60. I had a talk the other day with Churchill. He had talked in the summer about doing a deal with Lloyd George as to seats. He tells me he sounded L.G. on the subject, but got the reply that the Liberal party was set on fighting 500 seats. He said however that L.G. was all out against the Labour party and that he was very anxious to get an assurance that the P.M. would not resign directly after an election if things went badly. The position is that L.G. would sell himself on terms, but he is still sore over the old Carlton Club incident and his price would be stiff. I had a talk one day with Freddy Guest. He tells me that about 20 Liberals who are likely to get in are giving a definite pledge that they will not support a Labour Government.

CHAPTER 18 NOTES

1   Ernest Brown had been an M.P. only since 1927 and Arthur Green-wood had been only a junior minister in 1924 but was to be Minister of Health later in 1929.
2   Lord Stanley was Deputy Chairman of the Conservative party responsible for candidates and John Buchan was head of the Central Office Education Department.

Chapter 19   1930–35: Retirement in the House of Lords

7 February 1930   A long time since I wrote. Since then among other events I have become a peer. The defeat of our party did not come as a great surprise to me. I spoke in eleven divisions during the election. Everywhere what was going against us was the new assessment. To synchronise it with the election was the worst of tactics. It is curious that the harm was done by Neville, in many ways the ablest of the Ministers. I thought Baldwin made a mistake in resigning so soon. It would have been better tactics to throw on the Liberals the responsibility of turning him out. There is a great deal of dissatisfaction with his leadership just now. Besides that Rothermere and Beaverbrook are running a very vigorous protection campaign which always makes trouble in the party. Altogether I have not known so much grousing for more than 20 years. I wrote to Baldwin about the effect any proposal to tax food would have on our west country seats. He wrote me in reply to set my mind at rest. He was going to declare against Food Taxes, and all his colleages were with him except Amery. I think the Coliseum speech has been well received on the whole. The same evening, 5 February, S.B. let go against Rothermere at a dinner of the 1922 Club.[1]

8 April 1930   Baldwin's speech proposing a referendum before food taxes gave general satisfaction at the time. It has squared Beaverbrook. When declared it was acclaimed by the party. Since then there have been the negotiations between L.G. and Snowden. No one quite knows what the terms are but there is general agreement that there has been a deal. It is reported that franchise questions are involved. I have been sitting on the Ullswater committee on that subject, and up to now the Labour party have been more opposed than we have to any proposals made by Samuel and other Liberals for P.R. and alternative vote. I was at a dinner last night given by Gretton and Hannon to welcome Neville C. on his return to England. A curious gathering: Neville, Winston, Beaverbrook, Page Croft in the chair owing to Gretton's illness. I sat between Winston and Kingsley Wood. Both think the present policy fatal from the electioneering point of view. Winston says it will keep us out for seven years. The speeches were cautious. The idea of a deal between Liberals and Labour depresses even the stalwarts. But Beaverbrook announces that he is going to preach food taxes everywhere.

23 May 1930 I made my maiden speech in the Lords on the Land Drainage Bill at the request of the N.F.U. and the Land Union and since then have moved a large number of amendments, most of which were accepted by the Government. To my mind it is easier to speak there than in the Commons. You are not interrupted and every one who is there is out for business being done.

The long postponed decision in the Ullswater committee came yesterday. Herbert Samuel moved resolutions for P.R. being adopted if any change is made. The Conservatives supported that. Labour went strongly against it. Now it is said the Lib/Lab deal is off. It remains to be seen what L.G. will do next. It is said that an election would wipe out the Liberals. Personally I doubt that. Unemployment figures are up by half a million over a year ago. That is hitting the Labour party hard. They are having trouble in their own party. So are we. Beaverbrook has come out against the referendum proposal, after having agreed to it at first.

22 March 1931 The Beaverbrook squabble still goes on. After his man got in at Paddington, an offer was made to send him the whip. After consulting Rothermere B. declined this. Then Herbert Williams was put up as candidate against him. That of course exasperated B., and he is continuing the vendetta. The St George's election has been a knock to him.[2]

At the National Union Council meeting in December I moved on behalf of the Somerset Division a vote of confidence in Baldwin. I went out of my way to challenge the opposition. But the motion was carried unanimously. At the same time it must be said Philip Lloyd Graeme tells me the state of things is rather impossible. He says S.B. is so extraordinarily idle now. He also says he would never again work with Winston as Chancellor. He defeated all tariff proposals. Bridgeman says S.B. must go on because there is no one to take his place. The only possible suggestion made at present is that Hailsham should lead the party and Neville be leader in House of Commons. Winston has gone against the official Indian policy. This is a bid for the old Tory vote, and may well be successful. This real difference in policy is small. As stated by Lloyd in the Lords last week it really boils down to the question of whether provincial and federal governments should be set up at the same time or one after the other.

Everyone agrees that the Government position is very precarious. But they continue to carry on. There were strong rumours last week that they would break up. The Liberal party is now deliberating. L.G. wants to do a deal, but it is doubtful if his own party will let him, or if the Labour party would agree to it.

7 May 1931 The position of the Government seems stronger. L.G. is giving them quite steady support. The Alternative Vote Bill is the price.[3] The line at the moment is an attack on the Lords. We have had the committee stage of the Land Utilization Bill there lately and have handled it a little roughly. Hailsham was a little too outspoken in his demands for an assurance that the question of privilege should be waived. I have been called into council by the front bench all through. It is not quite easy to reconcile the dictates of wisdom and the feelings of Banbury and a few more.

The new land tax proposals have just been launched. They are still vague, but undoubtedly dangerous. I am afraid the Conservative opposition on this subject will want a bit of screwing up. Oliver Stanley told me he thought the Conservatives would in the end be glad to get the money that way.

Beaverbrook has come into line. The motive power is said to have been a movement organised in the City to boycott the *Evening Standard*.

15 May 1931 Opposition to the land tax proposals is hardening a bit. But the Government proposes to guillotine the discussion in committee. That always makes it more difficult to get reasonable amendments accepted.

Ferguson the Canadian High Commissioner stayed last weekend at Bayford.[4] He says the Government are much more pleased with their prospects than they were six months ago. He also told me that both Thomas and Graham[5] are very anxious to have some sort of preference proposals to put before the Conference at Ottawa.

Saw Sam Hoare today. He suggested that it may be wise for the Lords to pass the Alternative Vote Bill. According to usage a dissolution ought to follow as soon as a new register is ready.

11 June 1931 I attended a meeting summoned by S.B. last week to consider the Alternative Vote Bill. About a dozen ex-Ministers, etc. The House of Commons people strong against our throwing out the Bill on second reading. Hailsham anxious to do so, but overruled. No real argument as to what ought to be done afterwards, but there is a report that Ullswater means to move to insert P.R.[6] Agreed House of Lords should reject clauses about motors and restore plural vote for Universities and City of London.

5 July 1931 At the request of Sam Hoare I put down an amendment to the Representation of the People Bill with the object of substituting P.R.

for Alternative Vote. He thought that if carried it might split Liberals and Labour when it came to the House of Commons. Liberals are beginning to think A.V. will not help them much. I put down that amendment and we had quite a good debate last Thursday. But was evident the House was not for it. So at Hailsham's suggestion I withdrew. The peers looked on it as a tactical move and they seem rather against tactics at present.

12 May 1932 The excitements of last summer took place while I was down on Exmoor. I did a good deal of speaking at the election. In the west country it was curious. Most of the contests were between Conservatives and Liberals, both professing to support the Government, and followed the old fashioned lines of 1906. We had the Big and Little Loaf and all the old free trade stuff.[7] There was an unusual amount of rowdyism. In Bristol Central Apsley could not get a hearing. Our west country Agent Tydeman was not at all happy as to our prospects. But in the result we won all along the line.

The general attitude to the Government is one of unenthusiastic toleration. Personally I have been surprised that their fiscal policy has been so vigorous. The agreement to differ as to Samuel & Co. is of course absurd; the Conservatives all want to get rid of him but he won't go.

All reports as to the future are fearfully gloomy. S.B. spoke to the N.U. Executive yesterday. He said we could not expect an early recovery; it must be a matter of years. Any currency arrangement such as Horne and Winston suggest is possible only by agreement with America and there is no present chance of getting that.[8] Further economies are very desirable but the Government has not had time to think them out, and will not have till the House has risen. The same as to debt conversion. All very straight-forward, but somewhat naive. However, it went down very well.

Sam Hoare says that when he took on at the India Office every Indian he met assumed as a matter of course that we were going out of the country at an early date.

We again have a Second Chamber committee going. This time it is of both Houses with Salisbury in the chair. The differences of opinion seem as great as ever. Gretton is on it and seems to think that the present Conservative party in the House of Commons may be much more amenable than that of four or five years ago.

23 June 1932 The Second Chamber Committee has sat every week. We decided at an early date that the Parliament Act provision of two years should be altered to two Parliaments. Then we had a very long discussion as to composition. Salisbury very anxious for some form of nomination. This eventually crystallised into nomination by those members of the Privy Council who do not sit in the Lords. In addition to the nominated element half of the House to consist of peers elected by their fellow peers. It seemed at first as if this view would have a majority. Steel-Maitland, Sir John Withers and I pressed all through for election by county councils. We were asked to produce a scheme. Luckily I had one cut and dried among the old Bryce committee papers. Last Monday we divided on the question and our scheme was carried by one vote. Salisbury is now to draw up a report which is to be submitted to the Cabinet. As Baldwin promoted the committee he ought to get something done, but I am very doubtful.

I cannot make out that there is any real improvement in trade in spite of more or less hopeful speeches by some of the Ministers. Horne and Amery are advocating inflation without explaining how they mean to do it. There is a regular scramble to go to Ottawa. I don't know where they are all to stay. Ferguson stayed with me the other day. He does not seem very sanguine as to anything much being done, and I failed to find out what he thought Canada could offer.

There was a centenary dinner at the Carlton last night. It went off very well, but none of the Cabinet were there and not many M.P.s. A lot of old fossils. Bertie Horne in proposing the Chairman's health at the end said he really felt he must be in paradise, there were so many men present that he thought were dead!

31 July 1933 About the end of last year Stonehaven[9] asked me if I would take on the chairmanship of the Association of Conservative Clubs in place of Sir Herbert Nield who had just died. He told me the work was not great, chiefly involving the making of a few speeches each year in different parts of the country. Solbé the Secretary had been there for over twenty years and ran the whole thing very efficiently. The Central Office wanted someone they could trust as a figurehead. I agreed to take it on. Almost immediately Solbé died. I then had to go into the whole thing. It is a considerable affair. There are 1,500 clubs affiliated with a membership of 500,000. The Association has a staff of about 30 and an income of £12,000 a year, derived partly from voluntary subscriptions from the clubs and partly from fees for auditing and stock-taking. The governing body consists of about fifteen nominees from the six big London Conservative clubs. But the whole show has been run by the Secretary. I have luckily got a good successor to Solbé in E.M. Moyle. I am taking steps to get a committee formed on rather more representative lines, and have presided at four or five meetings in the country where the attendance has been very good.

In April I was elected President of the County Councils Association for the year. It fell to my lot to make a speech at the Annual Meeting. The C.C.A. had lately sent a deputation to the Ministry of Health urging relief works for unemployed and had got no encouragement. I took the opportunity of hoping the C.C.A. would not press for a policy of relief in aid of wages. I had begun by saying that I was expressing my own opinions only. It went down all right.

The National Union Executive Committee is going to nominate me as President of the N.U. next year when the annual meeting is at Bristol.

The Ottawa conference duly came off last autumn. I had an excellent account of it from Jack Gilmour and from Tony Muirhead who went out as his P.P.S. The Canadians seem to have been very troublesome. Bennett haggled till the very end and an agreement was only reached on the very last day. As far as I can make out our farmers have been rather let down. The Dominions get free entry for three years. The result in Somerset has been an enormous increase in the import of New Zealand cheese – this has hit the producers of Cheddar harder than anything in recent years. Elliott who has succeeded Gilmour has been wonderfully clever in dealing with the N.F.U. They seem to feed out of his hand. A wonderful experience for a Minister of Agriculture. He has succeeded in getting a voluntary rationing of certain imports, but so far has done nothing for milk products. The Marketing Bill may improve matters. It remains to be seen if big trading concerns organised by farmers can make good.

Gilmour told me he was put into the Home Office specially to organise the London police. Under Clynes and H. Samuel they had got entirely out of hand, and corruption is rampant. He took the office on S.B.'s definite assurance that he would see him through. He had a very difficult time with them at first.

India has been a very burning question in the country constituencies. The retired colonials are very 'Die Hard' on the subject. S.B. spoke out at a meeting of the N.U. Executive on the subject. He said that unless the White Paper's terms were given he believed we should lose India. Page Croft asked him how soon. He replied 25 or 50 years. On the whole the Die Hards are losing ground on the subject. Reading started a debate in the House of Lords the other day on a speech that Lloyd had delivered at Shrewsbury. Lloyd came out of it rather badly. I had a talk with Irwin about it one day. He said that where Winston and his friends were so foolish was in attacking the plan for a central parliament. That body with the Princes in it would be a very Tory Assembly. I saw Lindsay who was an English traders' representative in the present Indian Assembly. He told me the Aga Khan thought it would be absolutely fatal to upset the White Paper proposals. The result would be strong agitation for something much worse.

9 October 1933 Attended the N.U. Conference at Birmingham where I was elected President for the coming year. On the whole it was rather dull. There was the regular motion on India defeated by a majority of two to one. All polite and good tempered, but the pity is that the Die Hard element in the country is taking the line of telling their supporters not to subscribe to local party funds. There was a motion by Lloyd deploring the weakness of our forces. It was supported by Winston and Amery. No Government representative intervened and it was carried *nem. con.* At the meeting on Friday evening S.B. made a really alarmist speech about the European situation and stressed our obligations under the Locarno pact. It looks as if the whole thing was staged to impress Germany in view of the disarmament negotiations.

3 June 1934 The India Committee has not yet reported and there is less agitation on that subject. Bye elections have gone badly and Conservatives are less anxious to display internal differences. I had a few words with Baldwin the other day. He is very anxious about the German danger. Says it is not immediate but that in four or five years time it will be very great.

I was elected President of the Conservative National Union last month. The Conference this year is at Bristol. I have travelled a good deal to take the chair at meetings of the Association of Conservative Clubs. They have gone off very well and have shown no signs of the discontent with the Government which undoubtedly exists. One speech that I made about the need for a 'Boomster' attracted a good deal of attention. Punch had some verses about it.

The Second Chamber question is again to the fore. Salisbury introduced a bill in the House of Lords on the subject. A meeting of Conservative peers was rather inclined to withold its support. I succeeded in persuading them that we ought to back it and so was one of the small committee that was appointed to organise the debate. The Liberals were out against us and a lot of people thought we should be beaten. However, by dint of whipping we got a majority of more than two to one at the end of a three-day debate. The Government took no part and said they could give no facilities. Salisbury said that under the circumstances he would not go beyond second reading. I was all for that, but a good many did not like it.

We were engaged last week on the Tote Bill. I moved many amendments on behalf of the C.C.A. and the Conservative Clubs and got many of them accepted.

1 August 1934 House adjourned yesterday. Last week I moved the second reading of the Game Laws Bill. Its object is to codify and amend the Game Laws which want it badly. The Bill was produced by a committee of the Field Sports Society. I took no part in it. But several Lords did who were not ready to move, so I reluctantly undertook the job. It is a very long and complicated Bill, and I had to read my speech. It was not a very successful effort, but I got the second reading on the undertaking to go no further this session. Now we shall probably try to get some portions of it introduced separately in House of Commons next session.

Stanhope told me yesterday that in the last twelve months nine million people had died of starvation in South Russia.[10]

The position of the Government seems a little better than it was six months ago.

12 October 1934 I was President of the N.U. Conference at Bristol last week. In the course of the proceedings it was noticeable that resolutions were carried condemning several items of Government policy, notably as to housing. I took the chair at the mass meeting and pulled Baldwin's leg a bit. He made a good speech but told us nothing.

Muirhead my successor at Wells told me he had been staying at Clandon. Lothian was there and said L.G. would like to come into the present Government. He would be ready to serve under Baldwin but not under Ramsay.

21 April 1935 Until quite lately things have been going badly for the Government. The peace propaganda undoubtedly did them harm. Then came the muddle about the dole. It is hard to get at the rights and wrongs of that. Last year's Bill left the fixing of the dole rates to an independent committee with Betterton as chairman. I was told by Clifton Brown, M.P. for Hexham, that in some cases in Durham the Committee fixed the allowances lower than they had been fixed by the Ministry of Labour's own Commissioners. Anyway there was a row. I am told Stanley had not looked into the matter till the row was on him. Then he declared in a hurry that he must repeal the Act and legislate afresh. Betterton is very angry. The new Bill has not yet been produced. But it is sure to cost the country a lot of money. Things are looking up a bit just at present. Employment is improving. Chamberlain's budget has made a good impression. But the greatest point in the Government's favour has been Hitler's declaration as to German rearmament. Bobby Monsell told me Hitler made his increased estimates for the Navy quite easy to obtain. I never knew our Central Office people so rattled as they were in February. They looked on no seat as safe.

Baldwin made a very good impromptu speech at the N.U. Executive ten days ago. He said Hitler showed some sense of responsibility but Goring and Goebbels were merely gangsters. He spoke of an agreement for all powers to make it known that they would unite against Germany if she became aggressive.

I spoke in a debate in House of Lords on ribbon development the other day. The Government were evasive at first but the feeling was so strong that eventually they promised to introduce a Bill very soon.

CHAPTER 19 NOTES

1 On 5 February, Baldwin spoke on the tariff question at the London Coliseum, calling for a free hand in safeguarding and a more Imperial economic policy. K. Middlemas & J. Barnes, *Baldwin*, pp. 561–2.
2 See C.P. Cook and J. Ramsden, *By-Elections in British Politics*, pp. 78–108.
3 The Electoral Reform Bill which abolished the university seats and brought in the alternative vote was undoubtedly the price of Liberal support but it was not clear if Labour was prepared to pay it. Like other Bills it was mutilated by the House of Lords. R. Skidelsky, *Politicians and the Slump*, p. 357.
4 This was Bayford Lodge, Wincanton, from which Sanders had taken his title in 1929. Hon Howard Ferguson had been the Conservative Prime Minister of Ontario before becoming Ambassador to London in 1931, and was a keen huntsman.
5 William Graham as President of the Board of Trade and J.H. Thomas as Secretary of State for the Dominions were the Ministers most responsible for the coming Imperial Economic Conference.
6 1st Viscount Ullswater, Speaker of the House of Commons 1905–21, had been Chairman of the 1915–17 and 1929–30 Electoral Reform Conferences and so his views would be expected to carry great weight.
7 The Big Loaf and the Little Loaf was a favourite Liberal campaigning cry against tariffs: a large (free trade) loaf was contrasted with a small one (baked under a tariff system), a graphic political visual aid of the Edwardian era.
8 The Exchange Equalisation Account was set up in April 1932, but soon ran into difficulties as it was in competition with U.S. interests rather than in cooperation. Only with the U.S. and French decisions to go off gold and a tripartite currency agreement was it possible to restore stability in 1936.
9 Lord Stonehaven, previously Sir John Baird M.P., was Chairman of the Conservative party 1931–6.
10 7th Earl Stanhope was the Under Secretary at the Foreign Office, so this presumably reflects F.O. thinking. It seems likely that three or

four millions died in the worst year of famine although it has been calcuated that some ten million Russians 'demographically disappeared' in 'the terrible early thirties'. Alec Nove, *An Economic History of the U.S.S.R.*, p. 180.

Index